ALSO AVAILABLE

The *Original*

Lean and Luscious

Now, you can also own the original volume that started the **Lean and Luscious** series. One of the best-selling low-calorie, low-fat cookbooks ever, this popular volume with its over-400 recipes can enlarge your collection of delicious recipes that are good for you.

Available in Bookstores Everywhere!

Or, if you cannot find **Lean and Luscious** in your bookstore, or if you prefer receiving a copy in your home, turn to the last page of this book for ordering information.

more LEAN AND LUSCIOUS

VOLUME II IN
THE LEAN AND LUSCIOUS SERIES

BOBBIE HINMAN & MILLIE SNYDER

ILLUSTRATIONS BY VONNIE CRIST

Prima Publishing & Communications
P.O. Box 1260MLL
Rocklin, CA 95677
(916) 624-5718

Typography by Miller Freeman Publications
Production by Robin Lockwood, Bookman Productions
Editing by Helen Duncanson
Cover design by The Dunlavey Studio
Place setting on cover courtesy of William Glen,
    Sacramento, California

Prima Publishing & Communications
Rocklin, CA

Library of Congress Cataloging-in-Publication Data

Hinman, Bobbie.
    More lean and luscious / Bobbie Hinman and Millie Snyder.
        p.   cm.
    Includes index.
    ISBN 0-914629-49-2 : $13.95
    1. Low-fat diet—Recipes.   2. Low-carbohydrate diet—Recipes.
I. Snyder, Millie. II. Title.
RM237.7.H56 1988   88-17811
641.5'635—dc19   CIP

90   91—10   9   8   7   6   5   4

Printed in the United States of America

To Harry,
For your unconditional love and support. This one's for you.

To Harvey,
Grow on through the years with me, for the best is yet to be.

Important

This book is not intended as a promotion or recommendation for any specific diet, nor as a substitute for your physician's advice. Its purpose is to show you how you can follow a balanced diet and enjoy tasty, nutritious meals.

Contents

About the Authors

BOBBIE HINMAN

Bobbie Hinman was an avid gourmet cook when she discovered, 18 years ago, that there was a history of high cholesterol in her family. So, at a time when information and recipes on low-fat cooking were scarce, Bobbie became a pioneer. She found that by substituting certain ingredients and using exciting combinations of everyday spices, she could greatly reduce the fat content of recipes while actually enhancing their flavor. She has become a whiz at creating wonderfully tasty recipes that don't rely on high-fat ingredients for their flavor.

With her B.S. Degree in Education, Bobbie is right at home teaching the many cooking classes she is now called upon to teach. She also travels extensively, speaking to hospital groups, cardiac centers, and many private weight-loss organizations.

Since the publication of the first volume, Bobbie has made quite a few television appearances, including several complete cable series. In addition, she now writes a monthly cooking column for a Maryland magazine.

Even with her busy schedule, Bobbie still finds time to read as many health publications as possible. Her goal is to keep abreast of the latest advances in food and health issues so that she can continue to help people to eat healthfully and still enjoy their food.

Bobbie resides in Maryland with her husband Harry and their four children.

MILLIE SNYDER

Because of her concern for people, Millie Snyder has established a reputation for helping men and women enhance the quality of their lives by learning how to change. Through her twenty-two-year association in the field of weight-control service, Millie takes the position that change in the right direction is only a matter of personal choice. Her busy lifestyle includes being the creator and distributor of a large line of reduced-calorie foods. In addition, she has been actively involved in this exciting collection of recipes for *More Lean and Luscious*. Millie believes that humor is a requirement for change. Perhaps that is one reason why she has become a much sought-after public speaker on the subject of self-image and weight control. This quintessential contemporary American woman shares her life with husband Harvey and two teenage children, Jennifer and Craig. Listed in *Who's Who of American Women* and *Who's Who of Finance and Industry*, Millie always finds time to let people know they can do whatever they want to do.

Foreword by
Steven J. Jubelirer, M.D.

Medical Director
Cancer Care Center of Southern West Virginia
at CAMC

As an oncologist, many patients have asked me about the influence of diet on cancer. I have often been asked why it is so important for people with cancer to eat well. A number of studies have indicated that patients who eat well during their treatment period are better able to withstand any side effects of various treatments, particularly chemotherapy, radiation therapy, and even surgery. Patients with cancer who eat well can often tolerate higher doses of chemotherapeutic drugs than those who do not.

You have probably heard that a high-fiber, low-fat diet can help reduce the risk of certain types of cancer. Both the National Cancer Institute and the American Cancer Society have recommended such a diet. Of course, there is no overwhelming evidence at this time that changes in your diet will prevent cancer, but until more data are available, I feel it is very practical to follow these dietary guidelines. Following these guidelines may ultimately be shown to prevent certain types of cancer and, to be sure, are important to one's well-being in itself.

In addition to providing introductory tips on lowering calories, fats, and cholesterol, the recipes in this book by Millie Snyder and Bobbie Hinman represent gourmet cooking. To make matters easier, each recipe gives the number of calories, and the content of sodium, cholesterol, proteins, carbohydrates, and fats as well as equivalents on the diet exchange lists. This is important because it makes compliance with a diet much easier.

The recipes provided in this book are not only therapeutic and indeed healthful, but most important, extremely appetizing!

Foreword by
Harold Selinger, M.D.

Medical Director
The Heart Institute of West Virginia

Once again Millie and Bobbie have written a book and have done me the honor of asking me to write an introduction.

It seems clear to us physicians that the American people have taken our advice and are trying to modify their diets, get involved in exercise programs, and stop smoking in order to reduce their risk of heart attacks. It is also clear that this is working since for several years now the mortality rate from heart attacks has been going down. Unfortunately, not all the things that physicians recommend are as enjoyable as what we have done before. As an example, many individuals think that aerobic exercises such as jogging do not actually prolong your life but make it seem much longer. Those who do jog know that that's not true. Certainly many of those foods that we are told to avoid or limit obviously are the most delicious. Therefore, anything that can be done to make these modifications more attractive to us is a great favor to us and deserves much credit.

As before, Millie and Bobbie are attempting to make these changes in diet which are so essential to weight and cholesterol reduction as palatable and appetizing as possible. Having eaten at my friend Millie's home frequently, I can assure you that she always does this. Now, they are trying to tell those of us who are not as expert in preparing foods how to do the same. Therefore, once again I would like to express my thanks to Millie and Bobbie for all their efforts in writing this book to help us enjoy our dietary regimen.

Good healthful eating!

About Our Book

BACK BY POPULAR DEMAND

Why a second book? Two reasons: First, the response to our first volume was overwhelming, and second, we have hundreds of new ideas and recipes to share with you. *More Lean and Luscious* is not just a continuation of the first book. Rather it is an expression of the expanding knowledge of the health professionals in our country. With mounting medical evidence pointing to the importance of reducing our intake or fats, cholesterol, and sodium and increasing our intake of fiber, we have responded to the challenge. Our quest for finding new and interesting ideas has become an adventure, and the new American eating style has become our passion.

As in our first book, we have always tried to keep in mind that foods have their own built-in flavors. We have used spices and extracts to enhance, not hide, these flavors. We use basic ingredients and show you how to trim the fat from your favorite foods, and add fiber, without sacrificing flavor. In addition, we have developed a style of cooking that is especially loved by people who love good food but don't always have a lot of time to devote to cooking.

Like our first volume, *More Lean and Luscious* is not a diet book. It is a collection of recipes that will allow you to enjoy your favorite foods without adding unnecessary calories and fat. We have added more fiber to our dishes and have included more recipes using whole grains, fruits, and vegetables.

Another exciting feature of this book is the inclusion of many lists of "Hints" that will help you to adapt your own favorite recipes and make them lower in fat, cholesterol, and sodium, and higher in fiber.

In response to our many requests, we have also included ideas for entertaining and lots of menu suggestions for every type of meal, from family breakfasts to formal dinner parties.

Most of these new recipes are our own, a result of countless hours of cooking and tasting. We have also included some traditional favorites and others that have been graciously given to us by loving friends and family members. We have lowered the calorie and fat content of these recipes and converted them in a way that makes them available to the greatly expanding health-conscious population.

OUR USE OF SWEETENERS

In our recipes we have left the choice of which sweetener to use up to each individual. We have greatly reduced the amount of sweetener called for, so that, even if you use sugar, you will only find a small amount in each recipe. We have heightened the flavor of our sweet dishes by using extracts, instead of an excessive amount of sugar. Each recipe was tested using all sugar, and again using half sugar and half artificial sweetener. The calorie count for each recipe was based on the use of sugar. In general, we have found that cakes and cookies made entirely with artificial sweeteners often do not have as pleasant a taste and texture as those made with some sugar.

It is important to note that NutraSweet should only be used in recipes that do not require cooking, or in those that have the sweetener added after cooking. This is because the sweetening power of this particular sweetener is lost during prolonged exposure to high temperatures.

FOOD FAMILIES

Our highly successful concept of dividing foods into basic food groups has been repeated in this volume. The foods found in each family are comparable in nutritional and calorie values.

If you are currently following a weight reduction organization diet, this will allow our recipes to be easily adapted to your program. As with the first volume, we recommend that if you wish to lose weight, you should consult your physician or other weight control expert regarding the number of servings from each Food Family that would be the best for your particular daily needs.

Family #1 — Proteins

The Protein Family is made up of meats, poultry, seafood, eggs, cheese, legumes, and tofu. All of these foods are valuable sources of protein. Legumes and tofu are not of animal origin and so, while high in protein, they contain no cholesterol and low amounts of saturated fat.

For additional information on proteins, please see the Hints at the beginning of our sections on Poultry, Seafood, Meats, Eggs and Cheese, Legumes, and Tofu.

One serving from the Protein Family contains approximately 70 calories.

Family #2 — Breads

The Bread Family is made up of breads, crackers, cereals, grains, and starchy vegetables. We have included starchy vegetables in this Family because their carbohydrate levels are about the same as an equivalent serving of bread. The Bread Family is a good source of fiber in the diet.

For additional information on breads, please see the Hints at the beginning of our sections on Breads and Muffins, Starchy Vegetables, and Grains.

One serving from the Bread Family contains approximately 75 to 85 calories.

Family #3 — Vegetables

The Vegetable Family consists of fresh, canned, or frozen vegetables, other than the Starchy Vegetables. This family provides valuable sources of vitamins, minerals, and fiber.

For additional information on Vegetables, please see the Hints at the beginning of our Vegetable section.

One serving from the Vegetable Family contains approximately 25 to 30 calories.

Family #4 — Fats

The Fat Family is made up of margarine, mayonnaise, vegetable oils, and salad dressings. Most health professionals recommend using polyunsaturated fats, rather than saturated fats, whenever possible.

For additional information on Fats, please see the Hints at the beginning of our sections on Salads, and Desserts.

One serving from the Fat Family contains approximately 40 to 45 calories.

Family #5 — Fruit

The Fruit Family consists of fruits and fruit juices. This Family provides valuable sources of vitamins, minerals, and fiber. Fruits may be fresh, canned, dried, or frozen. Be sure, when choosing canned or frozen fruits, that the fruit has been packed in water or unsweetened fruit juice and that no sugar has been added.

For additional information on Fruits, please see the Hints at the beginning of our Fruit section.

One serving from the Fruit Family contains approximately 40 to 50 calories.

Family #6 — Milk

The Milk Family is made up of milk and milk products, such as buttermilk and yogurt. This Family is an excellent source of vitamins, minerals, protein, and calcium. In order to cut down on calories and fats, choose skim milk and other dairy products that are derived from skim milk, such as lowfat or nonfat yogurt.

For additional information on Milk, please see the Hints at the beginning of our sections on Eggs and Cheese, and Desserts.

One serving from the Milk Family contains approximately 80 to 90 calories.

Family #7 — Free Foods

The Free Food Family consists of foods that appear in our recipes, but provide no nutritional value. They are used to enhance the taste of each dish. Included in this Family are spices, extracts, unflavored gelatin, vinegar, artificial sweeteners, lemon juice, mustard, Worcestershire sauce, and soy sauce. While we call them "Free," some of these foods are very high in sodium and should only be used in moderate amounts.

Each serving from the Free Food Family contains a negligible amount of calories.

Family #8 — Additional Calories

The Additional Calories Family consists of foods that appear in our recipes in small amounts, and while they do not appreciably alter the nutritional value of each dish, they do add calories. Among these foods are sugar, honey, molasses, ketchup, jams and jellies, nuts and seeds, bacon bits, cocoa, broth mix, flour, cornstarch, egg whites, and coconut.

In each recipe we have figured the Additional Calories for you. They appear at the end of each list of Food Family servings where applicable.

HOW TO USE THE NUTRITIONAL INFORMATION FOUND IN THIS BOOK

After each recipe you will find a box that contains the nutritional information for that particular recipe:

Each serving provides:

85 Calories*

2	Protein Servings	4	g	Protein
1	Vegetable Serving	2	g	Fat
4	Additional Calories	12	g	Carbohydrate
	(plus 4 more calories if	76	mg	Sodium
	sugar is used as	2	mg	Cholesterol
	sweetener)			

*If sugar is used as sweetener

If you are following a weight reduction organization diet or are interested in choosing foods wisely from our Food Families, you can tell at a glance how many servings from each Food Family one portion contains. In this example, each serving contains 2 servings from the Protein Family, 1 serving from the Vegetable Family, and 4 calories from the Additional Calories Family. However, if you used sugar as the sweetener in the recipe, you would need to count the sugar calories as Additional calories, bringing the total number of Additional calories to 8 (1 teaspoon of sugar contains 16 calories).

If you are counting calories, the information in this box tells you that each serving contains 85 calories. The asterisk tells you that these calories were figured with sugar as the sweetener. If you are following any type of restrictive diet, such as diabetic, low sodium, or low cholesterol, the information provided will give you a nutritional analysis of each serving that will help you to choose the best recipes for your particular diet. All of the numbers in our analysis have been rounded to the nearest whole number, and a zero listed before a nutrient indicates that a serving of that recipe contains a negligible amount of that particular ingredient. Be sure to see the Hints at the beginning of each section for lots of ideas on further reducing the amounts of sodium, cholesterol, etc. in each recipe.

If you are not on any particular diet, just enjoy the delicious taste of each of our recipes and know that you are embarking on a healthful way of eating.

Enjoy!

Hints and Menus for Family Meals

One of the major obstacles in planning nutritious, low-fat meals seems to be boredom. There are an abundance of cookbooks devoted entirely to entertaining menus, and these books are filled with wonderful ideas. However, when it comes right down to the day-to-day planning of countless breakfasts, lunches, and dinners, even the most inventive people can run short of ideas. To ease the monotony of daily planning and to help prevent falling into the possible rut of cereal for breakfast, bologna sandwiches for lunch, and meatloaf and mashed potatoes for dinner, we have included the following hints and menus to help you and your family enjoy delicious food without extra calories and fat. For more ideas, be sure to see the Hints at the beginning of each section.

What's for Breakfast?

- Since carbohydrates are our bodies' main source of fuel, an ideal breakfast should be planned around whole grains and fresh fruit.
- Read the labels on cereal boxes and avoid the ones that have added fat, sugar, and salt.
- Choose cereals that are made from whole grains, such as whole wheat or whole oats.
- Use skim milk on cereal, or for a delicious alternative try fruit juice.
- Be sure the fruit juice you buy has no added sugar.
- For toast, use whole grain breads.
- In place of butter, choose a margarine that is high in polyunsaturated fats.
- If you are watching your cholesterol, try using egg substitutes or just egg whites in place of eggs.
- Be aware that sausage and bacon are very high in both saturated fat and sodium.
- Bagels and English muffins generally are low in fat and make a better choice than most other bakery items.
- Try some of our delicious breads and muffins (See Breads and Muffins). They're all quick and easy.
- Use left-over grains as a cereal. They're good hot or cold, with added fruit and skim milk.
- Mix left-over rice with part-skim ricotta cheese and add cinnamon, vanilla, and raisins.

- Combine plain lowfat yogurt with your choice of fresh fruit. Sweeten lightly and add your favorite cereal.
- Before you go to bed, fill your crockpot with oats, rice, grits, millet, or any grain or combination of grains. Add water, raisins, cinnamon, and vanilla. You'll wake up to a delicious breakfast. (A general guideline is 3 cups of water to 1 cup of grains. You may have to change this, according to taste.)
- A baked potato topped with yogurt or a little margarine makes a very nutritious breakfast. It can be made quickly in the microwave or baked ahead and reheated in a toaster oven or microwave.
- Try a baked sweet potato topped with cinnamon and a little margarine.
- Try a breakfast milkshake made from skim milk, fruit, and ice in the blender.
- Top a rice cake with lowfat cottage cheese, apple butter (unsweetened), and a sprinkling of sunflower seeds.

Family Breakfast Menus

Apple Strudel Omelet (page 74)
Whole Wheat Toast
with
Peach Butter (page 349)

Skim Milk

❀   ❀   ❀

Fruit Salad
with
Lowfat Cottage Cheese
Bran Muffin (page 341)

❀   ❀   ❀

Apple Tapioca Dessert (page 353)
with
Creme Topping (page 449)
over
Cooked Brown Rice

❀   ❀   ❀

Peanut Butter spread on Sliced Apple

Granola (page 432)
topped with Lowfat Yogurt

Hints for Lunch

- Remember that a high-fat lunch will usually leave you feeling sluggish and a low-fat lunch will give you more energy.
- Be aware that lunch meats, such as bologna and salami, are extremely high in saturated fat and sodium.
- Add a whole grain, such as whole wheat bread or crackers, and a piece of fresh fruit for a really nutritious lunch.
- Break away from the idea that lunches have to mean sandwiches. Buy some plastic containers that will fit into a lunch bag, and you can pack almost anything.
- Having a salad with your lunch will add vitamins and fiber and will help to fill you up.
- If possible, keep a bottle of your favorite reduced-calorie dressing at work.
- If you have to eat out, find a salad bar and eat only the fresh vegetables and fruits. Avoid the potato salad, macaroni salad, and other salads that are laden with fat.
- In a fast food restaurant, a baked potato is a good alternative to a hamburger or other high-fat entree. Ask for it dry, with margarine on the side. That way *you* are in control of the amount of fat used.
- If you have access to a microwave, make extra portions of your favorite low-fat entrees and freeze them in plastic containers.

Easy-to-Pack Lunch Menus

Sesame, Broccoli, and Cauliflower Salad (page 42)

Sliced Turkey Breast with
French Honey Mustard (page 69)
on
Whole Wheat Bread

Fresh Fruit

❀   ❀   ❀

Tossed Salad
with
Lowfat Dressing

Hearty Bean Soup (page 34)

Oatmeal Bread (page 331)

Fresh Fruit

❀   ❀   ❀

Baked Potato
with
Vegetable Chili (page 263)

Fresh Fruit

❀   ❀   ❀

Cut Fresh Vegetables
with
Dilly Dip (page 447)

Whole Wheat Zucchini Bread (page 327)
with
Peanut Butter   Fresh Fruit

Hints for Children's Lunches

- Pack a whole grain muffin in place of a cupcake.
- Save the small containers from lowfat yogurt. They can be used for packing items such as fruit salad or cottage cheese and then discarded.
- Let children help pack their favorite items in the containers.
- Help children to cut and wrap their own fresh fruits and vegetables. They will be more likely to eat them if they do.
- Vary the fillings in children's sandwiches. Try peanut butter with raisins, bananas, or chopped apples for a change.
- For children who resist whole wheat bread, make a sandwich with one slice each of white and whole wheat bread and call it a "special" sandwich.
- For variation, make sandwiches on whole grain muffins instead of bread.

- Pack fresh or dried fruit for dessert. It's sweet and it's healthful.
- Buy whole wheat pretzels instead of fat-laden potato chips or taco chips.
- Core an apple and fill the center with peanut butter. It makes a wonderful lunch box treat.

Children's Lunch Menus

Carrot and Celery Sticks

Banana Oat Muffin (page 339)
with Peanut Butter

Orange Juice

❊   ❊   ❊

Container of Tuna Salad

Whole Wheat Zucchini Bread (page 327)
with Apple Butter

Cinnamon Popcorn (page 442)

Apple Juice

❊   ❊   ❊

Celery
stuffed with
Peanut Butter-Bean Spread (page 216)

Tropical Fruit Salad (page 55)

Cinnamon Bread Sticks (page 433)

Skim Milk

❊   ❊   ❊

Sliced Turkey with Lettuce and Tomato
on
Whole Wheat Bread

Raspberry Tapioca (page 364)

Skim Milk

Hints for Family Dinners

- Don't announce to your family that they are about to have a "diet" meal.
- Starting your meal with a low-fat soup or salad will help fill you up.
- Serve chicken and fish more often than red meats.
- For added vitamins, minerals, and fiber, try serving smaller portions of your protein and larger portions of vegetables.
- Adding a whole grain, such as brown rice, barley, or bulgur to your dinner, adds important nutrients as well as interesting flavors and textures.
- Remember that carbohydrates have fewer calories than fats. It is generally not the potatoes that cause weight gain. Rather, it is the fat that is spread on them.
- Pasta mixed with a small amount of poultry, seafood, or meat makes a very filling meal that is lower in fat than a dinner consisting of all meat.
- It's a good idea to make enough so that there will be leftovers for lunches or another dinner.
- For information on lowering the fat and calories in your favorite recipes, please see the Hints in the beginning of our Poultry, Seafood, and Meat sections.
- Have some "meatless" meals. For delicious vegetarian entrees, please see our Legumes and Tofu sections.
- Remember that food is always more appealing when served attractively.

Family Dinner Menus

Tossed Salad
with
Zesty Tomato Dressing (page 66)

Cheese Pie with Potato Crust (page 90)

Steamed Broccoli

Vanilla Ice Milk

Blueberry and Apple Delight (page 360)

❁   ❁   ❁

Spiced Tomato Soup (page 30)

Oven-Fried Chicken (page 157)

Steamed Green Beans

Herbed Rice Toss (page 298)

Fruit Salad
with
Brown Sugar Dip (page 450)

❄   ❄   ❄

Tossed Salad
with
Thousand Island Dressing (page 63)

Italian Beans and Cheese (page 199)

Baked Potato

Mystery Custard Pie (page 404)

❄   ❄   ❄

Sliced Tomatoes, Onions, and Cucumbers
with
Creamy Bacon Dip (page 445)

Meat and Potato Loaf (page 184)

Steamed Broccoli

Best Carrot Cake (page 387)

Hints for Adding Fiber to Your Meals

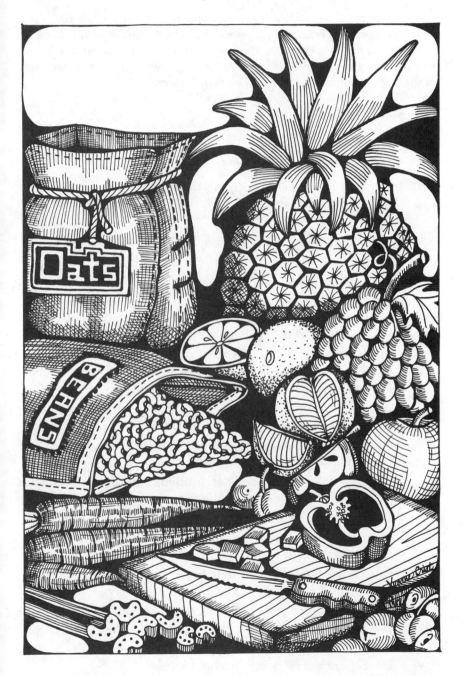

According to many health experts, the "typical" American diet is too low in fiber. It is believed that fiber, which itself is not digested, helps to remove many of the toxic substances found in our food supply. Fiber also aids in weight control by providing bulk. High fiber foods fill the stomach and satisfy hunger with the intake of fewer calories.

Foods that are generally high in fiber are:
- *Fresh fruits*
- *Fresh vegetables*
- *Whole grains*
- *Legumes (beans, peas, and lentils)*

Following are hints that will help you to add fiber to your meals without adding unnecessary fats and calories. There also are many wonderful high-fiber recipes throughout this book.

- Leave the skin on fruits and vegetables whenever possible.
- Make fresh fruit or fruit salad your first choice for dessert.
- Eat vegetables raw or crisp-cooked.
- Try cooking combinations of fresh fruits and vegetables, such as carrots with apples, squash with apples or pineapple, beets with oranges, or red cabbage with apples.
- Make tossed salads out of a wide variety of vegetables. A good guide is color. If you use a vegetable of every color, you generally have a nutritious salad.
- Replace half the flour in a recipe with whole wheat flour.
- Choose 100 % whole wheat bread, not "wheat bread."
- Other good choices are rye bread and corn bread, provided they are made with whole grains.
- Be aware that when grains are milled, most of the bran and germ, and therefore most of the fiber, is removed.
- Read bread labels and make sure the whole grain is listed first.
- Make your own bread crumbs and croutons out of toasted whole grain bread.
- Choose breakfast cereals that list a whole grain as the first ingredient.
- Use rolled oats in place of bread crumbs in your next meat loaf.
- Serve Granola (see Grains) as a topping for ice milk, lowfat yogurt, or fruit.
- Use oat bran to thicken soups and sauces.

- Add cooked brown rice or another whole grain to your dinner. They'll complement your favorite entree.
- Try stir-fried vegetables over cooked brown rice. It's great for lunch or dinner.
- For interesting texture and flavor, buy a variety of grains and serve them in different combinations.
- Put a cup of uncooked brown rice or mixed grains in the crock-pot at night. Add cinnamon, vanilla, and 3 cups of water. You'll love your breakfast!
- Have leftover grains for breakfast. They're great hot or cold with skim milk, raisins, and cinnamon.
- Try whole wheat pasta in place of the regular type.
- Read the labels on bakery items. You're usually better off making your own.
- Add cooked legumes (beans, peas, or lentils) to your favorite spaghetti sauce and serve over whole wheat pasta.
- Cooked legumes also make a tasty and nutritious addition to any soup or stew.
- Make burgers out of mashed, cooked beans or add them to your favorite burger or meat loaf recipe.
- Use wheat germ in place of bread crumbs for dishes such as oven-fried chicken.
- Roll cheese logs in wheat germ instead of ground nuts.

Spice Up Your Life

If you look at the vast array of spices and extracts on your grocer's shelf, you'll realize that there's no need for food to ever be dull and unexciting. Spices and extracts can greatly enhance the flavor of food and the combinations are endless. These fat-free wonders add only one thing—flavor, wonderful flavor. No one will ever notice that the fat has been removed from a recipe if the spices are right. The recipes throughout this book use many delicious combinations of spices that you will be able to enjoy and adapt to your own favorite recipes.

If a recipe calls for dried spices and you wish to substitute fresh ones, you will usually need to use two to three times the amount called for.

Following are some hints to guide you. Remember, when trying a new flavor, to go easy. You can always add more.

Flavorful Seafood

- Try dill weed and lemon peel on baked or broiled fish.
- For a Chinese flavor, marinate seafood in a small amount of soy sauce and sprinkle with garlic powder and ginger.
- For an Italian flavor, combine one 16-ounce can of tomatoes (drained and chopped) with 2 tablespoons of onion flakes, 1/8 teaspoon garlic powder, and 1/4 teaspoon each of basil and oregano. Spoon over fish or shrimp and bake.
- Sprinkle fish with thyme and pepper before baking.
- Make a tuna or salmon pâté by mashing 8 ounces of the fish with 1/2 teaspoon tarragon, 1/8 teaspoon pepper, 1 teaspoon dill weed, 1/8 teaspoon garlic powder, and 2 teaspoons reduced-calorie mayonnaise.

Flavorful Poultry

- Combine chopped tomatoes, onion, and green peppers and add garlic and oregano. Spoon over chicken and bake.
- Sauté turkey cutlets in a nonstick skillet with a small amount of oil. Sprinkle with garlic powder, oregano, and poultry seasoning.
- Combine reduced-calorie mayonnaise with Dijon mustard and spread on chicken. Sprinkle with rosemary and bake.
- For the taste of sausage, to 1 pound of ground turkey add 1/8 teaspoon ground savory, and 1/4 teaspoon each of ground sage, thyme, marjoram, pepper, and salt, and 1/2 teaspoon crushed fennel seeds. Make into patties and sauté in a nonstick skillet.

- Chicken marinated in soy sauce with sherry extract, garlic powder, and ginger makes a wonderful Oriental entree.

Flavorful Meats

- Steaks marinated in soy sauce, sherry extract, garlic powder, and ginger are wonderful on the grill.
- Lemon juice or lime juice with garlic powder and rosemary makes a delicious marinade for beef or pork.
- Curry powder and minced onion flakes can turn an ordinary meat loaf into a gourmet treat.
- Baked pork chops are delicious when spread with Dijon mustard and sprinkled with rosemary or dill weed.

Flavorful Eggs

- Try scrambling eggs (or an egg substitute) in a nonstick skillet and sprinkling with oregano and garlic powder.
- A scrambled egg folded over sliced apples that have been cooked in a nonstick skillet with cinnamon makes a delicious crepe.
- Dill weed adds a spark to egg salad made with reduced-calorie mayonnaise.
- Vary French toast by adding different extracts and cooking on a nonstick skillet with a minimal amount of margarine. (Try lemon, coconut, etc.)

Flavorful Fruits

- Cook sliced, unpeeled apples in a saucepan or microwave until tender. For 4 apples add 1/2 teaspoon vanilla extract, 1/4 teaspoon each of cinnamon and nutmeg, and sweetener to taste. (Try with pears, too.)
- Combine 1/4 cup each of plain lowfat yogurt and unsweetened applesauce. Add 1/4 teaspoon apple pie spice and sweeten to taste.
- Sprinkle grapefruit halves with cinnamon and a small amount of brown sugar. Broil until bubbly.
- Sauté fresh sliced peaches, apples, or pineapple (or a combination of the three) in a nonstick skillet with cinnamon, nutmeg, and a few drops of vanilla extract.
- Broil banana halves after sprinkling with cinnamon and nutmeg.

Flavorful Vegetables

- Try cinnamon and orange peel on cooked carrots.
- Dill weed is delicious on cooked broccoli, cauliflower, or carrots.
- Lemon peel and pepper spark up any cooked vegetable.
- Cooked spinach is delicious with a hint of nutmeg and garlic.
- Pumpkin pie spice is delicious on cooked squash.
- Add a small amount of imitation butter flavor to skim milk and use as a topper for a baked potato.
- In a nonstick skillet, cook chopped tomatoes, eggplant, onions, and green pepper with garlic powder, oregano, and pepper.
- Sauté sliced zucchini in a nonstick skillet. Sprinkle with dill weed, salt, and pepper.
- Sprinkle tomato halves with garlic powder and oregano. Then bake or broil.
- For a Mexican treat, cook cabbage, tomatoes, onions, and green pepper with cumin and garlic.

Flavorful Vegetarian Entrees

- Stir-fry fresh vegetables and sliced tofu in a nonstick skillet with soy sauce, garlic powder, and ginger. Serve over brown rice.
- Mash tofu with part-skim Mozzarella cheese. Add garlic powder and oregano and use as a topper for pizza.
- Cook onions and green pepper in a nonstick skillet with a small amount of oil. Add tomatoes, cooked kidney beans, garlic, and oregano. Top with part-skim Mozzarella cheese.
- Mash cooked beans or lentils with basil and thyme and make into patties or "meatless" loaves.
- Sprinkle cooked beans with minced onion flakes and garlic powder. Top with lowfat cheese and bake until bubbly.

Flavorful Grains

- Mix leftover cooked grains with vanilla extract and cinnamon for a delicious breakfast treat.

- When cooking rice, add sage and thyme and chopped celery and onions to the water.
- For Oriental rice, add soy sauce, ginger, and garlic powder.
- Any cooked grain in the blender with crushed pineapple and coconut extract makes an instant "Piña colada" pudding.
- Add garlic powder, basil, and oregano to tomato sauce and serve over any cooked grain.

Flavorful Dairy Dishes

- Cinnamon and vanilla add a new flavor to lowfat cottage cheese, part-skim ricotta cheese, or plain lowfat yogurt.
- Yogurt makes a good salad dressing base. To 1 cup plain lowfat yogurt add 1/2 teaspoon each oregano and dill weed, 1/8 teaspoon garlic powder, and 1 tablespoon minced onion flakes.
- Lowfat cottage cheese in the blender makes a creamy salad dressing. After blending, mix with 2 tablespoons ketchup, 2 teaspoons pickle relish, 1 tablespoon finely minced green pepper, and 1 teaspoon minced onion flakes.
- For the taste of cheesecake, to 1/2 cup part-skim ricotta cheese add 1 teaspoon vanilla extract and sweeten to taste. Add other flavored extracts as desired.
- Mix 1 packet instant beef-flavored broth mix and 1 tablespoon minced onion flakes with 1 cup plain lowfat yogurt for a delicious dip for vegetables.

Miscellaneous

- Spread a small amount of reduced-calorie margarine on whole wheat toast. Sprinkle with cinnamon and sweetener for delicious cinnamon toast.
- For garlic bread, sprinkle with garlic powder and oregano.
- Make popcorn with a hot air popper, spray with nonstick cooking spray, and sprinkle with your favorite spice.

Hints and Menus for Entertaining

Entertaining doesn't have to be the downfall of a healthful eating plan. All too often, people who are careful to choose nutritious foods for themselves and their families find that when they entertain, they feel they must "go all out" for their guests. This usually means stocking the house with the very foods they have been avoiding. It may also mean cooking very fatty meals. This is unfortunate for several reasons: First, it leaves food in the house that "someone" has to finish; and second, it often jeopardizes the guests' eating plans. Many well-meaning people don't stop to think that perhaps their guests are trying to eat healthier, too.

Entertaining can be fun, and the food can be delicious. Yes, there is life on a healthful eating plan! Here are some hints that will help you to get started, and on the following pages are some menus that will help you to stay on the right track.

- Don't prepare anything you wouldn't want to eat yourself.
- Remember that your guests don't have to leave feeling "stuffed to the gills."
- Fill the room with low-fat munchies, such as fresh fruits and vegetables, instead of nuts and potato chips.
- Never apologize or make excuses for preparing a low-fat meal, and avoid using the words "diet" or "low-fat."
- Accept compliments with a gracious "thank you" instead of "thank you, but can you tell it's a diet recipe?"
- For an alcoholic beverage that's on the light side, try a wine spritzer (half white wine and half club soda with a twist of lemon or lime).
- Water, served in a pretty glass with a twist of lemon, makes a good beverage choice.
- To add variety to any meal, serve several different vegetables and/or salads.
- When serving vegetables, make large quantities rather than skimpy ones. All too often, hosts serve huge platters of meat and put out tiny little bowls of vegetables.
- For a sweet after-dinner touch, serve a flavored coffee.
- Remember that food is more appealing when served attractively.
- To summarize: Feed your guests the way you want to feed yourself.

Cocktail Party For a Crowd

Fresh Vegetable Platter
with
Dijon Dip (page 444)
and
Creamy Bacon Dip (page 445)
Dilled Carrots (page 45)
Marinated Mushrooms (page 44)
Marinated Mozzarella (page 50)
Mushroom Pâté (page 239)
Chicken Mousse (page 162)
Pepper and Onion Kuchen (page 262)
Mini Rice Cakes
Bagel Crackers (page 441)
Tropical Fruit Salad (page 55)
Peanut Butter Meringues (page 420)
Almond Macaroons (page 422)

Elegant Dinner Party #1

Dijon Dip (page 444)
with
Vegetable Dippers
Tossed Salad
Elegant Stuffed Chicken Breasts (page 146)
Baked Potato
with
Dilly Dip (page 447)
Steamed Broccoli
Berries Romanoff (page 362)

Elegant Dinner Party #2

Spinach Dip (page 446)
with
Vegetable Dippers

Tossed Salad
with
Marinated Mushrooms (page 44)

Shrimp in Cheddar Sauce (page 131)

Herbed Rice Toss (page 298)

Steamed Green Beans

Applesauce Ambrosia (page 354)

Weekend Brunch #1

Tropical Fruit Salad (page 55)

Bran Muffins (page 341)

Eggs Suzette with Strawberry Sauce (page 73)

Weekend Brunch #2

Buckwheat Pancakes (page 307)

Baked Pears with Cinnamon Creme Sauce (page 361)

Tailgate Picnic #1

Chicken 'n Pasta Primavera (page 165)

Tossed Salad
with
Classic Italian Dressing (page 65)

Applesauce Wheat Bars (page 388)

Fresh Fruit

Tailgate Picnic #2

Easiest Shrimp Salad (page 132)

Lettuce and Sliced Tomato

Whole Grain Bread

Marinated Mushrooms (page 44)

Piña Colada Upside-Down Cake (page 378)

Football Sunday Supper Buffet #1

Fresh Vegetable Platter
with
Cottage Cheese and Olive Dip (page 443)

Vegetable Chili (page 263)

Zucchini and Cheese Bread (page 332)

Lemon Dream Parfaits (page 409)

Almond Macaroons (page 422)

Football Sunday Supper Buffet #2

Tossed Salad
with
French Tomato Dressing (page 64)

Turkey Joes (page 170)

Double Corn Bread (page 335)

Mock Coconut Custard Pie (page 398)

Fresh Fruit Platter

Outdoor Barbecue #1

Spinach Salad (page 48)

Marinated Lamb Roast (page 190)

Pasta and Broccoli (page 317)

Grilled Onions (page 261)

Tropical Fruit Salad (page 55)

Outdoor Barbecue #2

Pepper Burgers (page 182)

Sliced Tomatoes and Onions

Whole Grain Buns

Veggie Packets (page 265)

Strawberry Fruit Sherbet (page 363)

INTERNATIONAL FARE

Chinese Dinner

Egg White Drop Soup (page 31)

Oriental Turkey Patties (page 166)

Steamed Brown Rice

Steamed Broccoli and Pea Pods

Vanilla Ice Milk
with
Yogurt Marmalade Dip (page 148)

Italian Dinner

Romaine Lettuce
with
Marinated Tomato Salad (page 49)

Italian Tofu Squares (page 227)

Italian Barley (page 312)

Steamed Green Beans

Citrus Fluff (page 356)

Jewish Dinner

Tossed Salad

Crispy Onion Chicken (page 155)

Kasha and Bow Ties (page 306)

Baked Carrots (page 244)

Apple Tapioca Dessert (page 353)

Special Holiday Dinner #1

Herbed Turkey Roll (page 173)

Sweet Potato Pudding (page 283)

Broiled Tomatoes (page 256)

Steamed Green Beans

Cranberry Party Mold (page 59)

Pumpkin Pie (page 402)

Special Holiday Dinner #2

Roast Turkey

Corn Bread Stuffing (page 308)

Mashed Sweet Potatoes and Apples (page 280)

Cranberry Raisin Relish (page 54)

Steamed Broccoli and Cauliflower

Pumpkin Custard Cups (page 412)

Casual Luncheon #1

Tossed Salad
with
Number 1 Dressing (page 62)
"Almost" Lasagna (page 86)
Orange-Pineapple-Carrot Mold (page 60)
Molasses Brown Bread (page 333)

Casual Luncheon #2

Gazpacho (page 36)
Tuna, Broccoli, and Shells (page 129)
Fresh Strawberries and Pineapple Wedges
Fruity Oat and Bran Bread (page 336)

Soups

Hints for Soups

- When making soup with a homemade stock, chill the soup before serving so that the fat can be easily skimmed off the top.

- If oil is called for, choose a polyunsaturated oil, such as safflower, sunflower, corn, or soybean oil. Or use olive oil, which is monounsaturated and has been shown to lower blood cholesterol.

- Avoid animal fats such as butter and lard. When a recipe calls for butter, use margarine instead. The calories are the same, but butter is high in saturated fat and cholesterol.

- When a recipe calls for cooking the vegetables in oil, generally a few teaspoons are all that are needed. If more seems to be needed, add water instead.

- When adding meat to a soup, cook the meat on a rack first to allow the fat to drip off, and then add it to the soup.

- For cream soups, use evaporated skim milk in place of the cream.

- For added nutrition, any leftover cooked grain makes a nice addition to almost any soup.

- For extra protein and fiber, add cooked beans to your favorite soup.

- Cooked pasta makes another wholesome addition to soup.

- Tofu, cut into small cubes, is another way to add protein to your soup.

- Experiment with new combinations of spices. They will spark up your soup without adding calories.

- If you are watching your sodium intake, when a recipe calls for broth mix, choose the low-sodium variety.

- For a buttery taste, add a small amount of imitation butter flavor.

- For cheese soups, choose the lowfat version of the cheese that is called for.

- When sprinkling soup with Parmesan cheese, use 1/3 or 1/4 of the amount called for. The strong flavor goes a long way.

Creamy Carrot Soup

This unusual soup is both light and creamy.

Makes 6 servings

2   tablespoons vegetable oil
1   cup chopped onions
3   cups chopped carrots
4   cups water
3   packets instant chicken-flavored broth mix
2   teaspoons tomato paste
1   ounce uncooked white or brown rice
1-1/2 cups evaporated skim milk
    Salt and pepper to taste

Heat oil in a large saucepan over medium heat. Add onions and cook until tender, adding water, if necessary, to prevent drying.

Add carrots, water, broth mix, tomato paste, and rice. Reduce heat to low, cover and simmer 30 to 40 minutes, until rice and carrots are tender. (Brown rice will take slightly longer to cook than white rice.)

Pour soup through a strainer into another saucepan. Place about 1/2 cup of the vegetables back in the broth. Place remaining vegetables in a blender container. Blend until smooth. Add to broth.

Stir in milk and salt and pepper. Heat, stirring frequently until heated through.

Each serving provides:

149 Calories

1-1/3	Vegetable Servings	7	g	Protein
1	Fat Serving	5	g	Fat
1/2	Milk Serving	19	g	Carbohydrate
23	Additional Calories	665	mg	Sodium
		3	mg	Cholesterol

Split Pea Soup

Hot, hearty, and full of protein, this soup is perfect on a cold winter night. Add a salad and a slice of crusty whole grain bread and your meal is complete.

Makes 8 servings

6   ounces uncooked split peas (1 cup)
6   cups water
1   cup chopped onions
1/2   cup chopped celery
1/2   cup chopped carrots
1   clove garlic, minced
1/2   teaspoon dried thyme
       Salt and pepper to taste

Place peas and water in a large saucepan over medium heat. Bring to a boil.

Add remaining ingredients, reduce heat to low, cover and simmer until peas are soft, about 2 hours. Stir occasionally while cooking.

For a thicker soup, mash cooked peas with a fork or potato masher.

Each serving provides:

84 Calories

1	Protein Serving	6 g	Protein
1/2	Vegetable Serving	0 g	Fat
		15 g	Carbohydrate
		13 mg	Sodium
		0 mg	Cholesterol

Leftover Bean Soup

This soup provides an excellent use for leftover beans. It works well with any type or any combination of beans. And you can add any spice you like.

Makes 4 servings

12	ounces cooked beans
2	cups evaporated skim milk
	Salt and pepper to taste
1/8	teaspoon garlic powder
1/8	teaspoon dried thyme

In a blender container, combine all ingredients. Blend until smooth.

Pour mixture into a small saucepan. Heat, stirring frequently, until hot. Add water if desired, for a thinner consistency.

Each serving provides:

22 Calories

1-1/2	Protein Servings	17	g	Protein
1	Milk Serving	1	g	Fat
		37	g	Carbohydrate
		1	mg	Sodium
		5	mg	Cholesterol

Spiced Tomato Soup

Make lots of this deliciously spiced soup in the summer when fresh tomatoes are plentiful. Freeze it and enjoy it all year long.

Makes 6 servings

6   cups chopped, peeled tomatoes
1/2   cup chopped onions
1   tablespoon mixed pickling spices
2   tablespoons margarine
       Salt and pepper to taste
1   tablespoon sugar (or sweetener equivalent to 3 teaspoons
          sugar)
3   tablespoons all-purpose flour

In a blender container, combine tomatoes and onions. Blend until smooth. Pour through a strainer into a medium saucepan.

Place mixed pickling spices in a tea strainer or tie into a piece of cheesecloth. Add to saucepan with margarine, salt, pepper, and sugar.

In a small bowl, stir flour into a small amount of soup mixture until blended. Add to soup. Cook, uncovered, over low heat 30 minutes, stirring frequently.

Each serving provides:

95 Calories*

1-1/6	Vegetable Servings	2	g	Protein
1	Fat Serving	4	g	Fat
17	Additional Calories	14	g	Carbohydrate
	(plus 8 more calories if	59	mg	Sodium
	sugar is used as	0	mg	Cholesterol
	sweetener)			

*If sugar is used as sweetener

Egg White Drop Soup

This is our low cholesterol version of the Chinese favorite. It also works well with an egg substitute in place of the egg whites.

Makes 4 servings

4   cups water
4   packets instant chicken-flavored broth mix
4   egg whites
2   tablespoons chopped green onion (green part only)

In a medium saucepan, combine water and broth mix. Bring to a boil over medium heat.

Beat egg whites with a fork until slightly frothy.

Gradually pour egg whites into boiling soup, stirring briskly with the other hand, in a circular motion.

Pour into individual soup bowls. Garnish with green onion.

Each serving provides:

33 Calories

30	Additional Calories	4	g	Protein
		1	g	Fat
		2	g	Carbohydrate
		1,165	mg	Sodium
		1	mg	Cholesterol

Curried Lima Soup

Serve a salad and some whole-grain crackers with this rich high-protein soup for a complete and nutritious lunch.

Makes 4 servings

1	10-ounce package frozen lima beans, thawed
2	cups water
2	packets instant chicken-flavored broth mix
1	tablespoon plus 1 teaspoon margarine
1	teaspoon curry powder
1	tablespoon minced onion flakes
1	small bay leaf
	Salt and pepper to taste
1/2	cup evaporated skim milk
1	tablespoon dried chives

In a medium saucepan, combine beans, water, broth mix, margarine, curry powder, onion flakes, bay leaf, and pepper. Bring to a boil over medium heat. Reduce heat to low. Cover and simmer until beans are tender, about 20 minutes. Remove and discard bay leaf.

Place soup mixture in a blender container. Blend until smooth. Return to saucepan.

Stir in milk. Heat, stirring, until heated through. Do not boil.

Spoon soup into individual serving bowls. Garnish with chives.

Each serving provides:

147 Calories

1-1/4	Protein Servings	8	g	Protein
1	Fat Serving	5	g	Fat
1/4	Milk Serving	14	g	Carbohydrate
5	Additional Calories	680	mg	Sodium
		2	mg	Cholesterol

Creamy Vegetable Chowder

This rich, flavorful soup is really a meal-in-one.

Makes 4 servings

1	tablespoon plus 1 teaspoon vegetable oil
1/4	cup chopped onions
1/4	cup chopped green pepper
1/4	cup chopped celery
1/4	cup chopped carrots
1	clove garlic, minced
2/3	cup lowfat cottage cheese
1	1-pound can tomatoes, undrained
1/2	cup water
1/8	teaspoon dried thyme
1/2	teaspoon dried oregano
1/4	teaspoon dried basil
	Salt and pepper to taste
1	cup cooked brown rice

Heat oil in a medium saucepan over medium heat. Add onions, green pepper, celery, carrots, and garlic. Cook until vegetables are lightly browned. Add small amounts of water, if necessary, to prevent drying.

In a blender container, combine cottage cheese, tomatoes, water, and spices. Blend until smooth. Add to vegetable mixture.

Stir in rice.

Reduce heat to low. Cook, stirring, until heated through. Do not boil.

Each serving provides:

159 Calories

1/2	Protein Serving	7	g	Protein
1/2	Bread Serving	6	g	Fat
1-1/2	Vegetable Servings	21	g	Carbohydrate
1	Fat Serving	348	mg	Sodium
		2	mg	Cholesterol

Hearty Bean Soup

This flavorful soup is chock full of beans and vegetables. It can easily be served as a meal in itself, and welcomes such additions as chunks of cooked chicken or seafood.

Makes 6 servings

2	tablespoons vegetable oil
1/2	cup chopped onions
1/2	cup chopped celery
1/2	cup chopped carrots
1/2	cup chopped green pepper
1	clove garlic, minced
12	ounces cooked navy or Great Northern beans
2	cups water
1	1-pound can tomatoes, chopped, undrained
1/2	teaspoon dried basil
1/2	teaspoon dried oregano
1	bay leaf
	Salt and pepper to taste
2	tablespoons grated Parmesan cheese

Heat oil in a large saucepan over medium heat. Add onions, celery, carrots, green pepper, and garlic. Cook until tender, about 10 minutes. Add small amounts of water, if necessary, to prevent drying.

Add beans, water, tomatoes, and spices. Reduce heat to low, cover, and cook 1 hour. Remove and discard bay leaf.

Spoon soup into individual serving bowls. Sprinkle with Parmesan cheese.

Each serving provides:

157 Calories

1	Protein Servings	7	g	Protein
1-1/3	Vegetable Servings	6	g	Fat
1	Fat Serving	21	g	Carbohydrate
10	Additional Calories	168	mg	Sodium
		1	mg	Cholesterol

Vegetarian Chowder

This exquisite blend of flavors makes this soup a perfect starter for any meal.

Makes 6 servings

2	tablespoons olive oil
1	cup chopped onions
1/2	cup chopped carrots
1	cup chopped celery
2	cloves garlic, minced
9	ounces potato, cut into small cubes
1	1-pound can tomatoes
2	cups water
1	small bay leaf
1	teaspoon dried thyme
1/2	teaspoon dried basil
	Salt and pepper to taste
1-1/2 cups cooked macaroni

Heat oil in a large saucepan over medium heat. Add onions, carrots, celery, and garlic. Cook, stirring frequently, 10 minutes. Add small amounts of water, if necessary, to prevent drying.

Add remaining ingredients, *except* macaroni. Reduce heat to low, cover, and simmer 40 minutes.

Add macaroni. Heat through.

Remove and discard bay leaf before serving.

Each serving provides:

146 Calories

1	Bread Serving	3	g	Protein
1-1/2	Vegetable Servings	5	g	Fat
1	Fat Serving	23	g	Carbohydrate
		148	mg	Sodium
		0	mg	Cholesterol

Gazpacho

Gazpacho is a spicy Spanish soup that is served cold. It tastes best when made with fresh, vine-ripened tomatoes and is a cooling summer treat.

Makes 8 servings

4	cups tomato juice
1/8	teaspoon garlic powder
2	green onions, chopped
2	medium cucumbers, peeled and seeded
2	tablespoons wine vinegar
1	tablespoon plus 1 teaspoon olive oil
1/4	teaspoon Worcestershire sauce
1	teaspoon dried basil
1	teaspoon dried parsley flakes
	Salt and pepper to taste
1	cup finely chopped green pepper
1	cup finely chopped tomato
1/2	cup finely chopped onions

In a blender container, combine all ingredients, *except* chopped green pepper, tomato, and onions. Blend until smooth.

Chill several hours to blend flavors. Also chill reserved chopped vegetables.

To serve, spoon cold soup into individual serving bowls. Sprinkle reserved vegetables on top.

Each serving provides:

61 Calories

1	Vegetable Serving	2	g	Protein
1/2	Fat Serving	2	g	Fat
1/2	Fruit Serving	10	g	Carbohydate
		449	mg	Sodium
		0	mg	Cholesterol

Potato-Leek Soup

There are many ways to make this classic soup. In ours, the fat has been greatly reduced, while the flavor has actually been enhanced.

Makes 6 servings

3	tablespoons margarine
1	cup sliced leeks (white part only)
1/2	cup chopped onions
18	ounces diced, peeled potatoes
6	cups water
4	packets instant chicken-flavored broth mix
	Salt and pepper to taste
1-1/2	cups evaporated skim milk
	Dried parsley

Melt margarine in a large saucepan over medium heat. Add leeks and onions and cook until tender, about 5 minutes.

Add potatoes, water, broth mix, and salt and pepper. Reduce heat to low. Cover and simmer 20 minutes, until potatoes are tender.

Pour soup into a blender container. Blend until smooth. Return to saucepan.

Stir in milk. Cook, stirring, until heated through. Do not boil.

To serve, spoon soup into individual serving bowls and sprinkle with parsley.

Each serving provides:

194 Calories

1	Bread Serving	8	g	Protein
1/2	Vegetable Serving	7	g	Fat
1-1/2	Fat Serving	27	g	Carbohydrate
1/2	Milk Serving	892	mg	Sodium
7	Additional Calories	3	mg	Cholesterol

Chicken Corn Soup

A take-off on a traditional Pennsylvania Dutch recipe, this thick, hearty soup provides a terrific use for leftover chicken.

Makes 4 servings

1   1-pound can cream-style corn
1-1/2 cups water
1   package instant chicken-flavored broth mix
1   cup cooked noodles
4   ounces cooked chicken, shredded or cubed
       Salt and pepper to taste

In a medium saucepan, combine all ingredients. Heat over medium-low heat, stirring frequently, until soup boils.

Each serving provides:

190 Calories

1	Protein Serving	12	g	Protein
1-1/2	Bread Servings	3	g	Fat
3	Additional Calories	30	g	Carbohydrate
		627	mg	Sodium
		38	mg	Cholesterol

Salads and Salad Dressings

Hints for Salads and Dressings

The word "salad" doesn't necessarily mean low in calories or fat. In fact, salads that are heavily-laden with creamy, oily dressings can contain more fat and calories than a piece of cake or pie. Following are some useful hints for lowering the calories and fat in salads and salad dressings.

- Choose an oil that is low in saturated fat and high in polyunsaturated fat, such as safflower oil, sunflower oil, corn oil, or soybean oil. Although the calories are the same as in saturated oils, polyunsaturated oils seem to lower blood cholesterol levels.

- Recent studies show that olive oil, a monounsaturated oil, may also have a cholesterol-lowering effect. This flavorful oil is good in salad dressings that are used with vegetables. Its distinctive taste, however, does not blend as well with fruit salads.

- When a recipe calls for oil, try using half the amount and substituting water for the other half.

- Reduced-calorie mayonnaise is whipped with water and has half the amount of calories as regular mayonnaise. It works well in any salad dressing.

- Read the labels carefully on bottled dressings. Many are high in saturated fat, calories, and sodium.

- Experiment with vinegar or lemon juice and different spices on a tossed salad. (Examples: lemon peel, oregano, basil, dill weed, pepper.)

- Dijon mustard adds a delicious spark to oil and vinegar dressings.

- When a recipe calls for sour cream, substitute plain lowfat or nonfat yogurt.

- Make mayonnaise-type salads, such as cole slaw, a day ahead, using less mayonnaise than the recipe calls for. You'll be amazed at how much liquid is drawn out of the vegetables while they marinate overnight.

- If using canned fruit in a salad, always choose the variety packed in water or fruit juice.

- Mix lowfat or nonfat yogurt with unsweetened fruit juice concentrate for a flavorful dressing for fruit salad.

Chunky Greek Salad

This dish is perfect for a luncheon. Add some tuna salad and a whole grain muffin and your meal is complete.

Makes 6 servings

2	cups thinly sliced cucumbers
2	cups tomatoes, cut into chunks
1/4	cup chopped onions
6	ounces feta cheese, cut into small cubes
12	black olives, preferably Greek-style
1/4	cup vegetable oil
2	tablespoons dried oregano

Combine all ingredients in a large bowl. Toss until well blended.

Chill several hours to blend flavors.

Each serving provides:

205 Calories

1	Protein Serving	5	g	Protein
1-1/2	Vegetable Servings	18	g	Fat
2	Fat Servings	7	g	Carbohydrate
10	Additional Calories	585	mg	Sodium
		25	mg	Cholesterol

Sesame, Broccoli, and Cauliflower Salad

The sesame oil gives this salad a wonderful Oriental flavor that will spark up any meal. Try this delicious oil in other salads, too, but remember to go easy so the flavor will not be overpowering.

Makes 6 servings

1	10-ounce package frozen broccoli flowerets
1	10-ounce package frozen cauliflower
1	tablespoon plus 1 teaspoon soy sauce
1	tablespoon vegetable oil
1	tablespoon sesame oil
2	teaspoons red wine vinegar
1	tablespoon toasted sesame seeds
2	teaspoons sugar (or equivalent amount of sweetener)
	Salt and pepper to taste

Cook vegetables according to package directions, cooking until just tender-crisp. Drain.

In a small bowl, combine remaining ingredients. Pour over vegetables. Toss to coat evenly.

Chill several hours to blend flavors. Stir occasionally while chilling.

Each serving provides:

81 Calories*

1-1/3	Vegetable Servings	3	g	Protein
1	Fat Serving	6	g	Fat
10	Additional Calories	7	g	Carbohydrate
	(plus 5 more calories if	250	mg	Sodium
	sugar is used as	0	mg	Cholesterol
	sweetener)			

*If sugar is used as sweetener

Confetti Pasta Salad

Not only does it taste good, but it's so pretty and colorful. This salad is a perfect addition to your next cookout.

Makes 4 servings

2	cups cooked elbow macaroni
1/2	cup thinly sliced celery
1/4	cup finely chopped green pepper
1/4	cup finely chopped carrots
1	tablespoon chopped pimiento
1/4	cup reduced-calorie mayonnaise
1	tablespoon minced onion flakes
1/8	teaspoon dry mustard
1/2	teaspoon dill weed
1	teaspoon sugar (or equivalent amount of sweetener)
	Salt and pepper to taste

In a large bowl, combine macaroni, celery, green pepper, carrots, and pimiento.

Combine remaining ingredients, mixing well. Add to macaroni. Toss until well mixed.

Chill.

Each serving provides:

133 Calories*

1	Bread Serving	3	g	Protein
1/2	Vegetable Serving	4	g	Fat
1-1/2	Fat Servings	21	g	Carbohydrate
4	Additional Calories (if	130	mg	Sodium
	sugar is used as	5	mg	Cholesterol
	sweetener)			

*If sugar is used as sweetener

Marinated Mushrooms

Add these to a tossed salad or enjoy them alone. Either way, you're in for a real treat.

Makes 4 servings

2	cups small, fresh mushrooms, cut in half
2	tablespoons lemon juice
2	tablespoons vegetable oil
2	tablespoons water
1	tablespoon dried chives
1	teaspoon dried parsley flakes
1/4	teaspoon dried oregano
1/8	teaspoon garlic powder
1	teaspoon grated Parmesan cheese
1/8	teaspoon pepper
	Salt to taste

Combine all ingredients in a shallow bowl. Mix well.
Cover and refrigerate overnight, stirring several times.

Each serving provides:

73 Calories

1	Vegetable Serving	1	g	Protein
1-1/2	Fat Servings	7	g	Fat
3	Additional Calories	2	g	Carbohydrate
		11	mg	Sodium
		0	mg	Cholesterol

Dilled Carrots

These carrots will delight the pickle-lovers in your family.

Makes 4 servings

1	pound carrots, cut into 4-inch julienne strips
1	cup vinegar
1	cup water
2	teaspoons salt
1-1/2	teaspoons dill seed
3/4	teaspoon mustard seed
1	clove garlic, cut in half
2	tablespoons sugar (or sweetener equivalent to 6 teaspoons sugar)

Cook carrots, covered, in 1 inch of boiling water 3 to 4 minutes, until tender-crisp. Drain. Place carrots in a bowl or jar.

In a small saucepan, combine remaining ingredients. Bring to a boil over medium heat. Reduce heat to low and simmer 5 minutes.

Pour mixture over carrots.

Cover and refrigerate for 1 week.

Each serving provides:

87 Calories*

2	Vegetable Servings	2	g	Protein
24	Additional Calories (if	1	g	Fat
	sugar is used as	22	g	Carbohydrate
	sweetener)	1,141	mg	Sodium
		0	mg	Cholesterol

*If sugar is used as sweetener

Dijon Sprout Salad

This tangy recipe also works well with alfalfa sprouts in place of the bean sprouts.

Makes 4 servings

1/2	cup thinly sliced zucchini, unpeeled
1/2	cup thinly sliced cucumber
1/2	cup fresh bean sprouts
1/2	cup sliced mushrooms
2	tablespoons chopped radishes
2	tablespoons chopped carrots
2	tablespoons wine vinegar
1	tablespoon plus 1 teaspoon vegetable oil
1	tablespoon water
1	teaspoon Dijon mustard
1/8	teaspoon garlic powder

In a large bowl, combine all vegetables. Toss.

In a small bowl, combine remaining ingredients. Pour over vegetables. Toss until evenly coated.

Chill.

Each serving provides:

55 Calories

1	Vegetable Serving	1	g	Protein
1	Fat Serving	5	g	Fat
		3	g	Carbohydrate
		42	mg	Sodium
		0	mg	Cholesterol

Basil Bean Salad

Spicy and delicious, the flavor of this salad is reminiscent of the popular Italian pasta with pesto sauce.

Makes 4 servings

1	10-ounce package frozen green beans
1/2	cup very thinly sliced onions
2	tablespoons red wine vinegar
1	tablespoon plus 1 teaspoon olive oil
3	tablespoons water
1/8	teaspoon garlic powder
1	teaspoon dried basil
1	tablespoon grated Parmesan cheese
1/8	teaspoon pepper
	Salt to taste

Cook beans according to package directions, cooking until just tender-crisp. Drain.

Combine beans and onions in a large bowl.

Combine remaining ingredients and pour over beans. Toss until well blended.

Chill several hours or overnight, stirring occasionally.

Each serving provides:

78 Calories

1-1/4	Vegetable Servings	2	g	Protein
1	Fat Serving	5	g	Fat
8	Additional Calories	7	g	Carbohydrate
		26 mg		Sodium
		1 mg		Cholesterol

Spinach Salad

To feed one person or a crowd, this salad is always a hit. To feed more than one, simply multiply the ingredients by the number of people you're serving.

Makes 1 serving

1-1/2 cups fresh spinach leaves, washed and torn
5   medium, fresh mushrooms, sliced
1   hard-cooked egg, chopped
1   slice onion, broken into rings
1   teaspoon imitation bacon bits
2   teaspoons vegetable oil
1-1/2 teaspoons red wine vinegar
1/4   teaspoon dry mustard
1   teaspoon water

Place spinach on a salad plate. Top with mushrooms, egg, onion, and bacon bits.

Combine remaining ingredients in a small bowl. Pour over salad.

Enjoy!

Each serving provides:

218 Calories

1	Protein Serving	12	g	Protein
4	Vegetable Servings	16	g	Fat
2	Fat Servings	10	g	Carbohydrate
10	Additional Calories	183	mg	Sodium
		274	mg	Cholesterol

Marinated Tomato Salad

Like most salads that get their flavor from herbs, this one tastes best when made a day ahead.

Makes 4 servings

1-1/2 cups thinly sliced tomatoes
1/2   cup thinly sliced red onions
1-1/2 teaspoons dried basil
3/4   teaspoon dried tarragon
1/4   teaspoon dried oregano
1/4   cup red wine vinegar
2   tablespoons plus 2 teaspoons vegetable oil
       Salt and pepper to taste

Place tomatoes and onions in a shallow bowl, overlapping slightly.

In a small bowl, combine remaining ingredients. Pour over vegetables.

Chill several hours to blend flavors.

Each serving provides:

105 Calories

1	Vegetable Serving	1	g	Protein
2	Fat Servings	1	g	Fat
		5	g	Carbohydrate
		6	mg	Sodium
		0	mg	Cholesterol

Marinated Mozzarella

Serve with toothpicks as an hors d'oeuvre, or on a bed of lettuce. The flavor improves with age.

Makes 8 servings

8	ounces part-skim Mozzarella cheese, cut into 1/2-inch cubes
2	tablespoons plus 2 teaspoons vegetable oil
1/2	cup chopped green pepper
3	tablespoons red wine vinegar
1/2	cup water
2	teaspoons dried oregano
1/2	teaspoon dried basil
1/4	teaspoon dried thyme
1/8	teaspoon garlic powder
1/2	teaspoon sugar

Place cheese in a 1-quart jar.

Combine remaining ingredients in a small saucepan. Bring to a boil over medium heat. Remove from heat and cool 10 minutes.

Pour liquid over cheese in jar.

Refrigerate 1 to 2 weeks.

Each serving provides:

117 Calories

1	Protein Serving	7	g	Protein
1	Fat Serving	9	g	Fat
		2	g	Carbohydrate
		132	mg	Sodium
		16	mg	Cholesterol

Pickled Onions

This recipe is an old family favorite that is slightly sweet, slightly tangy, and just plain delicious.

Makes 16 servings

8	cups small white onions, peeled
9	cups boiling water
1/3	cup salt
1-1/2	tablespoons whole allspice
1-1/2	tablespoons whole white mustard seed
1-1/2	tablespoons whole peppercorns
2	tablespoons sugar (or sweetener equivalent to 6 teaspoons sugar)
2	tablespoons horseradish
2	cups white vinegar

Place peeled onions in a large bowl.

Dissolve salt in 3 cups of the boiling water and pour over onions. Cover and let stand 24 hours. Drain.

Cover with 3 more cups of boiling water. Let stand 10 minutes. Drain.

Place onions in two 1-quart jars.

In a medium saucepan combine 3 cups of water with remaining ingredients. Bring to a boil over medium heat. Boil 3 minutes. With a slotted spoon remove allspice and peppercorns.

Pour liquid over onions in jars. Cover and chill 1 to 2 weeks.

Each serving provides:

46 Calories*

1	Vegetable Serving	1	g	Protein
6	Additional Calories (if sugar is used as sweetener)	0	g	Fat
		11	g	Carbohydrate
		423	mg	Sodium
		0	mg	Cholesterol

*If sugar is used as sweetener

Carrot and Orange Salad

This delicious combination of carrots and oranges has a lively tropical flavor that you'll love. Serve it on a bed of lettuce with a scoop of lowfat cottage cheese for a cool, light summer lunch.

Makes 4 servings

3	cups finely shredded carrots
2	small oranges, peeled and sectioned
1/4	cup raisins
1/2	cup plain lowfat yogurt
1/2	teaspoon coconut extract
1/2	teaspoon vanilla extract
1	tablespoon honey

In a large bowl, combine carrots, orange sections, and raisins.

In a small bowl, combine remaining ingredients, mixing well. Spoon over carrot mixture. Toss to combine.

Chill to blend flavors. Mix occasionally while chilling.

Each serving provides:

128 Calories

1-1/2	Vegetable Servings	3	g	Protein
1	Fruit Serving	1	g	Fat
1/4	Milk Serving	29	g	Carbohydrate
15	Additional Calories	50	mg	Sodium
		2	mg	Cholesterol

Cheddar-Apple Salad

Inspired by our favorite Waldorf salad, this salad makes a tasty luncheon dish when served on a bed of lettuce with a whole grain muffin.

Makes 6 servings

4	small, sweet apples, unpeeled, diced
2	tablespoons lemon juice
1-1/2	cups diced celery
1	cup canned pineapple chunks (unsweetened), drained
6	ounces lowfat Cheddar cheese, cut into 1/2-inch cubes
1-1/2	ounces chopped walnuts
1/2	cup reduced-calorie mayonnaise
1/2	cup plain lowfat yogurt
1	tablespoon plus 1 teaspoon sugar (or sweetener equivalent to 4 teaspoons sugar)

Sprinkle the lemon juice over the apple cubes. Toss.

Add celery, pineapple, cheese, and walnuts. Toss gently, but thoroughly.

In a small bowl, combine remaining ingredients and mix well. Add to the apple mixture, mixing well.

Chill several hours to blend flavors.

Each serving provides:

265 Calories*

1	Protein Serving	8	g	Protein
1/2	Vegetable Serving	14	g	Fat
2	Fat Servings	31	g	Carbohydrate
1	Fruit Serving	280	mg	Sodium
63	Additional Calories	16	mg	Cholesterol
	(plus 11 more calories if sugar is used as sweetener)			

*If sugar is used as sweetener

Cranberry Raisin Relish

When cranberries are available, buy several extra bags and keep them in the freezer so you can enjoy this holiday treat all year round.

Makes 8 servings

3/4   cup raisins
1/2   cup orange juice (unsweetened)
1/3   cup water
1/4   cup sugar (or sweetener equivalent to 12 teaspoons sugar)
1   tablespoon lemon juice
1   cup cranberries
1   teaspoon grated orange peel

In a small saucepan, combine raisins, orange juice, water, sweetener, and lemon juice. (If using NutraSweet as sweetener, it should be added *after* cooking.)

Bring to a boil over medium-high heat.

Reduce heat to low. Simmer 5 minutes.

Add cranberries and orange peel. Cook until cranberry skins pop. Then simmer 20 minutes, stirring frequently.

Chill.

Each serving provides:

79 Calories*

1	Fruit Serving	1	g	Protein
24	Additional Calories (if sugar is used as sweetener)	0	g	Fat
		21	g	Carbohydrate
		2	mg	Sodium
		0	mg	Cholesterol

*If sugar is used as sweetener

Tropical Fruit Salad

Cool and refreshing, this salad can be made with a variety of fruits. Use whatever is in season.

Makes 4 servings

1/2	cup fresh strawberries, cut in half
1/2	cup melon balls
1/2	cup canned pineapple chunks (unsweetened)
1/2	cup grapes, cut in half
1/2	cup orange juice (unsweetened)
1	teaspoon rum extract
1	teaspoon coconut extract
2	teaspoons honey

Combine all ingredients in a bowl. Mix well.
Chill several hours to blend flavors, stirring occasionally.

Each serving provides:

76 Calories

1	Fruit Serving	1	g	Protein
20	Additional Calories	0	g	Fat
		18	g	Carbohydrate
		3	mg	Sodium
		0	mg	Cholesterol

Caribbean Rice and Fruit

This elegant, low-calorie rice salad is reminiscent of a tropical island. Serve it as an appetizer, a dessert, or as a brand new breakfast idea.

Makes 4 servings

1	cup plain lowfat yogurt
3	tablespoons sugar (or sweetener equivalent to 9 teaspoons sugar)
1/4	teaspoon coconut extract
1	teaspoon vanilla extract
1	cup cooked brown rice
1/2	cup canned crushed pineapple (unsweetened), drained
2	tablespoons juice from pineapple
1	medium, ripe banana, sliced
1	small orange, peeled and sectioned

In a large bowl, combine yogurt, sugar, and extracts. Mix well.
Add remaining ingredients. Toss until well blended.
Chill.
Toss before serving.

Each serving provides:

198 Calories*

1/2	Bread Serving	5	g	Protein
1	Fruit Serving	1	g	Fat
1/2	Milk Serving	43	g	Carbohydrate
36	Additional Calories (if sugar is used as sweetener)	40	mg	Sodium
		3	mg	Cholesterol

*If sugar is used as sweetener

Lemon Rice Salad

Slightly sweet, this versatile salad goes with almost any entree. It looks great on a buffet table, too.

Makes 8 servings

4	cups cooked rice
2	small apples, unpeeled, diced into 1/4-inch pieces
1/4	cup raisins
1	cup finely diced zucchini, unpeeled
2	tablespoons plus 2 teaspoons vegetable oil
2	tablespoons lemon juice
1/2	teaspoon ground cinnamon
2	teaspoons sugar (or equivalent amount of sweetener)

In a large bowl, combine rice, apples, raisins, and zucchini. Toss to blend.

In a small bowl, combine remaining ingredients. Pour over rice mixture. Mix well.

Chill overnight to blend flavors.

Each serving provides:

188 Calories*

1	Bread Serving	2	g	Protein
1/4	Vegetable Serving	5	g	Fat
1	Fat Serving	34	g	Carbohydrate
1/2	Fruit Serving	2	mg	Sodium
4	Additional Calories (if sugar is used as sweetener)	0	mg	Cholesterol

*If sugar is used as sweetener

Strawberry-Apple Mold

Quick, easy, and unusually tasty, this salad's flavor boost comes from the cinnamon.

Makes 4 servings

1   package sugar-free strawberry-flavored gelatin
1/4   teaspoon ground cinnamon
2   small apples, unpeeled, coarsely shredded

Prepare gelatin according to package directions. Stir in cinnamon.
Chill until slightly thickened.
Stir in apples. Pour mixture into a small bowl.
Chill until firm.

Each serving provides:

39 Calories

1/2	Fruit Serving	1	g	Protein
8	Additional Calories	0	g	Fat
		8	g	Carbohydrate
		60	mg	Sodium
		0	mg	Cholesterol

Cranberry Party Mold

This is a salad that is slightly tart, slightly sweet, crunchy, and delicious. It's great for parties, but also good for no particular occasion at all.

Makes 8 servings

2	packages sugar-free raspberry-flavored gelatin
1	cup plain lowfat yogurt
3	cups fresh cranberries
1/2	cup sugar (or sweetener equivalent to 24 teaspoons sugar)
1-1/2	cups canned crushed pineapple (unsweetened), drained
1/2	cup finely chopped celery
1	ounce chopped walnuts
2	small apples, unpeeled, chopped into 1/4-inch pieces

Prepare gelatin according to package directions. Add yogurt. Stir until blended. Chill until slightly thickened.

Place cranberries and sweetener in a blender container. Blend until berries are chopped.

Add cranberries and remaining ingredients to thickened gelatin. Spoon into a large bowl. Chill until firm.

(If you wish to make this salad in a mold, use 1/2 cup *less* water than the directions call for.)

Each serving provides:

194 Calories*

1/8	Vegetable Serving	3	g	Protein
1	Fruit Serving	3	g	Fat
1/4	Milk Serving	32	g	Carbohydrate
24	Additional Calories (if	88	mg	Sodium
	sugar is used as	2	mg	Cholesterol
	sweetener)			

*If sugar is used as sweetener

Orange-Pineapple-Carrot Mold

This quick, easy salad can also double as a nutritious dessert.

Makes 4 servings

1   package sugar-free orange-flavored gelatin
1   cup coarsely shredded carrots
1   cup canned crushed pineapple (unsweetened), drained

Prepare gelatin according to package directions. Chill until gelatin is syrupy.

Stir remaining ingredients into gelatin. Pour into a small bowl or mold. Chill until firm.

Each serving provides:

57 Calories

1/2	Vegetable Serving	2	g	Protein
1/2	Fruit Serving	0	g	Fat
8	Additional Calories	13	g	Carbohydrate
		70	mg	Sodium
		0	mg	Cholesterol

Banana Mold

The riper the bananas, the sweeter this mold will be.

Makes 6 servings

2	envelopes unflavored gelatin
1-1/2	cups water
3	medium, ripe bananas
1	teaspoon lemon juice
1-1/2	cups plain lowfat yogurt
1/4	teaspoon banana extract
1	teaspoon vanilla butternut flavor
1/4	cup sugar (or sweetener equivalent to 12 teaspoons sugar)
1/2	cup cold water
1	cup non-dairy whipped topping

Sprinkle gelatin over water in a medium saucepan. Let soften a few minutes. Heat, stirring frequently, over low heat, until gelatin is completely dissolved. Remove from heat.

Mash bananas with lemon juice.

Add bananas, yogurt, extracts, sweetener, and water. Beat on low speed of an electric mixer until blended. Chill until slightly thickened.

Fold whipped topping into thickened mixture. Spoon into a large serving bowl. Chill until firm.

Each serving provides:

156 Calories*

1	Fruit Serving	6	g	Protein
1/2	Milk Serving	3	g	Fat
34	Additional Calories (if	28	g	Carbohydrate
	sugar is used as	51	mg	Sodium
	sweetener)	5	mg	Cholesterol

*If sugar is used as sweetener

Number 1 Dressing

This recipe got its name from the proportions of each ingredient. It can be made in any quantity. Simply multiply 1 by the number of servings desired. It's quick and easy and enhances the flavor of any mixed salad.

Makes 1 serving
(1-1/2 tablespoons each serving)

1   teaspoon vegetable oil
1   teaspoon wine vinegar
1   teaspoon water
1   teaspoon Dijon mustard
1   teaspoon plain lowfat yogurt
1   dash garlic powder

In a small bowl, combine all ingredients, stirring until blended. Serve right away or chill for a later serving.

Each serving provides:

50 Calories

1	Fat Serving	0	g	Protein
4	Additional Calories	5	g	Fat
		1	g	Carbohydrate
		153	mg	Sodium
		0	mg	Cholesterol

Thousand Island Dressing

For a variation, try adding imitation bacon bits to this classic favorite. The result is a creamy bacon-tomato dressing.

Makes 4 servings
(2 tablespoons each serving)

1/4	cup reduced-calorie mayonnaise
3	tablespoons ketchup
1/8	teaspoon garlic powder
1	teaspoon lemon juice
1	tablespoon sweet pickle relish

In a small bowl, combine all ingredients, stirring until blended. Chill to blend flavors.

Each serving provides:

60 Calories

1-1/2 Fat Servings
19 Additional Calories

0 g Protein
4 g Fat
6 g Carbohydrate
273 mg Sodium
5 mg Cholesterol

French Tomato Dressing

This recipe was borrowed from my mother. It's the one her guests always ask for. When you try it, you'll see why.

Makes 6 servings
(2 tablespoons each serving)

1/2	cup tomato juice
2	tablespoons vegetable oil
2	tablespoons reduced-calorie mayonnaise
1/4	teaspoon salt
1/4	teaspoon pepper
1	teaspoon Dijon mustard
1/2	teaspoon Worcestershire sauce
1/2	teaspoon dried oregano
1/4	teaspoon dried basil
1	teaspoon sugar (or equivalent amount of sweetener)

In a small bowl, combine all ingredients. Beat with a fork or wire whisk until smooth.

Chill to blend flavors.

Each serving provides:

62 Calories*

1-1/2	Fat Servings	0	g	Protein
4	Additional Calories (if	6	g	Fat
	sugar is used as	2	g	Carbohydrate
	sweetener)	230	mg	Sodium
		2	mg	Cholesterol

*If sugar is used as sweetener

Classic Italian Dressing

We've lowered the calories in this all-time favorite by replacing some of the oil with water. We always make a lot because it keeps well in the refrigerator and the flavor seems to increase.

Makes 12 servings
(1-1/2 tablespoons each serving)

1/4	cup red wine vinegar
1/4	cup water
1/2	cup vegetable oil
2	teaspoons minced onion flakes
1	teaspoon dried oregano
1/2	teaspoon dried basil
1/2	teaspoon dry mustard
2	teaspoons grated Parmesan cheese
1	teaspoon sugar (or equivalent amount of sweetener)
	Salt and pepper to taste

Combine all ingredients in a jar. Shake well.
Chill to blend flavors.

Each serving provides:

85 Calories*

2	Fat Servings	0	g	Protein
2	Additional Calories (if	9	g	Fat
	sugar is used as	1	g	Carbohydrate
	sweetener)	5	mg	Sodium
		0	mg	Cholesterol

*If sugar is used as sweetener.

Zesty Tomato Dressing

To lower the amount of sodium in this dressing, choose the low-salt variety of tomato sauce and reduce the amount of Worcestershire sauce to 1/2 teaspoon.

Makes 8 servings
(2 tablespoons each serving)

1	8-ounce can tomato sauce
2	tablespoons wine vinegar
1	teaspoon Worcestershire sauce
1/2	teaspoon dill weed
1/2	teaspoon dried oregano
1/2	teaspoon dried basil
1/2	teaspoon onion powder
1/8	teaspoon pepper

In a small bowl, combine all ingredients. Beat with a fork or wire whisk until smooth.

Chill to blend flavors.

Each serving provides:

11 Calories

6	Additional Calories	0	g	Protein
		0	g	Fat
		3	g	Carbohydrate
		179	mg	Sodium
		0	mg	Cholesterol

Chili Dressing

*In addition to topping mixed salads, try serving this tasty dressing as a
dipping sauce for steamed shrimp.*

*Makes 4 servings
(2 tablespoons each serving)*

1/4	cup reduced-calorie mayonnaise
1/4	cup chili sauce
1	tablespoon capers
1	teaspoon prepared mustard
1/8	teaspoon garlic powder
1	tablespoon minced onion flakes

In a small bowl, combine all ingredients, mixing until well
blended.

Chill to blend flavors.

Each serving provides:

62 Calories

1-1/2	Fat Servings	1	g	Protein
16	Additional Calories	4	g	Fat
		6	g	Carbohydrate
		412	mg	Sodium
		5	mg	Cholesterol

Herb Mayonnaise

More than just a dressing, this sauce has many uses. Try it on a turkey sandwich or on a pita bread filled with cheese and alfalfa sprouts. It's also great to keep in the refrigerator for Thanksgiving leftovers.

Makes 16 servings
(1 tablespoon each serving)

1   cup reduced-calorie mayonnaise
2-1/2 teaspoons fines herbes*

In a small bowl, combine mayonnaise and fines herbes. Chill several hours to blend flavors.

*Fines herbes is a pre-blended mixture of spices. If not available, create your own by using 1/2 teaspoon *each* of dried thyme, oregano, sage, rosemary, marjoram, and basil.

Each serving provides:

41 Calories

1-1/2 Fat Servings

0	g	Protein
4	g	Fat
1	g	Carbohydrate
112	mg	Sodium
5	mg	Cholesterol

French Honey Mustard

This versatile, tangy dressing is a great flavor-enhancer for sandwiches as well as salads.

Makes 12 servings
(1 tablespoon each serving)

1/2   cup Dijon mustard
1/4   cup honey

In a small bowl, combine mustard and honey.
Chill several hours to blend flavors.

Each serving provides:

53 Calories

17	Additional Calories	0	g	Protein
		1	g	Fat
		7	g	Carbohydrate
		297	mg	Sodium
		0	mg	Cholesterol

Orange-Peanut Dressing

This delicious dressing keeps well in the refrigerator and makes a wonderful after-school treat when spooned over cut-up fruits or vegetables. If chilling makes it too thick, just stir in a little water or a little more orange juice.

Makes 8 servings
(1-1/2 tablespoons each serving)

1/4	cup peanut butter
1/2	cup orange juice (unsweetened)
1	tablespoon lemon juice
1/2	teaspoon ground cinnamon

In a small bowl, gradually stir orange juice into peanut butter. Add remaining ingredients. Stir until smooth.
Spoon over fresh fruit salad.

Each serving provides:

55 Calories

1/2	Protein Serving	2	g	Protein
1/2	Fat Serving	4	g	Fat
8	Additional Calories	3	g	Carbohydrate
		38	mg	Sodium
		0	mg	Cholesterol

Eggs and Cheese

Hints for Eggs and Cheese

The following hints will help you to adapt your own favorite egg and cheese recipes and lower their calories, fat content, and cholesterol. Included are ideas for other dairy products as well.

- To lower the cholesterol content of a recipe, use an egg substitute in place of the eggs, or replace each whole egg with 2 egg whites. (The cholesterol is in the yolk.)
- Use lowfat cottage cheese (1%) in recipes calling for cottage cheese.
- Use part-skim ricotta in place of whole milk ricotta cheese.
- Look for the new lowfat versions of other cheeses, such as Swiss, Cheddar, and Mozzarella.
- If a recipe calls for Parmesan cheese, and you love the distinctive taste, try using only 1/3 or 1/4 of the amount called for. The strong flavor goes a long way.
- Try Sapsago, a lowfat cheese that, when grated, has a taste very much like Parmesan cheese.
- If you are using Cheddar cheese in a recipe, try using half the amount called for. Use part-skim Mozzarella cheese for the other half. You'll love the results.
- Use plain lowfat or nonfat yogurt in place of sour cream.
- Replace cream in a recipe with evaporated skim milk.
- Use skim milk in place of whole milk.
- Read the labels carefully when using non-dairy substitutes such as whipped topping or coffee creamers. They often contain coconut oil or palm kernel oil, both of which are very high in saturated fat.
- Use margarine in place of butter. The calories are the same, but butter is high in both saturated fat and cholesterol. Your best bet is a margarine that lists either liquid safflower oil or corn oil as its main ingredient.
- Reduced-calorie margarines are generally whipped with water. These tub-style margarines have fewer calories per serving and work well for spreading on bread, sautéing vegetables, or for use in sauces. In cakes and cookies, however, their high water content may alter the texture of the recipe.

Eggs Suzette with Strawberry Sauce

This fancy dish makes a wonderful company breakfast. And it's so easy.

Makes 4 servings

4	eggs
2	teaspoons vanilla extract
1	tablespoon sugar (or sweetener equivalent to 3 teaspoons)
1/2	teaspoon ground cinnamon

Strawberry Sauce

1	tablespoon cornstarch
1/2	cup water
2	tablespoons reduced-calorie strawberry spread (8 calories per teaspoon)
1	tablespoon sugar (or sweetener equivalent to 3 teaspoons)

Combine sauce ingredients in a small saucepan. Set aside. (If using NutraSweet as sweetener, add it after sauce is cooked.)

Beat each egg separately with 1/2 teaspoon of the vanilla.

Cook eggs one at a time by placing in a small nonstick skillet over medium heat. Spray skillet with a nonstick cooking spray before preparing each egg. Tilt pan back and forth so that the egg is evenly distributed and forms a thin pancake. Cook until set. Do not turn.

As each egg is finished, slide it onto a serving plate.

Combine the sugar and cinnamon and sprinkle evenly over the eggs. Fold each egg into quarters. Cover and keep warm.

Stir sauce ingredients to dissolve cornstarch. Bring to a boil over medium heat, stirring constantly. Boil 1 minute, stirring. Spoon over eggs.

Each serving provides:

130 Calories

1	Protein Serving	6	g	Protein
20	Additional Calories	6	g	Fat
	(plus 24 more calories if	13	g	Carbohydrate
	sugar is used as	69	mg	Sodium
	sweetener)	274	mg	Cholesterol

*If sugar is used as sweetener

Apple Strudel Omelet

This recipe turns an ordinary egg into an elegant dish. For more servings, just increase the amounts of each ingredient according to the number of servings needed.

Makes 1 serving

1/4   cup applesauce (unsweetened)
2   teaspoons reduced-calorie orange marmalade (8 calories per teaspoon)
1/4   teaspoon coconut extract
1/4   teaspoon ground cinnamon
1   teaspoon sugar (or equivalent amount of sweetener)
1   egg, beaten

Topping
1/4   teaspoon ground cinnamon
1   teaspoon sugar (or equivalent amount of sweetener)

Combine applesauce, marmalade, coconut extract, cinnamon, and sugar. Set aside.

Place egg in a small nonstick skillet over medium heat. Tilt pan back and forth so that egg is evenly distributed and forms a thin pancake. When egg is set, slide it gently onto serving place. Do not turn.

Spread applesauce mixture evenly over egg. Roll like a jelly roll.

Combine remaining cinnamon and sugar and sprinkle over egg.

Each serving provides:

158 Calories*

1	Protein Serving	6 g	Protein
1/2	Fruit Serving	6 g	Fat
16	Additional Calories	21 g	Carbohydrate
	(plus 32 more calories if	71 mg	Sodium
	sugar is used as	274 mg	Cholesterol
	sweetener)		

*If sugar is used as sweetener

Pennsylvania Dutch Apple Spoon Omelet

This recipe can be increased to serve as many people as you like. It works best in individual bowls and makes an interesting and unique brunch dish.

Makes 2 servings

2	eggs
1/2	cup applesauce (unsweetened)
1	teaspoon vanilla extract
1/4	teaspoon almond extract
1/4	teaspoon ground cinnamon
1	tablespoon plus 1 teaspoon sugar (or sweetener equivalent to 4 teaspoons sugar)

Preheat oven to 350°.

Combine all ingredients in a small bowl. Beat with a fork or wire whisk until blended.

Pour mixture into a small baking dish or oven-proof bowl that has been sprayed with a nonstick cooking spray.

Bake, uncovered, 35 minutes.

Each serving provides:

147 Calories*

1	Protein Serving	6	g	Protein
1/2	Fruit Serving	6	g	Fat
32	Additional Calories (if	17	g	Carbohydrate
	sugar is used as	70	mg	Sodium
	sweetener)	274	mg	Cholesterol

*If sugar is used as sweetener

Deviled Eggs 'n Dill

For a crowd, these can't be beat. Garnish with a few sprigs of fresh dill for a festive and aromatic touch.

Makes 9 servings

9   hard-cooked eggs
3   tablespoons reduced-calorie mayonnaise
1   packet instant chicken-flavored broth mix
1   tablespoon finely minced onion
1   teaspoon dill weed

Cut eggs in half, lengthwise. Carefully remove yolks and place in a bowl.
Add remaining ingredients to yolks. Mix well.
Carefully stuff mixture into whites, mounding it slightly.
Chill.

Each serving provides:

95 Calories

1	Protein Serving	6	g	Protein
1/2	Fat Serving	7	g	Fat
1	Additional Calorie	1	g	Carbohydrate
		231	mg	Sodium
		276	mg	Cholesterol

Egg Casserole

This casserole is so unusual and so delicious. Serve it over cooked brown rice for a meal that's high in protein, high in fiber, and so inexpensive.

Makes 4 servings

2   tablespoons plus 2 teaspoons reduced-calorie margarine
3   tablespoons all-purpose flour
1/3   cup nonfat dry milk
3/4   cup water
1   packet instant chicken-flavored broth mix
2   teaspoons imitation bacon bits
1/2   teaspoon dill weed
       Pepper to taste
2   tablespoons finely chopped onions
4   hard-cooked eggs, chopped

Preheat oven to 350°.

In a medium saucepan, melt margarine over medium heat. Stir in flour.

Slowly stir in milk. Bring mixture to a boil, stirring constantly. Continue to boil and stir for 1 minute. Remove from heat.

Add remaining ingredients, mixing well.

Pour into a 1-quart baking dish that has been sprayed with a nonstick cooking spray.

Bake, uncovered, 30 minutes, until hot and bubbly.

Each serving provides:

165 Calories

1	Protein Serving	9	g	Protein
1/4	Bread Serving	10	g	Fat
1	Fat Serving	9	g	Carbohydrate
1/4	Milk Serving	481	mg	Sodium
8	Additional Calories	275	mg	Cholesterol

Eggs in Tomato Cups

Colorful and delicious, these eggs are good for breakfast, lunch, or dinner.

Makes 4 servings

4   medium tomatoes
4   eggs
3   tablespoons dry bread crumbs
2   tablespoons grated Parmesan cheese
1-1/2 teaspoons dried parsley flakes
1/8   teaspoon pepper
1/4   teaspoon dried oregano
         Salt to taste

Preheat oven to 425°.

Cut a slice from the stem end of each tomato. Scoop out pulp carefully with a spoon. (Save pulp for use in a salad.)

Place tomatoes, cut-side up, in a small, shallow baking pan that has been sprayed with a nonstick cooking spray.

Crack an egg into each tomato.

In a small bowl, combine remaining ingredients then sprinkle evenly over eggs.

Bake 15 to 20 minutes, until eggs are set.

Each serving provides:

121 Calories

1	Protein Serving	8	g	Protein
1/4	Bread Serving	7	g	Fat
1	Vegetable Serving	7	g	Carbohydrate
15	Additional Calories	155	mg	Sodium
		276	mg	Cholesterol

Egg Foo Yung

For an Oriental treat, and a dinner your family will love, serve this dish over cooked brown rice, with steamed broccoli. Spoon a little of the sauce over the broccoli.

Makes 4 servings

Sauce

1	packet instant chicken-flavored broth mix
3/4	cup water
1	tablespoon cornstarch
1	tablespoon soy sauce

Pancakes

4	eggs, beaten
8	ounces cooked, diced shrimp or chicken
1-1/2	cups bean sprouts, fresh or canned
1/2	cup sliced mushrooms
1	tablespoon minced onion flakes
2	tablespoons sliced green onions

In a small saucepan, combine sauce ingredients. Stir until blended. Bring mixture to a boil over medium heat, stirring constantly. Cook 2 minutes, stirring, until mixture is thick and clear. Cover and remove from heat.

In a medium bowl, combine eggs with remaining pancake ingredients.

Heat a small nonstick skillet over medium heat. Spray with a nonstick cooking spray. Pour egg mixture, 1 cup at a time, into skillet. Cook until brown on both sides, turning carefully.

Serve with sauce.

Each serving provides:

166 Calories

3	Protein Servings	20	g	Protein
1	Vegetable Serving	6	g	Fat
10	Additional Calories	7	g	Carbohydrate
		735	mg	Sodium
		385	mg	Cholesterol

Huevos Rancheros (Cowboy Eggs)

This is our low-fat version of an old-time favorite. We've taken out some of the oil and cheese and added the whole wheat toast for fiber.

Makes 8 servings

1	tablespoon plus 1 teaspoon vegetable oil
1	clove garlic, crushed
1	cup chopped onions
1	cup chopped green pepper
1	cup peeled, chopped fresh tomatoes
1/4	teaspoon salt
1/4	teaspoon pepper
2	teaspoons chili powder
1/4	teaspoon dried oregano
1/8	teaspoon ground cumin
1	8-ounce can tomato sauce
8	eggs
8	slices thin-sliced whole wheat bread (40 calories per slice), toasted
3	tablespoons grated Parmesan cheese

In a large nonstick skillet, heat oil over medium-high heat. Add garlic, onions, and green pepper. Cook until soft.

Add tomatoes, spices, and tomato sauce. Cover, reduce heat to low, and simmer until slightly thickened, about 20 minutes.

Crack eggs gently into sauce, cover and poach until eggs are cooked as desired. Spoon sauce over eggs from time to time while cooking.

To serve, scoop eggs out of skillet onto toast. Sprinkle with Parmesan cheese.

Each serving provides:

161 Calories

1	Protein Serving	9	g	Protein
1/2	Bread Serving	9	g	Fat
1-1/4	Vegetable Servings	12	g	Carbohydrate
1/2	Fat Serving	463	mg	Sodium
11	Additional Calories	276	mg	Cholesterol

Italian Frittata

This easy, inexpensive dish can be served for breakfast, lunch, or dinner. It also works well with other vegetable combinations, so you can customize it to your own taste.

Makes 8 servings

2	tablespoons plus 2 teaspoons reduced-calorie margarine
1/2	cup chopped onions
1/2	cup chopped green pepper
1	1-pound can tomatoes, drained and chopped
1	cup broccoli, cut into flowerets
1	cup zucchini, cut into 1-inch chunks
1	4-ounce can mushroom pieces, drained (or 1/2 pound fresh mushrooms, sliced)
1/8	teaspoon garlic powder
1	teaspoon dried oregano
	Salt and pepper to taste
8	eggs
1/2	cup plain lowfat yogurt
3	tablespoons grated Parmesan cheese

Preheat oven to 375°.

Melt margarine in a heavy ovenproof skillet over medium heat. Add onions, green pepper, tomatoes, broccoli, zucchini, and mushrooms. Cook until vegetables are tender, adding small amounts of water if necessary, to prevent drying.

Stir in garlic powder, oregano, and salt and pepper.

In a medium bowl, combine eggs, yogurt, and *half* of the Parmesan cheese. Sprinkle with remaining Parmesan cheese.

Heat over low heat for 3 minutes.

Place skillet in oven. Bake 20 minutes, until eggs are set.

Cut into pie-shaped wedges to serve.

Each serving provides:

138 Calories

1	Protein Serving	9	g	Protein
1-1/4	Vegetable Servings	9	g	Fat
1/2	Fat Serving	6	g	Carbohydrate
23	Additional Calories	293	mg	Sodium
		276	mg	Cholesterol

Almost Eggs Benedict

Our luscious version of this popular dish uses lowfat Cheddar cheese for flavor. We've also eliminated the butter that's usually called for in the traditional recipe.

Makes 2 servings

2	ounces shredded lowfat Cheddar cheese
2/3	cup nonfat dry milk
1/2	cup water
1/4	teaspoon dry mustard
1	tablespoon imitation bacon bits
1	English muffin, split, toasted
2	eggs, poached

In the top of a double boiler, over boiling water, combine cheese, dry milk, water, and mustard. Cook, stirring, until cheese is melted.

Sprinkle bacon bits evenly on English muffin halves. Top each half with a poached egg. Spoon sauce over eggs.

Each serving provides:

312 Calories

2	Protein Servings	23	g	Protein
1	Bread Serving	11	g	Fat
1	Milk Serving	33	g	Carbohydrate
15	Additional Calories	569	mg	Sodium
		285	mg	Cholesterol

Cottage Cheese Dijon

For a change-of-pace lunch, you'll love this tangy cheese blend in a pita bread with lettuce and tomato.

Makes 2 servings

1-1/3 cups lowfat cottage cheese
1/2   medium cucumber, peeled, seeded, and diced
1/4   cup shredded carrot
1/4   cup shredded zucchini, unpeeled
2   teaspoons minced onion flakes, reconstituted in a small
         amount of water
1   teaspoon Dijon mustard
1/4   teaspoon Worcestershire sauce

Combine all ingredients. Mix well.
Chill to blend flavors.

Each serving provides:

131 Calories

2	Protein Servings	19	g	Protein
1	Vegetable Serving	2	g	Fat
		9	g	Carbohydrate
		700	mg	Sodium
		6	mg	Cholesterol

Creamy Spinach 'n Cheese

For a quick, nutritious lunch or dinner, spoon this creamy dish over rice or a baked potato.

Makes 4 servings

2	tablespoons plus 2 teaspoons reduced-calorie margarine
1/2	cup skim milk
1/8	teaspoon ground nutmeg
1/2	teaspoon onion powder
	Salt and pepper to taste
3	ounces shredded Muenster cheese
1	ounce grated Parmesan cheese
2	10-ounce packages frozen, chopped spinach, thawed and drained

In a medium saucepan, combine all ingredients, *except* spinach. Heat over medium heat, stirring, until cheese is melted.

Reduce heat to low.

Stir in spinach. Heat, stirring, until spinach is heated through.

Each serving provides:

190 Calories

1	Protein Serving	13	g	Protein
2	Vegetable Servings	13	g	Fat
1	Fat Serving	8	g	Carbohydrate
13	Additional Calories	467	mg	Sodium
		27	mg	Cholesterol

Welsh Rarebit

This recipe brings back memories of childhood. It's a lunch that children love.

Makes 2 servings

4	ounces shredded lowfat Cheddar cheese
1/3	cup nonfat dry milk
1/4	cup water
1/4	teaspoon dry mustard
1	teaspoon Worcestershire sauce
	Dash pepper
2	slices whole wheat or rye bread, toasted

Combine all ingredients, *except* toast, in the top of a double boiler over boiling water.

Cook, stirring, until cheese is melted and mixture is hot.

Spoon over toast.

Each serving provides:

242 Calories

2	Protein Servings	17	g	Protein
1	Bread Serving	9	g	Fat
1/2	Milk Serving	30	g	Carbohydrate
		386	mg	Sodium
		19	mg	Cholesterol

"Almost" Lasagna

In place of noodles, we've used thinly-sliced zucchini. The result is colorful and fun!

Makes 6 servings

4   cups zucchini, unpeeled, sliced 1/8-inch thick
1-1/4 cups part-skim ricotta cheese
6   ounces part-skim Mozzarella cheese, shredded
1   ounce grated Parmesan cheese
1   8-ounce can tomato sauce
1/8   teaspoon garlic powder
1   teaspoon dried oregano
1/2   teaspoon dried basil

Preheat oven to 350°.

Steam zucchini over boiling water until tender-crisp, about 5 minutes. Drain.

In a medium bowl, combine ricotta, Mozzarella, and Parmesan cheese, reserving 1 tablespoon of the Parmesan cheese for topping.

In a small bowl, combine tomato sauce, garlic powder, oregano, and basil.

Place a small amount of sauce in an 8-inch square baking pan that has been sprayed with a nonstick cooking spray. Top with a layer of zucchini, then dot with a layer of cheese.

Add a layer of sauce, then more zucchini, and remaining cheese.

Top with remaining zucchini, then remaining sauce.

Press mixture down gently with the back of a spoon.

Sprinkle with remaining Parmesan cheese.

Bake 30 minutes. Let stand 10 minutes before serving.

Each serving provides:

189 Calories

2	Protein Servings	16	g	Protein
2	Vegetable Servings	10	g	Fat
		9	g	Carbohydrate
		516	mg	Sodium
		36	mg	Cholesterol

Macaroni Verde

Although this recipe will work with any type of cooked pasta or noodles, for added fiber and nutrition choose a whole wheat pasta.

Makes 6 servings

1	tablespoon vegetable oil
1	10-ounce package frozen chopped spinach, thawed but *not* drained
1/4	teaspoon garlic powder
1/8	teaspoon pepper
2/3	cup lowfat cottage cheese
1	ounce grated Parmesan cheese
1/2	teaspoon dried basil
3	cups cooked macaroni

In a blender container, combine all ingredients, *except* macaroni. Blend until smooth. Pour into a medium saucepan.

Heat over medium-low heat until mixture is hot, stirring constantly. Remove from heat.

Add macaroni and stir until coated.

Each serving provides:

150 Calories

1/2	Protein Serving	9	g	Protein
1	Bread Serving	4	g	Fat
1/2	Vegetable Serving	19	g	Carbohydrate
1/2	Fat Serving	226	mg	Sodium
		5	mg	Cholesterol

Cheesy Noodles Almondine

The toasted almonds add an elegant touch and a wonderful crunch to this otherwise simple dish. Serve as a side dish for dinner or with a tossed salad for an appealing lunch.

Makes 6 servings

1-1/3 cups lowfat cottage cheese
1   ounce coarsely chopped toasted almonds
3   tablespoons margarine
2   ounces grated Parmesan cheese
3   cups cooked noodles
2   teaspoons dried parsley flakes

In a medium saucepan, combine cottage cheese, almonds, margarine, and Parmesan cheese. Heat through, stirring.

Add noodles. Gently stir and continue to heat until hot and bubbly.

Place noodles in a serving bowl and sprinkle with parsley.

Each serving provides:

258 Calories

1	Protein Serving	14 g	Protein
1	Bread Serving	13 g	Fat
1-1/2	Fat Servings	22 g	Carbohydrate
28	Additional Calories	448 mg	Sodium
		34 mg	Cholesterol

Potato-Cheese Casserole

This casserole is almost a meal in itself. Just add a vegetable, such as steamed broccoli or asparagus, for a colorful and nutritious dinner.

Makes 4 servings

4	eggs
1-1/3	cups lowfat cottage cheese
12	ounces cooked potatoes, peeled and mashed
2/3	cup nonfat dry milk
1/2	cup water
2	tablespoons minced onion flakes
3/4	teaspoon salt
1/4	teaspoon pepper
2	tablespoons plus 2 teaspoons reduced-calorie margarine

Preheat oven to 350°.

In a large bowl, beat eggs on medium speed of an electric mixer until frothy. Add remaining ingredients and blend well. Beat on high speed 1 minute.

Pour mixture into a casserole that has been sprayed with a non-stick cooking spray.

Bake, uncovered, 45 minutes.

Each serving provides:

286 Calories

2	Protein Servings	21	g	Protein
1	Bread Serving	10	g	Fat
1	Fat Serving	27	g	Carbohydrate
1/2	Milk Serving	933	mg	Sodium
		279	mg	Cholesterol

Cheese Pie with Potato Crust

Once you've tried this, you'll make it over and over again. It freezes well, so make an extra one!

Makes 4 servings

12   ounces coarsely shredded, unpeeled, baking potatoes
2/3   cup nonfat dry milk
1-1/3   cups lowfat cottage cheese
4   eggs, slightly beaten
4   ounces shredded lowfat Cheddar cheese
1   tablespoon minced onion flakes
1/8   teaspoon garlic powder
1   tablespoon all-purpose flour
1   tablespoon dried parsley flakes

Preheat oven to 350°.

Arrange shredded potato in the bottom and sides of a 10-inch pie pan that has been sprayed with a nonstick cooking spray, forming a crust.

Sprinkle dry milk evenly over potatoes.

Combine remaining ingredients in a bowl and mix with a fork or wire whisk until blended. (Mixture will be lumpy.) Spread evenly over potatoes.

Bake 35 to 40 minutes, until set.

Cool 5 minutes before serving.

Each serving provides:

318 Calories

3	Protein Servings	27	g	Protein
1	Bread Serving	11	g	Fat
1/2	Milk Serving	31	g	Carbohydrate
8	Additional Calories	531	mg	Sodium
		287	mg	Cholesterol

Cheese and Mushroom Pie

This dish is definitely party fare. The combination of garlic and rosemary is wonderful!

Makes 6 servings

Crust
3   tablespoons margarine, melted
1/2   cup plus 1 tablespoon dry bread crumbs

Filling
2   teaspoons reduced-calorie margarine
1/4   cup finely minced onions
3   cups sliced mushrooms
1   tablespoon lemon juice
3   eggs
1   cup lowfat cottage cheese
1/8   teaspoon garlic powder
1/2   teaspoon dried rosemary, crumbled
      Salt and pepper to taste

Preheat oven to 350°.

In a 9-inch pie pan, combine crust ingredients. Press crumbs onto bottom and sides of pan to form a crust.

Bake 8 minutes.

In a large nonstick skillet, sauté onions and mushrooms until tender, about 10 minutes.

Combine remaining ingredients in a blender container. Blend until smooth. Stir in mushrooms. Pour into crust.

Bake 30 minutes, until set.

Cool 5 minutes before cutting.

Each serving provides:

172 Calories

1	Protein Serving	10	g	Protein
1/2	Bread Serving	10	g	Fat
1	Vegetable Serving	11	g	Carbohydrate
1-1/2	Fat Servings	339	mg	Sodium
8	Additional Calories	139	mg	Cholesterol

Cheddar Bread Pudding

This is a great use for leftover bread. In fact, it works best with bread that's slightly stale.

Makes 4 servings

4	slices whole wheat bread, cubed
2	cups skim milk
4	eggs
4	ounces shredded lowfat Cheddar cheese
1	teaspoon dry mustard
1	tablespoon minced onion flakes
1/2	teaspoon sherry extract

Preheat oven to 350°.

Spread bread cubes evenly in an 8-inch square baking pan that has been sprayed with a nonstick cooking spray.

In a blender container, combine remaining ingredients. Blend until smooth.

Pour egg mixture evenly over bread cubes. Let stand for 5 minutes.

Bake 30 minutes, until set.

Let cool 10 minutes before serving.

Each serving provides:

256 Calories

2	Protein Servings	18	g	Protein
1	Bread Serving	11	g	Fat
1/2	Milk Serving	24	g	Carbohydrate
		342	mg	Sodium
		285	mg	Cholesterol

Cheese 'n Barley Bake

Choose whichever cheese you prefer for this hearty casserole. It tastes great either way.

Makes 4 servings

2	tablespoons plus 2 teaspoons reduced-calorie margarine
1/2	cup chopped onions
3	cups sliced mushrooms
2	cups cooked barley
6	ounces shredded lowfat Cheddar or Swiss cheese
2	eggs, beaten
2/3	cup nonfat dry milk
1	cup water
2	teaspoons Dijon mustard
	Dash garlic powder
	Salt and pepper to taste

Preheat oven to 350°.

Melt margarine in a large nonstick skillet over medium heat. Add onions and cook until tender, about 10 minutes.

Add mushrooms. Cook 5 minutes, stirring occasionally.

Place barley in a 6 x 10-inch baking pan that has been sprayed with a nonstick cooking spray. Spread onions and mushrooms evenly over barley.

Sprinkle with shredded cheese.

In a small bowl, combine remaining ingredients, mixing well. Pour evenly over cheese.

Bake, uncovered, 30 minutes.

Each serving provides:

344 Calories

2	Protein Servings	19	g	Protein
1	Bread Serving	14	g	Fat
1-3/4	Vegetable Servings	41	g	Carbohydrate
1	Fat Serving	388	mg	Sodium
1/2	Milk Serving	151	mg	Cholesterol

Parmesan Squash Casserole

Add a baked potato and a pretty green vegetable and your meal is complete.

Makes 4 servings

2   10-ounce packages sliced yellow summer squash (or 4 cups
      fresh squash)
1   tablespoon plus 1 teaspoon margarine, melted
1   tablespoon minced onion flakes
2   ounces grated Parmesan cheese
2   eggs
    Salt and pepper to taste

Cook squash according to package directions. Drain. (If using fresh squash, steam for 10 minutes, until tender.)

Preheat oven to 350°.

In a blender container, combine all ingredients. Blend until smooth.

Pour mixture into a 1-quart baking dish that has been sprayed with a nonstick cooking spray.

Bake, uncovered, 35 minutes.

Each serving provides:

168 Calories

1	Protein Serving	11 g	Protein
2	Vegetable Servings	11 g	Fat
1	Fat Serving	7 g	Carbohydrate
		345 mg	Sodium
		148 mg	Cholesterol

Cottage Cheese Patties

This unusual combination of ingredients makes a delightful side dish or a prize-winning dinner.

Makes 4 servings

1   cup lowfat cottage cheese
3   eggs, slightly beaten
1   packet instant chicken-flavored broth mix
1/4   teaspoon poultry seasoning
1   tablespoon minced onion flakes
1/4   teaspoon dill weed
1-1/2   ounces bran flakes cereal, slightly crushed

In a large bowl, combine all ingredients, mixing well.

Drop mixture onto a preheated nonstick skillet or griddle, over medium heat, making 8 small patties.

When edges are dry and bottoms are brown, turn patties gently to brown the other sides.

Each serving provides:

142 Calories

1-1/2	Protein Servings	13 g	Protein
1/2	Bread Serving	5 g	Fat
3	Additional Calories	11 g	Carbohydrate
		659 mg	Sodium
		208 mg	Cholesterol

Cottage Cheese Soufflé

This soufflé makes 4 very large meal-size portions. Add a colorful vegetable combination, such as steamed broccoli, carrots, and cauliflower, for a dinner that's pretty as well as tasty.

Makes 4 servings

2	cups lowfat cottage cheese
4	eggs, separated
1/4	cup plus 2 tablespoons all-purpose flour
1/4	teaspoon salt
1/4	teaspoon pepper
1/4	cup grated onion
1	4-ounce can mushroom pieces, drained and chopped

Preheat oven to 350°.

In a large bowl, beat cottage cheese on medium speed of an electric mixer, adding egg yolks one at a time. Beat until well blended.

Sift in the flour, half at a time, and continue beating.

Stir in salt, pepper, onion, and mushrooms, mixing well.

In a deep bowl, beat the egg whites on high speed of electric mixer until stiff. (Be sure to wash and dry beaters thoroughly first.)

Fold the egg whites into first mixture gently but thoroughly. Pour into a 1-1/2 quart casserole that has been sprayed with a non-stick cooking spray.

Bake 10 minutes. Then reduce heat to 300° and continue baking for 30 minutes, until set and golden brown.

Serve right away.

Each serving provides:

212 Calories

2-1/2	Protein Servings	22	g	Protein
1/2	Bread Serving	7	g	Fat
1/2	Vegetable Serving	13	g	Carbohydrate
		748	mg	Sodium
		279	mg	Cholesterol

Cheesy-Chicken Brunch Rolls

This easy brunch dish makes eggs into crepes. It also works well with tuna in place of the chicken.

Makes 6 servings

6   eggs
10 ounces cooked chicken, shredded
8   ounces shredded lowfat Cheddar cheese

Preheat oven to 375°.

Prepare eggs one at a time: Beat egg in a small bowl. Place in a preheated, small nonstick skillet over medium heat. Tilt pan back and forth so that egg is evenly distributed and forms a thin pancake. Cook until egg is set. Do not turn.

Slide each egg onto a piece of wax paper.

Combine chicken and cheese, mixing well. Divide mixture evenly among eggs, placing it across the center of each egg. Roll up the eggs.

Place rolls in a shallow baking pan that has been sprayed with a nonstick cooking spray.

Bake, uncovered, 15 minutes, until heated through.

Each serving provides:

263 Calories

4	Protein Servings	26	g	Protein
		14	g	Fat
		9	g	Carbohydrate
		227	mg	Sodium
		327	mg	Cholesterol

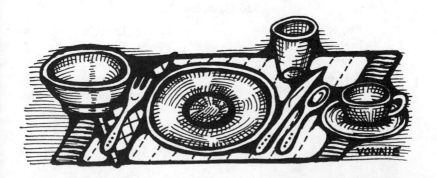

Triple Cheese and Rice

You can increase the nutritional value of this dish by using brown rice, and it adds wonderful "nutty" flavor.

Makes 4 servings

1	tablespoon plus 1 teaspoon vegetable oil
1	cup chopped onions
1	cup chopped celery
2	cups cooked rice
3/4	cup part-skim ricotta cheese
1	egg, beaten
1	teaspoon poultry seasoning
1/4	teaspoon ground sage
1/8	teaspoon garlic powder
	Salt and pepper to taste
2	ounces shredded lowfat Cheddar cheese
2	ounces shredded part-skim Mozzarella cheese

Preheat oven to 375°.

Heat oil in a medium nonstick skillet over medium heat. Add onions and celery and sauté until golden, about 15 minutes. Add small amounts of water, if necessary, to prevent drying.

Add rice, ricotta cheese, egg, and spices. Stir until blended.

Place *half* of this mixture in an 8-inch square baking pan that has been sprayed with a nonstick cooking spray.

Combine the Cheddar cheese and Mozzarella cheese. Sprinkle *half* over the first mixture.

Repeat, using the rest of each mixture.

Bake, uncovered, 30 minutes.

Each serving provides:

326 Calories

2	Protein Servings	15	g	Protein
1	Bread Serving	14	g	Fat
1	Vegetable Serving	35	g	Carbohydrate
1	Fat Serving	212	mg	Sodium
		95	mg	Cholesterol

Spinach and Feta Combo

This is our version of a Greek favorite. We've replaced the usual buttery pastry with nutritious potatoes, and the result is great!

Makes 4 servings

12	ounces potatoes, unpeeled, coarsely shredded
3	eggs, beaten
1	10-ounce package frozen chopped spinach, thawed and drained well
6	ounces feta cheese, crumbled
1/2	cup part-skim ricotta cheese
1/2	cup skim milk
1/8	teaspoon garlic powder
2	tablespoons minced onion flakes
1/4	teaspoon ground nutmeg
1	ounce grated Parmesan cheese
1	tablespoon plus 1 teaspoon reduced-calorie margarine
	Pepper to taste

Preheat oven to 375°.

Spread potatoes evenly in an 8-inch square baking pan that has been sprayed with a nonstick cooking spray.

In a large bowl, combine eggs, spinach, feta cheese, ricotta cheese, milk, garlic powder, onion flakes, and nutmeg. Mix well. Pour evenly over potatoes.

Sprinkle with Parmesan cheese. Dot with margarine.

Bake, uncovered, 40 minutes, until golden.

Cool 5 minutes before serving.

Each serving provides:

370 Calories

3	Protein Servings	22	g	Protein
1	Bread Serving	20	g	Fat
1	Vegetable Serving	24	g	Carbohydrate
13	Additional Calories	811	mg	Sodium
		259	mg	Cholesterol

Cheesy Peaches

What a delicious breakfast!

Makes 4 servings

4   medium, ripe peaches, peeled, sliced 1/4-inch thick
2   eggs
2/3   cup lowfat cottage cheese
2/3   cup nonfat dry milk
1/3   cup water
1-1/2   teaspoons vanilla butternut flavor
1/2   teaspoon maple extract
1   teaspoon ground cinnamon
3   tablespoons sugar (or sweetener equivalent to 9 teaspoons
            sugar)

Preheat oven to 350°.

Arrange peach slices in a shallow baking pan that has been sprayed with a nonstick cooking spray.

In a blender container, combine remaining ingredients. Blend until smooth. Pour mixture evenly over peaches.

Bake 40 minutes, until set.

Serve warm, or chill and serve cold.

Each serving provides:

208 Calories*

1	Protein Serving	13	g	Protein
1	Fruit Serving	3	g	Fat
1/2	Milk Serving	32	g	Carbohydrate
36	Additional Calories (if	251	mg	Sodium
	sugar is used as	141	mg	Cholesterol
	sweetener)			

*If sugar is used as sweetener

French Toast Cheese-Wich

This sandwich version of French toast has lots of variations. For example, try adding chopped chives or imitation bacon bits, or try making it with a different type of cheese.

Makes 1 serving

2   slices thin-sliced whole wheat bread (40 calories per slice)
1   ounce sliced American cheese
1   egg, beaten
1/4   cup skim milk
2   teaspoons reduced-calorie margarine

Place the cheese between the bread slices, making a sandwich.

In a shallow bowl, combine the egg and milk. Soak the sandwich in the egg mixture, turning carefully to soak both sides.

Melt half of the margarine in a nonstick skillet over medium heat. Place sandwich in skillet and brown lightly. Turn carefully, add remaining margarine, and brown the other side.

Each serving provides:

320 Calories

2	Protein Servings	18	g	Protein
1	Bread Serving	19	g	Fat
1	Fat Serving	22	g	Carbohydrate
1/4	Milk Serving	776	mg	Sodium
		302	mg	Cholesterol

Gourmet French Toast

The taste is gourmet, but the preparation is simple. For variations, try other extracts, such as almond, banana, or orange.

Makes 2 servings

1	egg
1/4	cup part-skim ricotta cheese
1	teaspoon vanilla extract
1/2	teaspoon lemon extract
1	tablespoon sugar (or sweetener equivalent to 3 teaspoons sugar)
2	slices whole wheat bread
2	teaspoons margarine
	ground cinnamon

In a blender container, combine egg, ricotta cheese, extracts, and sugar. Blend until mixture is just combined. Pour into a shallow pan.

Soak bread in egg mixture.

Melt margarine in a nonstick skillet over medium-high heat. Place bread in skillet and drizzle with any remaining egg mixture. Sprinkle with cinnamon.

Turn gently to brown both sides.

Each serving provides:

209 Calories*

1	Protein Serving	9	g	Protein
1	Bread Serving	10	g	Fat
1	Fat Serving	20	g	Carbohydrate
24	Additional Calories (if	239	mg	Sodium
	sugar is used as	147	mg	Cholesterol
	sweetener)			

*If sugar is used as sweetener

Cheese and Peanut Butter Treat

You'll have to try this to believe it! Our favorite way to enjoy this delectable spread is on rice cakes or graham crackers.

Makes 1 serving

1/4	cup part-skim ricotta cheese
1	tablespoon peanut butter
1/2	teaspoon vanilla extract
1	teaspoon cocoa (unsweetened)
1	teaspoon sugar (or equivalent amount of sweetener)

In a small bowl, combine all ingredients. Mix with a spoon until blended.

Enjoy!

Each serving provides:

208 Calories*

2	Protein Servings	12	g	Protein
1	Fat Serving	13	g	Fat
10	Additional Calories	12	g	Carbohydrate
	(plus 16 more calories if	153	mg	Sodium
	sugar is used as	19	mg	Cholesterol
	sweetener)			

*If sugar is used as sweetener

Fish and Seafood

Hints for Fish and Seafood

- For best flavor and tenderness, avoid overcooking seafood.
- Some of the mildest tasting fish are flounder, sole, scrod, and orange roughy.
- Low-calorie salad dressings make wonderful seafood marinades.
- Fruit juice and herb combinations also make excellent marinades. (Examples: orange juice with ginger and garlic, lime juice with dill weed, lemon juice with thyme.)
- As an alternative to fried fish, try dipping fillets in wheat germ or bread crumbs and baking them instead.
- Add leftover flaked fish to tuna salad for a delicious cold salad.
- Spread a thin layer of Dijon mustard on fish, sprinkle lightly with thyme, dill, or rosemary, and bake.
- For a Chinese flavor, marinate seafood in a small amount of soy sauce and sprinkle with garlic powder and ginger.
- For an Italian flavor, combine a 1-pound can of tomatoes (drained and chopped) with 2 tablespoons of minced onion flakes, 1/8 teaspoon garlic powder, and 1/4 teaspoon *each* of oregano and basil. Spoon over fish and bake.
- Try sprinkling fish with instant chicken-broth mix and garlic powder before baking or broiling.
- Try dill weed and lemon peel on fish for a flavorful combination.
- Sautéed onions, mushrooms, and green pepper (in a small amount of oil or margarine, in a nonstick skillet) make a delicious topping for any baked or broiled fish.
- Use water-packed tuna instead of the variety packed in oil.
- Fish can be substituted for other types of seafood in almost any recipe.
- Mix leftover seafood with reduced-calorie mayonnaise and herbs of your choice for a unique and delicious salad.

Parmesan Fish

This delicious dish is elegant enough for your most discriminating guests. They'll never believe it's so low in calories.

Makes 4 servings

1   pound scrod fillets (or any non-oily fish)
2   tablespoons plus 2 teaspoons reduced-calorie mayonnaise
2   teaspoons Worcestershire sauce
1   tablespoon minced onion flakes
1   teaspoon Dijon mustard
1   teaspoon sherry extract
1   ounce grated Parmesan cheese

Preheat oven to 350°.

Place fish in a shallow baking pan that has been sprayed with a nonstick cooking spray.

Combine remaining ingredients, *except* Parmesan cheese. Spread mixture evenly over fillets.

Sprinkle with Parmesan cheese.

Bake, uncovered, 30 minutes.

Each serving provides:

163 Calories

3-1/4	Protein Servings	23	g	Protein
1	Fat Serving	6	g	Fat
		2	g	Carbohydrate
		333	mg	Sodium
		58	mg	Cholesterol

Thyme for Fish

If crispier fish is desired, after baking place fish under the broiler for a few minutes.

Makes 4 servings

1-1/2 pounds flounder or sole fillets
2   tablespoons plus 2 teaspoons reduced-calorie mayonnaise
1/2   teaspoon dried thyme
1/8   teaspoon grated lemon peel
         Salt and pepper to taste
2   tablespoons dry bread crumbs (or wheat germ)

Preheat oven to 350°.
Place fish in a shallow baking pan that has been sprayed with a nonstick cooking spray.
Combine mayonnaise, thyme, lemon peel, and salt and pepper. Spread mixture evenly over fillets.
Sprinkle with bread crumbs.
Bake, uncovered, 30 minutes.

Each serving provides:

195 Calories

4	Protein Servings	33	g	Protein
1	Fat Serving	5	g	Fat
15	Additional Calories	3	g	Carbohydrate
		236	mg	Sodium
		85	mg	Cholesterol

Fish and Peppers

If you want to reduce the sodium content of this dish, use low-sodium tomato sauce and use half the amount of Worcestershire sauce.

Makes 4 servings

2	tablespoons plus 2 teaspoons vegetable oil
2	cups chopped green pepper
1/2	cup chopped onions
1	clove garlic, minced
1	8-ounce can tomato sauce
2	teaspoons Worcestershire sauce
1	tablespoon firmly-packed brown sugar (or sweetener equivalent to 3 teaspoons brown sugar)
	Salt and pepper to taste
1	pound scrod or orange roughy fillets (or any thickly sliced non-oily fish)

Preheat oven to 350°.

Heat oil in a large nonstick skillet over medium heat. Add green pepper, onions, and garlic. Cook, stirring frequently, until tender, about 10 minutes.

Stir in remaining ingredients, *except* fish.

Place fish in a baking dish that has been sprayed with a nonstick cooking spray. Spoon sauce evenly over fish.

Bake, uncovered, 30 minutes.

Each serving provides:

226 Calories*

3	Protein Servings	22	g	Protein
2-1/4	Vegetable Servings	10	g	Fat
2	Fat Servings	12	g	Carbohydrate
12	Additional Calories (if	435	mg	Sodium
	brown sugar is used as	49	mg	Cholesterol
	sweetener)			

*If brown sugar is used as a sweetener

Fillet of Sole in Sherry Creme Sauce

Look for lowfat Swiss cheese in the deli department of your grocery store. It tastes and melts just like the original, and it's lower in fat and sodium.

Makes 4 servings

2   tablespoons plus 2 teaspoons margarine
3   tablespoons all-purpose flour
1   cup evaporated skim milk
4   ounces lowfat Swiss cheese, shredded
2   teaspoons sherry extract
    Salt and pepper to taste
1   pound sole or flounder fillets

Melt margarine in a small saucepan over medium heat. Remove from heat.

Stir in flour.

Gradually stir in milk.

Add remaining ingredients, *except* fish. Cook over medium heat, stirring constantly, until sauce comes to a boil. Remove from heat.

Preheat oven to 350°.

Place fish in a baking dish that has been sprayed with a nonstick cooking spray. Spoon sauce evenly over fish.

Bake, uncovered, 30 minutes.

Place under broiler for 5 minutes.

Each serving provides:

350 Calories

4	Protein Servings	34 g	Protein
1/4	Bread Serving	15 g	Fat
2	Fat Servings	13 g	Carbohydrate
1/2	Milk Serving	380 mg	Sodium
		66 mg	Cholesterol

Oriental Fish with Almonds

Sesame oil is a delicious oil that is found in the Oriental section of most grocery stores.

Makes 4 servings

2   tablespoons sesame oil
1/2   cup chopped green onions
1   clove garlic, minced
1   ounce sliced almonds
1   pound scrod or orange roughy fillets (or any thickly-sliced
         non-oily fish)

Heat oil in a nonstick skillet over medium heat. Add onions, garlic, and almonds. Cook 5 minutes, stirring frequently.

Cut fish into 2-inch pieces. Place in skillet. Cook, turning fish carefully, until done, about 10 minutes.

Each serving provides:

199 Calories

3	Protein Servings	22	g	Protein
1/4	Vegetable Serving	11	g	Fat
1-1/2	Fat Servings	2	g	Carbohydrate
43	Additional Calories	63	mg	Sodium
		49	mg	Cholesterol

Baked Herbed Fish

You may want to make extra sauce and serve it over rice as a flavorful accompaniment to this dish.

Makes 4 servings

1-1/2 pounds thickly-cut fish steaks, such as haddock or grouper
1   8-ounce can tomato sauce
1/4   teaspoon dried thyme
1/4   teaspoon dried basil
1/8   teaspoon pepper
1/4   teaspoon salt
1/2   cup finely chopped onions
1   clove garlic, minced

Preheat oven to 350°.
Place fish in a shallow baking pan that has been sprayed with a nonstick cooking spray.
In a small bowl, combine remaining ingredients, mixing well. Spread evenly over fish.
Bake, uncovered, 40 minutes.

Each serving provides:

174 Calories

4	Protein Servings	33	g	Protein
1-1/4	Vegetable Servings	1	g	Fat
		6	g	Carbohydrate
		594	mg	Sodium
		97	mg	Cholesterol

Garlic Broiled Fillets

If you like garlic, you'll love this dish!

Makes 4 servings

1-1/2 pounds scrod or orange roughy fillets (or any thickly-sliced
      non-oily fish)
2   tablespoons plus 2 teaspoons olive oil
2   cloves garlic, sliced
1/4   teaspoon salt
1/8   teaspoon pepper
2   tablespoons lemon juice

Preheat broiler.

Place fish on a broiler pan that has been sprayed with a nonstick cooking spray.

In a blender container, combine remaining ingredients. Blend until smooth. Spread *half* of the mixture evenly over fish.

Broil 5 inches from heat for 8 to 10 minutes.

Turn fish carefully with a spatula, spread with remaining garlic mixture, and broil 8 to 10 more minutes, until done.

Each serving provides:

223 Calories

4	Protein Servings	30	g	Protein
2	Fat Servings	10	g	Fat
		1	g	Carbohydrate
		229	mg	Sodium
		73	mg	Cholesterol

Potato-Fish Combo

Serve with a salad and a green vegetable and your meal is complete.

Makes 4 servings

2   6-ounce potatoes, baked
12   ounces cooked flounder or sole fillets (or any non-oily fish)
1/4   cup skim milk
1/4   cup reduced-calorie margarine
2   tablespoons minced onion flakes
1/8   teaspoon garlic powder
       Salt and pepper to taste

Preheat oven to 350°.

Cut potatoes in half lengthwise. Carefully scoop out pulp.

Flake the fish and combine, in a large bowl, with the potato pulp and all remaining ingredients. Mix well.

Fill potato shells with fish mixture, dividing evenly.

Place potatoes in a shallow baking pan that has been sprayed with a nonstick cooking spray.

Bake, uncovered, 30 minutes, or until heated through.

Each serving provides:

224 Calories

3	Protein Servings	23	g	Protein
1	Bread Serving	7	g	Fat
1-1/2	Fat Servings	16	g	Carbohydrate
5	Additional Calories	224	mg	Sodium
		58	mg	Cholesterol

Cod à l'Orange

This recipe is also delicious with chicken in place of the fish.

Makes 4 servings

1	pound cod fillets (or any thickly-cut non-oily fish)
1/2	cup frozen orange juice concentrate (unsweetened), thawed
2	teaspoons sherry extract
3	tablespoons soy sauce
1/8	teaspoon garlic powder
1	tablespoon plus 1 teaspoon vegetable oil
3	tablespoons dry bread crumbs (or wheat germ)

Place fish in a shallow baking pan.

Combine remaining ingredients, *except* bread crumbs. Pour over fish. Marinate in the refrigerator for several hours, turning fish occasionally.

When ready to cook, let fish stand at room temperature for 15 minutes.

Preheat oven to 350°.

Sprinkle bread crumbs evenly over fish.

Bake, uncovered, 40 minutes.

Each serving provides:

223 Calories

3	Protein Servings	22	g	Protein
1/4	Bread Serving	6	g	Fat
1	Fat Serving	18	g	Carbohydrate
1	Fruit Serving	868	mg	Sodium
		49	mg	Cholesterol

Fillet of Sole Oregano

If you like Italian food, be sure to try this. It's great with a side dish of pasta and a tossed salad.

Makes 4 servings

2   tablespoons plus 2 teaspoons reduced-calorie margarine
1/2   cup chopped onions
2   cups sliced mushrooms
1-1/2   pounds sole or flounder fillets
2   tablespoons lemon juice
1   tablespoon dried parsley flakes
1-1/2   teaspoons dried oregano
1/8   teaspoon pepper
1/2   cup water
1   packet instant chicken-flavored broth mix

Melt margarine in a large nonstick skillet over medium heat. Add onions and mushrooms and cook until tender.

Push onion mixture to one side of skillet and add fish. Sprinkle with lemon juice, parsley, oregano, and pepper.

Arrange onion mixture over fish.

Combine water and broth mix and add to pan. Cover, reduce heat to low, and simmer 20 minutes.

Each serving provides:

215 Calories

4	Protein Servings	33 g	Protein
1-1/4	Vegetable Servings	6 g	Fat
1	Fat Serving	4 g	Carbohydrate
3	Additional Calories	501 mg	Sodium
		82 mg	Cholesterol

Herbed Salmon Steaks

The wonderful combination of basil, tarragon, and rosemary makes this an unforgettable dish.

Makes 4 servings

1-1/2 pounds salmon steaks (or any firm fish, such as haddock)
1   tablespoon all-purpose flour
2   tablespoons plus 2 teaspoons reduced-calorie margarine
2   tablespoons lemon juice
1/2 cup dry white wine
1   teaspoon dried basil
1/2 teaspoon dried tarragon
1/2 teaspoon dried rosemary, crumbled
2   tablespoons minced onion flakes
     Salt and pepper to taste

Rinse fish and pat dry.

Rub flour into both sides of fish.

Melt margarine in a large nonstick skillet over medium heat. Add fish and cook 5 minutes. Turn carefully and cook 5 more minutes.

Combine remaining ingredients and pour over fish.

Cook for about 10 minutes, or until fish is done, turning once during cooking time and basting frequently with pan juices.

Each serving provides:

292 Calories

4	Protein Servings	34	g	Protein
1	Fat Serving	15	g	Fat
32	Additional Calories	4	g	Carbohydrate
		159	mg	Sodium
		94	mg	Cholesterol

Mexican Salmon Pitas

If you pack your lunch, you can make the sandwich ahead of time and take the dressing along in a small container.

Makes 2 servings

Mexican Dressing
1/2   cup plain lowfat yogurt
2   tablespoons finely chopped onion
1/8   teaspoon garlic powder
1/4   teaspoon ground cumin
1/4   teaspoon dried oregano

Sandwich
4   ounces canned salmon, drained and flaked (Tuna may also
        be used.)
1/4   cup chopped green pepper
1/4   cup shredded carrot
2   tablespoons finely chopped onion
1   medium tomato, chopped
2   ounces lowfat Cheddar cheese, shredded
2   1-ounce pita breads, split at one end

In a small bowl, combine all dressing ingredients. Chill several hours to blend flavors.

In a medium bowl, combine remaining ingredients, *except* pitas. Divide mixture evenly and stuff into openings in pitas.

Add half of the dressing to each sandwich.

Each serving provides:

303 Calories

3	Protein Servings	24	g	Protein
1	Bread Serving	9	g	Fat
1-1/2	Vegetable Servings	35	g	Carbohydrate
1/2	Milk Serving	596	mg	Sodium
		34	mg	Cholesterol

Florentine Salmon Bake

For a complete meal that's easy and delicious, try this dish with a tossed salad and our Garlic Noodles on page 321.

Makes 4 servings

8	ounces canned salmon, drained and flaked
2/3	cup lowfat cottage cheese
1	egg, slightly beaten
1	packet instant chicken-flavored broth mix
1/4	cup finely chopped onion
1/4	teaspoon ground nutmeg
1	10-ounce package frozen chopped spinach, thawed and drained
	Salt and pepper to taste
2-1/2	ounces lowfat Swiss cheese, shredded
1/2	ounce grated Parmesan cheese

Preheat oven to 350°.

In a medium bowl, combine salmon, cottage cheese, egg, broth mix, onions, and nutmeg. Mix well. Spread mixture in a 6 x 10-inch baking pan that has been sprayed with a nonstick cooking spray.

Spread spinach evenly over salmon mixture.

Sprinkle with salt and pepper.

Top with Swiss and Parmesan cheese.

Bake, uncovered, 30 minutes.

Each serving provides:

231 Calories

3-1/2	Protein Servings	27	g	Protein
1	Vegetable Serving	10	g	Fat
3	Additional Calories	6	g	Carbohydrate
		923	mg	Sodium
		101	mg	Cholesterol

Salmon-Potato Patties

Ever wonder what to do with leftover mashed potatoes? Try these tasty patties.

Makes 4 servings

9	ounces drained, canned salmon, flaked
6	ounces potatoes, cooked, peeled, and mashed
2	eggs, slightly beaten
2	tablespoons grated onion
1	tablespoon lemon juice
1	teaspoon Worcestershire sauce
1	ounce grated Parmesan cheese
1/2	teaspoon grated lemon peel
	Salt and pepper to taste

In a large bowl, combine all ingredients, mixing well. Shape into 8 patties.

Preheat a nonstick griddle or skillet over medium heat. Spray lightly with a nonstick cooking spray.

Cook patties until lightly browned on both sides, turning carefully.

Each serving provides:

202 Calories

3	Protein Servings	20	g	Protein
1/2	Bread Serving	8	g	Fat
		10	g	Carbohydrate
		494	mg	Sodium
		167	mg	Cholesterol

Salmon Quiche

This luscious quiche is at home at any luncheon or dinner party. We've replaced the usual cream with nonfat dry milk, but we haven't replaced the flavor.

Makes 8 servings

Crust

3/4	cup all-purpose flour
1/4	cup reduced-calorie margarine
2	tablespoons ice water

Filling

9	ounces drained, canned salmon, flaked
4	ounces lowfat Swiss cheese, shredded
3	eggs, beaten
2/3	cup nonfat dry milk
1-1/3	cups water
1	tablespoon dried chives
1	teaspoon sherry extract
1	teaspoon Dijon mustard
	Salt and pepper to taste

Preheat oven to 375°.

In a medium bowl, combine all crust ingredients, mixing well to form a dough. With your hands, work dough into a ball. Place between 2 pieces of wax paper and roll into an 11-inch circle.

Place dough in a 9-inch pie pan. Fold the edges under and flute with a fork. Prick the bottom and sides of crust with a fork about 25 times.

Arrange salmon evenly in crust. Sprinkle evenly with cheese.

In a small bowl, combine remaining ingredients. Beat with a fork or wire whisk until blended. Pour over salmon and cheese.

Bake 40 minutes, until set. Let stand 10 minutes, then serve.

Each serving provides:

215 Calories

2	Protein Servings	16	g	Protein
1/2	Bread Serving	10	g	Fat
3/4	Fat Serving	13	g	Carbohydrate
1/4	Milk Serving	354	mg	Sodium
		121	mg	Cholesterol

Salmon Salad

For a delicious change-of-pace from tuna salad, try this with lettuce and tomato in a pita bread or piled on a toasted English muffin.

Makes 2 servings

5	ounces drained, canned salmon, flaked
1	tablespoon lemon juice
1	teaspoon Dijon mustard
1	tablespoon plus 1 teaspoon reduced-calorie mayonnaise
2	tablespoons finely chopped onion
2	tablespoons finely chopped celery
1/4	teaspoon dill weed
	Salt and pepper to taste

In a small bowl, combine all ingredients, mixing well. Chill several hours to blend flavors.

Each serving provides:

136 Calories

2-1/2	Protein Servings	15	g	Protein
1/4	Vegetable Servings	7	g	Fat
1	Fat Serving	3	g	Carbohydrate
		503	mg	Sodium
		31	mg	Cholesterol

Tuna-Stuffed Peppers

We like to serve this dish with our Rice Pilaf on page 300. The flavors complement each other nicely.

Makes 2 servings

2	large green peppers
6	ounces drained, water-packed tuna, flaked
1	slice whole wheat bread, crumbled
1/2	cup finely chopped celery
2	tablespoons finely chopped onion
1/2	cup tomato sauce
1	teaspoon poultry seasoning
1	tablespoon grated Parmesan cheese
	Salt and pepper to taste

Preheat oven to 350°.

Slice off the top of each pepper. Chop the slice and remove the seeds from the pepper. Place peppers in a pot of boiling water. Boil 5 minutes. Remove peppers from water and drain, upside-down, on paper towels.

In a medium bowl, combine tuna with the chopped green pepper and remaining ingredients.

Spoon mixture evenly into the peppers. Place in a shallow baking pan that has been sprayed with a nonstick cooking spray.

Bake, uncovered, 30 minutes.

Each serving provides:

204 Calories

3	Protein Servings	29	g	Protein
1/2	Bread Serving	2	g	Fat
2-1/2	Vegetable Servings	17	g	Carbohydrate
15	Additional Calories	809	mg	Sodium
		38	mg	Cholesterol

Tuna Loaf Florentine

You'll love the leftovers in sandwiches–either hot or cold.

Makes 4 servings

9	ounces drained, water-packed tuna, flaked
1	10-ounce package frozen chopped spinach, thawed and drained well
2	slices whole wheat bread, crumbled
1	tablespoon plus 1 teaspoon vegetable oil
2	tablespoons minced onion flakes
1	cup plain lowfat yogurt
2	eggs, slightly beaten
1/8	teaspoon garlic powder
1	packet instant chicken-flavored broth mix
1	ounce grated Parmesan cheese
1/8	teaspoon ground nutmeg
1/8	teaspoon dried basil
	Salt and pepper to taste

Preheat oven to 350°.

In a large bowl, combine tuna, spinach, and bread, mixing well. Add remaining ingredients. Mix until well blended.

Spoon mixture into a 4 x 8-inch loaf pan that has been sprayed with a nonstick cooking spray.

Bake 50 minutes, until set and lightly browned.

Let stand for 10 minutes. Then run a knife around the edges of the pan and invert loaf onto a serving plate.

Slice to serve.

Each serving provides:

287 Calories

3	Protein Servings	31	g	Protein
1/2	Bread Serving	11	g	Fat
1	Fat Serving	15	g	Carbohydrate
1/2	Milk Serving	825	mg	Sodium
3	Additional Calories	173	mg	Cholesterol

Tuna-Vegetable Pie

The Italian flavor of this unique dish makes it go well with pasta. Try it with our Garlic Noodles on page 321, add a salad, and your meal is complete.

Makes 6 servings

10	ounces drained, water-packed tuna, flaked
1	egg, slightly beaten
1	ounce grated Parmesan cheese
1	8-ounce can tomato sauce
1/2	teaspoon dried oregano
1/2	teaspoon dried basil
2	tablespoons dry bread crumbs or wheat germ
1/2	cup finely chopped green pepper
1/4	cup finely chopped onions
1/2	cup finely chopped zucchini, unpeeled
1	4-ounce can mushroom pieces, drained
	Dash garlic powder

Preheat oven to 350°.

In a large bowl, combine all ingredients. Mix well.

Spoon mixture into a 9-inch pie pan that has been sprayed with a nonstick cooking spray. Press down gently with a fork.

Bake, uncovered, 40 minutes, until lightly browned.

Cut into wedges to serve.

Each serving provides:

126 Calories

2	Protein Servings	18	g	Protein
1-1/2	Vegetable Servings	3	g	Fat
10	Additional Calories	6	g	Carbohydrate
		569	mg	Sodium
		69	mg	Cholesterol

Pasta and Tuna Bake

This slightly different version of the traditional tuna-noodle casserole is quick, easy, and delicious.

Makes 4 servings

2	cups cooked macaroni
10	ounces drained, water-packed tuna, flaked
2	ounces lowfat Swiss cheese, shredded
1/2	cup chopped green pepper
1/2	cup chopped green onions (green part only)
1/4	cup reduced-calorie mayonnaise
1/2	cup skim milk
1/4	cup plain lowfat yogurt
2	tablespoons dried parsley flakes
	Dash garlic powder

Preheat oven to 400°.

In a large bowl, combine macaroni, tuna, Swiss cheese, green pepper, and onions. Toss until well mixed.

In a small bowl, combine remaining ingredients, mixing well. Add to tuna mixture, tossing until combined.

Spoon into a 1-1/2 quart baking dish that has been sprayed with a nonstick cooking spray.

Bake, uncovered, 20 minutes, until hot and bubbly.

Stir before serving.

Each serving provides:

288 Calories

3	Protein Servings	29	g	Protein
1	Bread Serving	8	g	Fat
1/2	Vegetable Serving	22	g	Carbohydrate
1-1/2	Fat Servings	455	mg	Sodium
1/4	Milk Serving	41	mg	Cholesterol

Tuna Cheese Pie

Leftovers of this pie freeze nicely and can be reheated in a toaster-oven or microwave for a quick, delicious lunch.

Makes 6 servings

8   ounces drained, water-packed tuna, flaked
1   ounce grated Parmesan cheese, divided in half
1-1/3 cups lowfat cottage cheese
3   eggs
2   tablespoons all-purpose flour
1   teaspoon baking powder
1   tablespoon minced onion flakes
1   packet instant chicken-flavored broth mix
1   teaspoon Worcestershire sauce

Preheat oven to 350°.

Arrange tuna evenly in a 9-inch pie pan that has been sprayed with a nonstick cooking spray.

In a blender container, combine *half* of the Parmesan cheese with remaining ingredients. Blend until smooth. Pour mixture over tuna.

Top with remaining Parmesan cheese.

Bake, uncovered, 30 minutes, until set and lightly browned.

Let stand for 5 minutes before serving.

Each serving provides:

162 Calories

2-2/3	Protein Servings	23 g Protein
23	Additional Calories	5 g Fat
		5 g Carbohydrate
		727 mg Sodium
		159 mg Cholesterol

4 points per serving

Tuna Balls with Dill Sauce

We like to serve these with steamed broccoli or asparagus and spoon some of the sauce over the vegetables.

Makes 4 servings

12	ounces drained, water-packed tuna, flaked
3	slices enriched white or whole wheat bread, crumbled
2	eggs, slightly beaten
1/2	cup finely chopped celery
1/2	cup finely chopped onions
2	tablespoons dried parsley flakes
1	tablespoon lemon juice
	Salt and pepper to taste

Sauce

2	tablespoons plus 2 teaspoons margarine
3	tablespoons all-purpose flour
1/4	teaspoon paprika
1/4	teaspoon salt
2	cups skim milk
1-1/2	teaspoons dill weed

Preheat oven to 350°. In a large bowl, combine tuna with remaining ingredients, *except* those for sauce. Mix well.

Shape mixture into 12 balls. Place in a shallow baking pan that has been sprayed with a nonstick cooking spray.

Bake 25 minutes. While tuna is baking, prepare sauce:

Melt margarine in a medium saucepan over medium heat. Stir in flour, paprika, and salt. Gradually stir in milk and dill weed.

Cook until thickened, stirring constantly.

Spoon over tuna balls to serve.

Each serving provides:

344 Calories

3-1/2	Protein Servings	35	g	Protein
1	Bread Serving	12	g	Fat
1/2	Vegetable Serving	22	g	Carbohydrate
2	Fat Servings	733	mg	Sodium
1/2	Milk Serving	176	mg	Cholesterol

Pepper Tuna Loaf

A combination of red and green peppers makes a very colorful and attractive loaf.

Makes 4 servings

10	ounces drained, water-packed tuna, flaked
2	eggs plus 1 egg white
2	slices whole wheat bread, crumbled
1/3	cup water
1	cup chopped green pepper
1/4	cup chopped onions
1	tablespoon prepared mustard
1	tablespoon plus 1 teaspoon vegetable oil
	Dash garlic powder
	Salt and pepper to taste

Preheat oven to 350°.

In a large bowl, combine all ingredients, mixing well.

Place mixture in a 4 x 8-inch loaf pan that has been sprayed with a nonstick cooking spray. Press down gently with the back of a spoon.

Bake 1 hour, until golden.

Let stand 5 minutes; then invert onto a serving plate.

Each serving provides:

217 Calories

3	Protein Servings	27	g	Protein
1/2	Bread Serving	8	g	Fat
1/2	Vegetable Serving	8	g	Carbohydrate
1	Fat Serving	410	mg	Sodium
5	Additional Calories	167	mg	Cholesterol

Tuna, Broccoli, and Shells

Using whole wheat macaroni increases the nutritional value of this tasty dish and adds a slightly nutty flavor.

Makes 4 servings

2	cups broccoli, cut into flowerets
8	ounces drained, water-packed tuna, flaked
2	cups cooked macaroni shells
2	medium tomatoes, cut into chunks
1/4	cup finely chopped onions
2	teaspoons dried basil
1	teaspoon dried oregano
2	tablespoons plus 2 teaspoons vegetable oil
1/4	cup vinegar
	Salt and pepper to taste

Steam broccoli, covered, in 2 inches of boiling water until tender-crisp, about 5 minutes. Drain and cool slightly.

In a large bowl, combine broccoli with remaining ingredients. Toss gently until combined.

Chill several hours, stirring occasionally.

Each serving provides:

265 Calories

2	Protein Servings	21	g	Protein
1	Bread Serving	10	g	Fat
1-1/2	Vegetable Servings	23	g	Carbohydrate
2	Fat Servings	220	mg	Sodium
		24	mg	Cholesterol

Creamy Tuna Salad

The ricotta cheese is the key to the creaminess.

Makes 4 servings

10	ounces drained, water-packed tuna, flaked
1/2	cup part-skim ricotta cheese
2	tablespoons plus 2 teaspoons reduced-calorie mayonnaise
1	tablespoon sweet pickle relish
2	tablespoons finely chopped onion
1/4	cup finely chopped green pepper
1/4	cup finely chopped celery
	Salt and pepper to taste

In a medium bowl, combine all ingredients, mixing well.
Chill several hours to blend flavors.

Each serving provides:

172 Calories

3	Protein Servings	25	g	Protein
1/4	Vegetable Serving	6	g	Fat
1	Fat Serving	5	g	Carbohydrate
8	Additional Calories	400	mg	Sodium
		43	mg	Cholesterol

Shrimp in Cheddar Sauce

This is a heavenly dish! Serve it over rice and enjoy.

Makes 4 servings

2	tablespoons plus 2 teaspoons reduced-calorie margarine
1/4	cup finely chopped onions
1/2	cup finely chopped celery
3	tablespoons all-purpose flour
2	cups skim milk
2	teaspoons sherry extract
1	tablespoon lemon juice
4	ounces lowfat Cheddar cheese, shredded
8	ounces cooked, peeled shrimp

Melt margarine in a medium saucepan over medium heat. Add onions and celery and cook until tender, about 5 minutes. (Add a small amount of water, if necessary, to prevent drying.)

Reduce heat to low. Stir in flour.

Gradually stir in milk.

Add sherry extract and lemon juice. Stir until blended.

Add cheese and shrimp. Cover and cook 15 minutes, stirring occasionally.

Each serving provides:

239 Calories

3	Protein Servings	22	g	Protein
1/4	Bread Serving	9	g	Fat
1/3	Vegetable Serving	18	g	Carbohydrate
1	Fat Serving	373	mg	Sodium
1/2	Milk Serving	121	mg	Cholesterol

Easiest Shrimp Salad

*Served on a bed of lettuce or made into a sandwich, this salad makes a
wonderful, tasty lunch or light supper.*

Makes 4 servings

12   ounces cooked, peeled shrimp, cut into 1-inch pieces
1/4   cup reduced-calorie mayonnaise
2   tablespoons ketchup
1   teaspoon lemon juice
2   teaspoons minced onion flakes, reconstituted in a small
            amount of water
        Dash garlic powder
        Salt and pepper to taste

In a medium bowl, combine all ingredients and mix well. Chill
several hours to blend flavors.

Each serving provides:

136 Calories

3	Protein Servings	18 g	Protein
1-1/2	Fat Servings	5 g	Fat
7	Additional Calories	4 g	Carbohydrate
		393 mg	Sodium
		171 mg	Cholesterol

Shrimp Teriyaki

These shrimp are also delicious on an outdoor grill. If you thread them on a skewer, they won't fall through the openings in the rack.

Makes 4 servings

3	tablespoons soy sauce
1	tablespoon water
1	tablespoon plus 1 teaspoon sesame oil
2	teaspoons sherry extract
1/8	teaspoon garlic powder
1/4	teaspoon ground ginger
2	teaspoons honey

1-1/4 pounds peeled and deveined shrimp

Combine all ingredients, *except* shrimp, in a shallow bowl. Add shrimp and marinate in the refrigerator for several hours, turning shrimp occasionally.

Preheat broiler.

Remove shrimp from marinade and place on a broiler pan. Broil 3 inches from heat for 5 minutes. Turn and broil 4 to 5 minutes, until shrimp is just done.

Heat marinade and serve with shrimp.

Each serving provides:

209 Calories

4	Protein Servings	30	g	Protein
1	Fat Serving	7	g	Fat
10	Additional Calories	5	g	Carbohydrate
		982	mg	Sodium
		216	mg	Cholesterol

Barbecued Shrimp

A lovely way to serve these is to place all 4 skewers on a large platter of cooked rice.

Makes 4 servings

1	8-ounce can tomato sauce
1/2	cup chopped onions
1	tablespoon plus 1 teaspoon firmly-packed brown sugar (or sweetener equivalent to 4 teaspoons brown sugar)
2	tablespoons vegetable oil
1/4	cup lemon juice
1	tablespoon Worcestershire sauce
	Salt and pepper to taste
1	tablespoon prepared mustard
1/8	teaspoon garlic powder
1	cup unsweetened pineapple chunks, drained (save juice)
1/4	cup juice from pineapple
1	pound peeled and deveined shrimp
1	large green pepper, cut into 1-inch squares

In a small saucepan, combine tomato sauce, onions, sweetener, oil, lemon juice, Worcestershire sauce, salt, pepper, mustard, garlic powder, and juice from pineapple. Bring to a boil over medium heat. Reduce heat to low, cover, and simmer 15 minutes.

Pour sauce over shrimp in a shallow bowl and marinate in the refrigerator for several hours, turning shrimp occasionally.

Remove shrimp from marinade. Alternately thread shrimp, pineapple, and green pepper on 4 skewers. Place on broiler pan or barbecue grill.

Broil or grill for 10 to 15 minutes, turning several times.

Heat remaining marinade and serve with shrimp.

Each serving provides:

285 Calories*

3	Protein Servings	25	g	Protein
1-3/4	Vegetable Servings	9	g	Fat
1-1/2	Fat Servings	27	g	Carbohydrate
1/2	Fruit Servings	608	mg	Sodium
16	Additional Calories (if brown sugar is used as sweetener)	173	mg	Cholesterol

*If brown sugar is used as sweetener

Oriental Shrimp and Water Chestnuts

Over cooked rice or thin noodles, this makes a very tasty Oriental treat. You can lower the sodium count by using the low-sodium varieties of broth mix and soy sauce.

Makes 4 servings

1	pound peeled and deveined shrimp
1	clove garlic, minced
1/2	cup chopped onions
6	ounces canned water chestnuts, drained, sliced thin
2	cups sliced mushrooms
2	tablespoons cornstarch
2	teaspoons sherry extract
1	teaspoon sugar (or equivalent amount of sweetener)
1	tablespoon soy sauce
1	cup water
1	packet instant chicken-flavored broth mix
2	tablespoons plus 2 teaspoons vegetable oil

Combine shrimp, garlic, onions, water chestnuts, and mushrooms in a large bowl.

In a small bowl, combine cornstarch, sherry extract, sweetener, soy sauce, water, and broth mix. Stir to dissolve cornstarch.

Heat oil in a large nonstick skillet over high heat. (Or a wok may be used.) Add shrimp mixture and cook until shrimp is done, about 10 minutes, stirring frequently. Lower heat to medium.

Pour broth mixture over shrimp. Cook, stirring, until mixture thickens, about 3 to 5 minutes.

Each serving provides:

271 Calories*

3	Protein Servings	25	g	Protein
1/2	Bread Serving	11	g	Fat
1	Vegetable Serving	15	g	Carbohydrate
2	Fat Servings	709	mg	Sodium
14	Additional Calories			
	(plus 4 more calories if sugar is used as sweetener)	173	mg	Cholesterol

*If sugar is used as sweetener

Scallops Italiano

If you like Italian food and seafood, this combination can't be beat. Add some pasta and our Broiled Zucchini on page 254, and what a feast!

Makes 4 servings

1	pound scallops
2	tablespoons lemon juice
1/8	teaspoon garlic powder
1/8	teaspoon salt
1/8	teaspoon pepper
1	8-ounce can tomato sauce
1	4-ounce can mushroom pieces, drained
2	tablespoons minced onion flakes
1	teaspoon dried oregano
1/2	teaspoon dried basil
1/4	teaspoon dried thyme

Place scallops in a shallow baking pan that has been sprayed with a nonstick cooking spray. Sprinkle with lemon juice, garlic powder, salt, and pepper.

Broil for 3 minutes. Turn and broil 3 more minutes.

Combine remaining ingredients in a small bowl. Pour evenly over scallops. Broil 5 minutes on each side, or until done.

Each serving provides:

132 Calories

3	Protein Servings	20	g	Protein
1-1/2	Vegetable Servings	1	g	Fat
		9	g	Carbohydrate
		682	mg	Sodium
		37	mg	Cholesterol

Garlic Scallops

Garlic lovers, enjoy!

Makes 4 servings

3   tablespoons all-purpose flour
       Salt and pepper to taste
1   pound scallops
2   tablespoons plus 2 teaspoons margarine
2–3 cloves garlic, minced
2   tablespoons dried parsley flakes
2   tablespoons lemon juice

In a shallow bowl, combine flour and salt and pepper. Add scallops and toss to coat.

Melt margarine in a large nonstick skillet over medium-high heat. Add garlic and cook 2 minutes, stirring frequently.

Add scallops to skillet. Cook, turning several times, until cooked through, about 5 minutes.

Sprinkle with parsley and lemon juice.

Each serving provides:

194 Calories

3	Protein Servings	20 g	Protein
1/4	Bread Serving	9 g	Fat
2	Fat Servings	8 g	Carbohydrate
		275 mg	Sodium
		37 mg	Cholesterol

Crab and Cheese Meltwich

For a delicious alternative, instead of topping an English muffin, spoon crab mixture over a baked potato.

Makes 1 serving

2   ounces crab meat
1   ounce lowfat Cheddar cheese, shredded
1   tablespoon reduced-calorie mayonnaise
1/4 teaspoon sherry extract
1/2 English muffin, toasted

Combine crab meat, cheese, mayonnaise, and sherry extract in a double boiler over boiling water. Cook, stirring, until cheese melts and mixture is hot.

Spoon over muffin and serve.

Each serving provides:

238 Calories

3	Protein Servings	19 g	Protein
1	Bread Serving	10 g	Fat
1-1/2	Fat Servings	20 g	Carbohydrate
		503 mg	Sodium
		70 mg	Cholesterol

Crab and Noodle Casserole

The sherry extract blends with the garlic and lemon juice for a flavor that's truly divine.

Makes 4 servings

1/4	cup reduced-calorie margarine
2	tablespoons finely chopped onion
1/2	cup finely chopped celery
3	tablespoons all-purpose flour
1/2	teaspoon dry mustard
1/4	teaspoon salt
1/8	teaspoon pepper
1/8	teaspoon garlic powder
2/3	cup nonfat dry milk
1-1/2	cups water
1	tablespoon lemon juice
1	teaspoon sherry extract
8	ounces crab meat
1-1/3	cups lowfat cottage cheese
2	cups cooked noodles

Preheat oven to 350°.

Melt margarine in a small saucepan over medium-low heat. Add onion and celery. Cook until tender, about 10 minutes. Stir in flour, dry mustard, salt, pepper, and garlic powder.

Dissolve dry milk in water. Gradually add to onion mixture, stirring constantly. Cook until bubbly and slightly thickened, still stirring. Remove from heat. Stir in lemon juice and sherry extract.

Add crab meat, cottage cheese, and noodles. Gently stir until mixture is combined.

Spoon into a 1-1/2 quart casserole that has been sprayed with a nonstick cooking spray. Bake, uncovered, 30 to 40 minutes.

Each serving provides:

334 Calories

3	Protein Servings	29	g	Protein
1-1/4	Bread Servings	9	g	Fat
1/4	Vegetable Serving	32	g	Carbohydrate
1-1/2	Fat Servings	797	mg	Sodium
1/2	Milk Serving	87	mg	Cholesterol

Crab-Stuffed Mushrooms

This elegant dish makes a great appetizer, as well as an entree. If you like, add 2 tablespoons of finely minced green pepper with the onions.

Makes 6 servings

24	large mushrooms
1	tablespoon plus 2 teaspoons margarine
2	tablespoons finely chopped onion
12	ounces crab meat
1	tablespoon Dijon mustard
1/8	teaspoon pepper
2	tablespoons lemon juice
2	teaspoons Worcestershire sauce
1-1/2	teaspoons sherry extract
1/4	cup skim milk

Topping

2	tablespoons plus 2 teaspoons reduced-calorie mayonnaise
2	tablespoons skim milk

Preheat oven to 450°.

Carefully remove stems from mushrooms. Slice stems into thin slices.

Melt margarine in a medium nonstick saucepan over medium heat. Add sliced stems and onions. Cook until onions are tender, about 10 minutes.

Add remaining ingredients. Mix well.

Pile mixture evenly into mushroom caps.

Combine topping ingredients. Brush over crab filling.

Place mushrooms in a shallow baking pan that has been sprayed with a nonstick cooking spray.

Bake 15 minutes, until hot and lightly browned.

Each serving provides:

142 Calories

2	Protein Servings	14	g	Protein
2	Vegetable Servings	7	g	Fat
1-1/2	Fat Servings	7	g	Carbohydrate
5	Additional Calories	351	mg	Sodium
		59	mg	Cholesterol

Caribbean Chicken

Treat yourself to a special flavor and try this wonderfully seasoned chicken over wild rice.

Makes 4 servings

2   tablespoons vegetable oil
1   pound boned and skinned chicken parts
1   large onion, sliced (about 1 cup)
2   large tomatoes, chopped (about 1 cup each)
2   tablespoons soy sauce
1/4   cup water
1   clove garlic, minced
1/8   teaspoon pepper
2   teaspoons curry powder
1   tablespoon parsley flakes

Heat oil in a large nonstick skillet over medium heat. Add chicken and brown lightly on all sides, turning frequently. Reduce heat to low.

Add remaining ingredients, mixing well.

Cover and cook 1 hour, stirring occasionally. (Add small amounts of water, if necessary, to prevent drying.)

Each serving provides:

242 Calories

3	Protein Servings	26	g	Protein
1-1/2	Vegetable Servings	11	g	Fat
1-1/2	Fat Servings	10	g	Carbohydrate
		612	mg	Sodium
		79	mg	Cholesterol

Elegant Stuffed Chicken Breasts

The name says it all! The results are so elegant that no one will believe how easy they are to prepare.

Makes 4 servings

1-1/4	pounds boned and skinned chicken breasts
2	tablespoons plus 2 teaspoons reduced-calorie margarine
1/2	cup chopped onions
2	cups chopped mushrooms
1	cup coarsely shredded zucchini, unpeeled
1/4	teaspoon ground nutmeg
1/8	teaspoon garlic powder
3	tablespoons dry bread crumbs
1	egg white
	Salt and pepper to taste
	Paprika
	Parsley flakes

Preheat oven to 350°.

Place each chicken breast between 2 pieces of wax paper and flatten with a mallet until 1/4-inch thick.

Melt margarine in a medium nonstick skillet over medium heat. Add onions and mushrooms and cook until tender, about 10 minutes. Remove from heat.

Stir zucchini, nutmeg, garlic powder, bread crumbs, egg white, and salt and pepper into mushroom mixture. Divide mixture evenly onto the center of each chicken breast. Fold up the edges to enclose the stuffing and place, smooth-side-up, in a shallow pan. Sprinkle liberally with paprika and parsley flakes.

Cover pan tightly with aluminum foil and bake 40 minutes.

Each serving provides:

233 Calories

4	Protein Servings	36	g	Protein
1/4	Bread Serving	6	g	Fat
1-3/4	Vegetable Servings	8	g	Carbohydrate
1	Fat Serving	222	mg	Sodium
5	Additional Calories	83	mg	Cholesterol

Chicken in Red Wine

This is our low-fat version of a classic French dish. For a truly elegant meal, we like to add a baked potato and steamed asparagus.

Makes 4 servings

3	pounds skinned chicken parts
12	small white pearl onions, peeled
12	small whole mushrooms
1	tablespoon plus 1 teaspoon vegetable oil
1	cup dry red wine
1/2	cup water
1	packet instant chicken-flavored broth mix
1/2	teaspoon paprika
1/4	teaspoon pepper
1/2	teaspoon dried thyme
2	cloves garlic, minced
1	small bay leaf
1	tablespoon dried parsley flakes

Preheat oven to 350°.

Place chicken in an oven-proof casserole. Top with onions and mushrooms.

In a small bowl, combine remaining ingredients. Pour over chicken.

Cover and bake 1 hour.

Remove and discard bay leaf before serving.

Each serving provides:

261 Calories

4	Protein Servings	36	g	Protein
1	Vegetable Serving	10	g	Fat
1	Fat Serving	5	g	Carbohydrate
28	Additional Calories	412	mg	Sodium
		115	mg	Cholesterol

Chicken with White Wine and Tomatoes

We like this dish best when it's made a day ahead and reheated. The flavors really blend.

Makes 4 servings

1	tablespoon plus 1 teaspoon vegetable oil
2	teaspoons lemon juice
1	cup thinly sliced onions
2	cloves garlic, minced
2-1/4	pounds skinned chicken parts
1/2	cup dry white wine
1	1-pound can tomatoes, chopped, undrained
1/4	cup tomato paste
1	packet instant chicken-flavored broth mix
1	bay leaf
1/4	teaspoon dried thyme
1/4	teaspoon pepper
1-1/2	cups water
2	cups sliced mushrooms

In a Dutch oven, heat oil and lemon juice over medium heat. Add onions and garlic. Cook until onions are lightly browned, stirring frequently, and separating onions into rings. Add small amounts of water, if necessary, to prevent drying.

Add chicken.

Combine remaining ingredients, except mushrooms. Pour over chicken.

Cover, reduce heat to low, and simmer 1-1/4 hours, stirring occasionally.

Add mushrooms, cover, and cook 15 minutes longer.

Remove and discard bay leaf before serving.

Each serving provides:

243 Calories

3	Protein Servings	28	g	Protein
2-3/4	Vegetable Servings	9	g	Fat
1	Fat Serving	14	g	Carbohydrate
28	Additional Calories	685	mg	Sodium
		80	mg	Cholesterol

Chicken Continental

The delicious blend of spices is always a hit and makes this a wonderful party meal.

Makes 4 servings

2-1/4	pounds skinned chicken parts
	Salt and pepper to taste
2	tablespoons margarine
1/2	cup chopped onions
2	cups sliced mushrooms
1	medium green pepper, sliced
1	clove garlic, minced
1	1-pound can tomatoes, chopped, undrained
1/2	cup dry white wine
1/2	teaspoon dried basil
1/2	teaspoon dried marjoram
1/2	teaspoon dried thyme
1/2	teaspoon dried oregano
2	teaspoons all-purpose flour
1	cup plain lowfat yogurt

Preheat oven to 350°.

Place chicken in a baking dish that has been sprayed with a non-stick cooking spray. Sprinkle with salt and pepper.

Melt margarine in a large nonstick skillet over medium heat. Add onions, mushrooms, green pepper, and garlic. Cook, stirring frequently, for 10 minutes.

Stir tomatoes, wine, and spices into onion mixture. Spoon over chicken. Cover and bake 1 hour.

Remove chicken and place on a serving plate.

Stir flour into yogurt. Stir yogurt into tomato mixture. Heat in skillet until heated through. Do not boil. Serve over chicken.

Each serving provides:

274 Calories

3	Protein Servings	30	g	Protein
2-3/4	Vegetable Servings	11	g	Fat
1/2	Milk Serving	15	g	Carbohydrate
30	Additional Calories	383	mg	Sodium
		83	mg	Cholesterol

Spanish Chicken

For a delicious and colorful accompaniment, cook brown rice or cracked wheat in water with chicken-broth mix and a little saffron.

Makes 4 servings

2	tablespoons vegetable oil
1/2	cup chopped onions
1/2	cup chopped green pepper
1	clove garlic, minced
1/2	cup chopped carrots
1/2	cup chopped celery
1	1-pound can tomatoes, chopped, drained (Reserve juice.)
2-1/4	pounds skinned chicken parts
1/4	cup water
1	packet instant chicken-flavored broth mix
1/4	teaspoon chili powder
	Pinch of saffron

Preheat oven to 350°.

Heat oil in a large nonstick skillet over medium heat. Add onions, green pepper, garlic, carrots, and celery. Cook 10 minutes, stirring frequently. Stir in tomatoes. Remove from heat.

Place chicken in a baking dish that has been sprayed with a nonstick cooking spray.

Combine remaining ingredients with reserved tomato juice. Pour over chicken.

Cover and bake 1 hour.

Each serving provides:

243 Calories

3	Protein Servings	26	g	Protein
2	Vegetable Servings	11	g	Fat
1-1/2	Fat Servings	10	g	Carbohydrate
3	Additional Calories	572	mg	Sodium
		80	mg	Cholesterol

Lemon Special Chicken

This is a very tangy dish that goes well with noodles that have a light sprinkling of toasted sesame seeds.

Makes 4 servings

1/4	cup lemon juice
2	tablespoons Dijon mustard
1/4	teaspoon garlic powder
1/4	teaspoon pepper
2	tablespoons frozen orange juice concentrate (unsweetened), thawed
1	tablespoon plus 1 teaspoon vegetable oil
1	packet instant chicken-flavored broth mix
1	tablespoon dried parsley flakes
1	pound boned and skinned chicken parts, cut in large chunks
1	tablespoon plus 1 teaspoon cornstarch
1	cup water

In a large nonstick skillet, combine lemon juice, mustard, garlic powder, pepper, orange juice concentrate, oil, broth mix, and parsley flakes. Heat over medium heat until hot.

Add chicken. Cook, turning frequently, until chicken is cooked through, about 15 minutes.

Reduce heat to low, cover, and cook 10 more minutes.

In a small bowl, dissolve cornstarch in water. Add to chicken. Cook, stirring constantly, until mixture is slightly thick and boils 1 minute.

Each serving provides:

216 Calories

3	Protein Servings	25	g	Protein
1	Fat Serving	9	g	Fat
1/4	Fruit Serving	8	g	Carbohydrate
12	Additional Calories	593	mg	Sodium
		80	mg	Cholesterol

Chicken Breasts Française

In the French tradition, the white wine and tarragon really give this dish flair, and yet it's so easy to do.

Makes 4 servings

2   tablespoons margarine
1-1/4 pounds boned and skinned chicken breasts
1/2   cup dry white wine
1   teaspoon Dijon mustard
1/2   teaspoon dried tarragon
2/3   cup nonfat dry milk
1/2   cup water
        Salt and pepper to taste

Melt margarine in a large nonstick skillet over medium heat. Add chicken and cook, turning frequently, until chicken is lightly browned on all sides and no longer pink inside. Reduce heat to low.

Remove chicken from pan and set aside.

Add remaining ingredients to skillet. Stir to blend. Simmer, uncovered, for 10 minutes, stirring frequently.

Return chicken to skillet. Heat through.

Each serving provides:

251 Calories

4	Protein Servings	37	g	Protein
1-1/2	Fat Servings	8	g	Fat
1/2	Milk Serving	7	g	Carbohydrate
25	Additional Calories	260	mg	Sodium
		84	mg	Cholesterol

Yogurt Baked Chicken

Try this unique dish with our Spanish Green Beans on page 248. The results will be colorful and delicious.

Makes 4 servings

1-1/4 pounds boned and skinned chicken parts
1   cup plain lowfat yogurt
1/4 teaspoon garlic powder
1/2 teaspoon paprika
1/2 teaspoon dried basil
1   tablespoon soy sauce
2   teaspoons all-purpose flour
3   tablespoons grated Parmesan cheese

Preheat oven to 400°.

Place chicken in a shallow baking pan that has been sprayed with a nonstick cooking spray.

In a small bowl, combine 1/2 cup of the yogurt with the garlic powder, paprika, basil, and soy sauce. Spread on chicken.

Bake, uncovered, 30 minutes.

Stir flour into remaining yogurt. Spread over chicken. Sprinkle evenly with Parmesan cheese.

Bake 10 minutes longer, until hot and bubbly.

Each serving provides:

231 Calories

4	Protein Servings	35 g	Protein
1/2	Milk Serving	6 g	Fat
28	Additional Calories	6 g	Carbohydrate
		476 mg	Sodium
		106 mg	Cholesterol

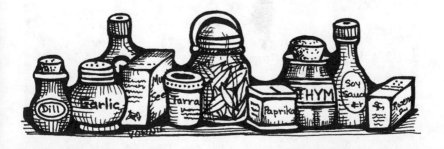

Oriental Stir-Fried Chicken

Serve this tasty dish over rice for a complete, and very filling, meal. To lower the sodium count use the reduced-sodium variety of soy sauce.

Makes 4 servings

3	tablespoons soy sauce
1/4	cup sherry
1/4	teaspoon ground ginger
2	teaspooons cornstarch
1	pound boned and skinned chicken parts, sliced into 1/2-inch strips
1	tablespoon plus 1 teaspoon vegetable oil
1	cup sliced celery
1	cup sliced mushrooms
1	cup snow pea pods
1/2	cup sliced onions
2	cloves garlic, minced
1/2	ounce sliced almonds
1/2	cup water

In a medium bowl, combine soy sauce, sherry, ginger, and cornstarch. Mix well. Add chicken and marinate several hours.

Heat a large skillet or wok over high heat. Add oil and tilt pan to coat. When oil is hot, add celery, mushrooms, pea pods, onions, garlic, and almonds. Stir and fry for 3 minutes. Remove vegetables with a slotted spoon and place in a large bowl.

Drain chicken, reserving marinade. Place chicken in pan and stir-fry for 4 minutes, until cooked throughout. Add to vegetables, stirring to combine.

Add marinade and water to pan. Stir until mixture boils, about 3 minutes. Add chicken and vegetables. Cook, stirring, until heated through.

Each serving provides:

249 Calories

3	Protein Servings	28	g	Protein
1-3/4	Vegetable Servings	10	g	Fat
1	Fat Serving	11	g	Carbohydrate
38	Additional Calories	890	mg	Sodium
		79	mg	Cholesterol

Crispy Onion Chicken

For an even crispier chicken, after baking place under the broiler for a few minutes.

Makes 4 servings

1-1/4 pounds boned and skinned chicken parts
2   tablespoons plus 2 teaspoons reduced-calorie mayonnaise
3   tablespoons dry bread crumbs
2   tablespoons minced onion flakes
1   packet instant beef-flavored broth mix

Preheat oven to 350°.
Place chicken in a shallow baking pan that has been sprayed with a nonstick cooking spray.
Spread mayonnaise evenly over chicken.
In a small bowl, combine remaining ingredients, mixing well. Sprinkle evenly over chicken. Press mixture down gently into the mayonnaise.
Bake, uncovered, 45 minutes.

Each serving provides:

223 Calories

4	Protein Servings	31	g	Protein
1/4	Bread Serving	7	g	Fat
1	Fat Serving	6	g	Carbohydrate
3	Additional Calories	474	mg	Sodium
		103	mg	Cholesterol

Grilled Orange Ginger Chicken

Be sure to watch the chicken carefully when grilling or broiling without the skin. Over-cooking can make it very tough and dry.

Makes 4 servings

1	pound boned and skinned chicken parts
1	tablespoon plus 1 teaspoon vegetable oil
1/4	cup frozen orange juice concentrate (unsweetened), thawed
1	tablespoon wine vinegar
1	tablespoon minced onion flakes
1/4	teaspoon ground ginger

Place chicken in a shallow bowl.

Combine remaining ingredients and pour over chicken. Marinate 4 to 5 hours, turning chicken several times.

Broil or grill until done, about 15 to 20 minutes. Turn chicken frequently and baste with marinade while grilling.

Each serving provides:

207 Calories

3	Protein Servings	25 g	Protein
1	Fat Serving	8 g	Fat
1/2	Fruit Serving	8 g	Carbohydrate
		89 mg	Sodium
		79 mg	Cholesterol

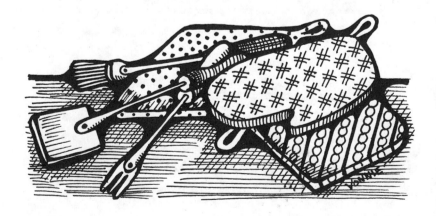

Oven-Fried Chicken

Simply changing the cooking method from deep-frying to baking greatly reduces the calories and fat content of this popular American favorite.

Makes 4 servings

2-1/4 pounds skinned chicken parts
2   tablespoons plus 2 teaspoons margarine, melted
2   teaspoons lemon juice
1/8   teaspoon garlic powder
1/4   teaspoon salt
1/8   teaspoon pepper
1/4   cup plus 2 tablespoons dry bread crumbs

Preheat oven to 350°.

Rinse chicken and pat dry.

In a small bowl, combine melted margarine and lemon juice.

In a shallow bowl, combine garlic powder, salt, pepper, and bread crumbs. Mix well.

Dip each piece of chicken first in margarine and then in crumbs. Turn to coat evenly.

Place chicken on a baking sheet that has been sprayed with a nonstick cooking spray. Drizzle with any remaining margarine.

Bake 1 hour, until brown.

Each serving provides:

241 Calories

3	Protein Servings	26	g	Protein
1/2	Bread Serving	12	g	Fat
2	Fat Servings	7	g	Carbohydrate
10	Additional Calories	381	mg	Sodium
		80	mg	Cholesterol

Pineapple Chicken

If you're in a hurry, canned carrots will work just fine, but be aware that they usually have added salt.

Makes 4 servings

1	pound boned and skinned chicken parts
2	cups cooked carrots, cut into chunks
1	cup canned pineapple chunks (unsweetened)
2	tablespoons soy sauce
2	tablespoons firmly-packed brown sugar (or sweetener equivalent to 6 teaspoons brown sugar)
1/4	cup plus 2 tablespoons dry bread crumbs
1	tablespoon plus 1 teaspoon reduced-calorie margarine

Preheat oven to 350°.

Place chicken in a 6 x 10-inch baking dish that has been sprayed with a nonstick cooking spray.

In a medium bowl, combine carrots, pineapple, soy sauce, and sweetener. Toss to combine. Spoon mixture over chicken.

Sprinkle bread crumbs evenly over pineapple mixture. Dot with margarine.

Bake, covered, 20 minutes. Uncover and continue to bake for 20 more minutes.

Each serving provides:

291 Calories*

3	Protein Servings	27	g	Protein
1/2	Bread Serving	6	g	Fat
1	Vegetable Serving	32	g	Carbohydrate
1/2	Fat Serving	765	mg	Sodium
1/2	Fruit Serving	80	mg	Cholesterol
24	Additional Calories (if brown sugar is used as sweetener)			

*If brown sugar is used as sweetener

Chicken Salad à l'Orange

The sweetness of the orange, combined with the tang of the vinegar and mustard, creates an enchanting blend of flavors. Served on a bed of lettuce, this dish makes a wonderful luncheon plate.

Makes 2 servings

6	ounces cooked chicken (or turkey), cubed
1	small orange, peeled and sectioned
1/4	cup sliced celery
6	sliced, pitted black olives
2	tablespoons reduced-calorie mayonnaise
2	tablespoons frozen orange juice concentrate (unsweetened), thawed
2	teaspoons vinegar
1/4	teaspoon dry mustard
	Salt and pepper to taste

Combine chicken, orange sections, celery, and olives.

In a small bowl, combine remaining ingredients. Mix well. Add to chicken mixture. Toss to combine.

Chill.

❋❋❋

Each serving provides:

285 Calories

3	Protein Servings	26	g	Protein
1/4	Vegetable Serving	13	g	Fat
1-1/2	Fat Servings	16	g	Carbohydrate
1	Fruit Serving	289	mg	Sodium
15	Additional Calories	81	mg	Cholesterol

❋❋❋

Curried Chicken Salad

For more servings, this recipe can easily be doubled or tripled.

Makes 4 servings

1/4	cup plain lowfat yogurt
1/4	teaspoon curry powder
1/8	teaspoon ground ginger
1/8	teaspoon salt
2	tablespoons plus 2 teaspoons reduced-calorie mayonnaise
6	ounces cooked chicken (or turkey), cubed
2	tablespoons finely minced onions
2	tablespoons finely minced green pepper
1	tablespoon raisins
1/4	cup canned crushed pineapple (unsweetened), drained

In a medium bowl, combine yogurt, curry powder, ginger, salt, and mayonnaise.

Add chicken and remaining ingredients. Mix well.

Chill for several hours to blend flavors.

Each serving provides:

136 Calories

1-1/2	Protein Servings	13	g	Protein
1/8	Vegetable Serving	6	g	Fat
1	Fat Serving	7	g	Carbohydrate
1/4	Fruit Serving	191	mg	Sodium
1/8	Milk Serving	42	mg	Cholesterol

Easy Chicken Barbecue

Served over rice or noodles, or on a bun, this is a quick and tasty way to use up leftovers.

Makes 4 servings

1	tablespoon plus 1 teaspoon vegetable oil
1/2	cup chopped onions
1/2	cup chopped green pepper
1	clove garlic, minced
1	8-ounce can tomato sauce
1	teaspoon Worcestershire sauce
1	tablespoon firmly-packed brown sugar (or sweetener equivalent to 3 teaspoons brown sugar)
1/2	teaspoon dry mustard
1	tablespoon sweet pickle relish
1/4	cup water
12	ounces cooked chicken (or turkey), shredded, skin removed

Heat oil in a large nonstick skillet over medium heat. Add onions, green pepper, and garlic. Cook until tender, about 10 minutes.

Add remaining ingredients, *except* chicken, and mix well. Reduce heat to low.

Stir in chicken. Cover and cook until hot and bubbly, about 10 minutes, stirring occasionally.

Each serving provides:

250 Calories*

3	Protein Servings	26	g	Protein
1-1/2	Vegetable Servings	11	g	Fat
1	Fat Serving	11	g	Carbohydrate
7	Additional Calories	459	mg	Sodium
	(plus 12 more calories if brown sugar is used as sweetener)	76	mg	Cholesterol

*If brown sugar is used as sweetener

Chicken Mousse

What a wonderful, tasty hors d'oeuvre for your next party! Spread it on crackers or melba toast, or on thin slices of zucchini or cucumber.

Makes 8 servings

1   envelope unflavored gelatin
1-1/2 cups water
12   ounces cooked chicken, cut into cubes, skin removed
1/4   cup plus 1 tablespoon plus 1 teaspoon reduced-calorie mayonnaise
1/8   teaspoon pepper
1   packet instant chicken-flavored broth mix
1/8   teaspoon garlic powder
1/2   teaspoon dill weed
1/4   cup finely minced onions

Sprinkle gelatin over water in a small saucepan. Heat over low heat until gelatin is completely dissolved.

In a blender container, combine gelatin mixture with remaining ingredients, *except* onions. Blend until smooth.

Stir in onions.

Pour mixture into a 3-cup mold that has been sprayed lightly with a nonstick cooking spray.

Chill until firm. Unmold to serve.

Each serving provides:

115 Calories

1-1/2	Protein Servings	13	g	Protein
1	Fat Serving	6	g	Fat
1	Additional Calorie	1	g	Carbohydrate
		252	mg	Sodium
		41	mg	Cholesterol

Chicken Chow Mein

This tastes so authentic! All you need is cooked rice and our Egg White Drop Soup on page 31 for a complete Chinese dinner.

Makes 4 servings

2	tablespoons vegetable oil
4	cups sliced onions
2	cups sliced celery
2	packets instant chicken-flavored broth mix
1-1/2	cups water
1	1-pound can bean sprouts, drained
8	ounces cooked chicken, cubed or shredded
1	tablespoon soy sauce
2	tablespoons water
2	tablespoons cornstarch
1	teaspoon sugar (or equivalent amount of sweetener)

Heat oil in a large saucepan over medium heat. Add onions, cover, and cook 5 minutes, stirring once.

Add celery, broth mix, and water. Cover and cook 5 minutes.

Stir in bean sprouts and chicken. Cover and cook 3 minutes.

In a small bowl, combine remaining ingredients, mixing until cornstarch is completely dissolved. Add to saucepan. Cook, stirring, 1 minute, until mixture thickens slightly and is hot and bubbly.

Each serving provides:

271 Calories*

2	Protein Servings	21	g	Protein
4	Vegetable Servings	12	g	Fat
1-1/2	Fat Servings	21	g	Carbohydrate
20	Additional Calories			
	(plus 4 more calories if	960	mg	Sodium
	sugar is used as	51	mg	Cholesterol
	sweetener)			

*If sugar is used as a sweetener.

Chicken Casserole Deluxe

This is a low-fat version of a delicious casserole, and it's still delicious. We replaced the cream with dry milk, and the butter with margarine and imitation butter flavor.

Makes 4 servings

1	cup lowfat cottage cheese
2/3	cup nonfat dry milk
1/2	cup water
3	eggs
1/4	cup plus 2 tablespoons all-purpose flour
2	tablespoons plus 2 teaspoons reduced-calorie margarine
1	tablespoon minced onion flakes
1/8	teaspoon pepper
1	packet instant chicken-flavored broth mix
1	teaspoon sherry extract
1/2	teaspoon imitation butter flavor
4	ounces cooked chicken, cut into cubes, skin removed
1	4-ounce can mushroom pieces, drained
2	ounces shredded lowfat Cheddar cheese

Preheat oven to 350°.

In a blender container, combine all ingredients, *except* chicken, mushrooms, and Cheddar cheese. Blend until smooth. Stir in chicken and mushrooms.

Pour mixture into a 1-1/2 quart casserole that has been sprayed with a nonstick cooking spray.

Sprinkle evenly with the Cheddar cheese.

Bake, uncovered, 30 minutes.

Let stand 5 minutes before serving.

Each serving provides:

323 Calories

3	Protein Servings	28	g	Protein
1/2	Bread Serving	13	g	Fat
1/2	Vegetable Serving	21	g	Carbohydrate
1	Fat Serving	856	mg	Sodium
1/2	Milk Serving	239	mg	Cholesterol
3	Additional Calories			

Chicken 'n Pasta Primavera

(Shown on Cover)

This pasta dish is pretty and colorful, as well as nutritious. Try it with the rainbow-colored vegetable pasta for a whole-meal salad your family will love.

Makes 4 servings

1	cup diced carrots
1	cup broccoli flowerets
2	cups cooked pasta
1/4	cup finely chopped green onion (green part only)
8	ounces cooked chicken, cut into cubes or strips
2	tablespoons plus 2 teaspoons reduced-calorie mayonnaise
1/2	cup plain lowfat yogurt
1	ounce grated Parmesan cheese
1/8	teaspoon pepper
1/2	teaspoon dried basil

Steam carrots and broccoli in a small amount of water until tender-crisp. Drain.

In a large bowl, combine pasta with carrots and broccoli. Toss gently.

In a small bowl, combine remaining ingredients, mixing well. Add to pasta mixture. Toss to combine.

Chill several hours to blend flavors.

Each serving provides:

290 Calories

2-1/4	Protein Servings	25	g	Protein
1	Bread Serving	10	g	Fat
1	Vegetable Serving	25	g	Carbohydrate
1	Fat Serving	297	mg	Sodium
1/4	Milk Serving	61	mg	Cholesterol

Oriental Turkey Patties

The delicious taste of this dish comes from the sesame oil, which has a unique Oriental flavor. Use it sparingly, or the flavor can be too overpowering.

Makes 4 servings

2	tablespoons sesame oil
2	cups sliced onions
1	4-ounce can mushroom pieces, drained
1	pound ground turkey
1/4	teaspoon ground garlic
1/4	teaspoon ground ginger
1	tablespoon soy sauce
1	tablespoon minced onion flakes
1	packet instant beef-flavored broth mix

Heat oil in a large nonstick skillet over medium heat. Add onions and mushrooms and cook until onions are tender, about 10 minutes.

Combine turkey with remaining ingredients, mixing well. Make into patties.

Place patties in pan with onion mixture and cook, turning several times, until patties are done.

Each serving provides:

286 Calories

3	Protein Servings	22	g	Protein
1-1/2	Vegetable Servings	18	g	Fat
1-1/2	Fat Servings	7	g	Carbohydrate
3	Additional Calories	704	mg	Sodium
		76	mg	Cholesterol

Curried Turkey Meatballs

This delectable dish has a mild curry flavor. For a stronger flavor and more tang, add more curry powder.

Makes 4 servings

1	tablespoon plus 1 teaspoon vegetable oil
1	cup sliced onions
1/4	cup raisins
1	pound ground turkey
1	tablespoon minced onion flakes
2	teaspoons curry powder
2	teaspoons lemon juice
	Salt and pepper to taste

Heat oil in a large nonstick skillet over medium heat. Add onions and raisins. Cover and cook until onions are slightly tender, about 5 minutes.

While onions are cooking, combine remaining ingredients, mixing well. Shape into balls.

Add meatballs to onion mixture. Cover and cook until meat is cooked through, stirring occasionally.

Each serving provides:

271 Calories

3	Protein Servings	21	g	Protein
1/2	Vegetable Serving	16	g	Fat
1	Fat Serving	12	g	Carbohydrate
1/2	Fruit Serving	109	mg	Sodium
		76	mg	Cholesterol

Turkey Noodle Casserole

The sodium content of this delicious casserole can be reduced by using the low-sodium varieties of canned tomatoes and tomato sauce.

Makes 6 servings

1	tablespoon vegetable oil
1/2	cup chopped onions
1/2	cup chopped green pepper
1	pound ground turkey
2	1-pound cans tomatoes, chopped, drained
1	8-ounce can tomato sauce
5	ounces shredded part-skim Mozzarella cheese
1	teaspoon chili powder
1	teaspoon dried oregano
1/2	teaspoon dried basil
1/4	teaspoon garlic powder
1/4	teaspoon dried thyme
	Salt and pepper to taste
3	cups cooked noodles or macaroni
1	ounce grated Parmesan cheese

Preheat oven to 375°.

Heat oil in a large nonstick skillet over medium heat. Add onions and green pepper and cook until slightly tender, about 5 minutes. Add turkey. Cook, stirring frequently, until turkey is lightly browned. Remove from heat and pour off any pan juices.

Add tomatoes, tomato sauce, Mozzarella cheese, and spices. Mix well. Stir in noodles.

Spoon mixture into an 8-inch square pan that has been sprayed with a nonstick cooking spray. Press mixture down gently with the back of a spoon. Sprinkle with Parmesan cheese.

Bake, uncovered, 30 minutes.

Each serving provides:

375 Calories

3	Protein Servings	27	g	Protein
1	Bread Serving	17	g	Fat
2-1/3	Vegetable Servings	31	g	Carbohydrate
1/2	Fat Serving	750	mg	Sodium
		93	mg	Cholesterol

Sweet and Spicy Turkey Loaf

A perfect accompaniment to this sweet and spicy loaf is our Potato Flapjack on page 272.

Makes 4 servings

1	pound ground turkey
	Salt to taste
1/4	teaspoon pepper
1/4	teaspoon ground nutmeg
1/16	teaspoon ground cloves
1/8	teaspoon garlic powder
1	tablespoon dried parsley flakes
1	tablespoon sweet pickle relish
3	tablespoons ketchup
1	teaspoon prepared mustard
1/2	cup finely chopped onions

Preheat oven to 350°.

In a large bowl, combine turkey with remaining ingredients. Mix well.

Shape into a loaf and place on a rack in a shallow baking pan. Bake, uncovered, 1 hour.

Each serving provides:

212 Calories

3	Protein Servings	21	g	Protein
1/4	Vegetable Servings	12	g	Fat
15	Additional Calories	6	g	Carbohydrate
		285	mg	Sodium
		76	mg	Cholesterol

Turkey Joes

*While the traditional way to serve this dish is on a hamburger bun, we also
love to spoon it over a baked potato.*

Makes 4 servings

1   tablespoon plus 1 teaspoon vegetable oil
1   cup chopped onions
1   cup chopped green pepper
1   clove garlic, minced
1   pound ground turkey
1   teaspoon dried oregano
     Salt and pepper to taste
1   1-pound can tomatoes, drained (Reserve liquid.)
1   4-ounce can mushroom pieces, drained
1   tablespoon all-purpose flour

Heat oil in a large nonstick skillet over medium heat. Add onions, green pepper, and garlic. Cook until tender, about 10 minutes.

Add turkey, oregano, and salt and pepper. Cook, stirring, until
turkey is cooked through. Reduce heat to low.

Add tomatoes and mushrooms.

Stir flour into reserved tomato liquid. Pour over turkey mixture.
Simmer, uncovered, 20 minutes, stirring frequently.

Each serving provides:

282 Calories

3	Protein Servings	23	g	Protein
2-1/2	Vegetable Servings	16	g	Fat
1	Fat Serving	11	g	Carbohydrate
8	Additional Calories	377	mg	Sodium
		76	mg	Cholesterol

Cheese-Stuffed Turkey Franks

This is sure to become a favorite last-minute dinner for kids of all ages.

Makes 6 servings

14	ounces turkey (or chicken) frankfurters
4	ounces shredded lowfat Cheddar cheese
1/2	teaspoon dry mustard
1/2	teaspoon onion powder
1	teaspoon Worcestershire sauce
1	8-ounce can tomato sauce
2	teaspoons minced onion flakes
1	teaspoon chili powder
1	teaspoon honey

Preheat oven to 350°.

Make a lengthwise slit in each frankfurter, being careful not to go all the way through.

In a medium bowl, combine cheese, mustard, onion powder, and *half* of the Worcestershire sauce. Stuff frankfurters with the cheese mixture.

Placed in a shallow baking pan that has been sprayed with a nonstick cooking spray.

Combine tomato sauce, onion flakes, chili powder, honey, and remaining Worcestershire sauce. Spoon evenly over frankfurters.

Bake, uncovered, 25 minutes, until hot and bubbly.

Each serving provides:

216 Calories

3	Protein Servings	12	g	Protein
2/3	Vegetable Serving	15	g	Fat
3	Additional Calories	10	g	Carbohydrate
		969	mg	Sodium
		62	mg	Cholesterol

Franks in Pungent Sauce

You really have to try this one to believe it! Serve it over rice for an easy and inexpensive meal.

Makes 4 servings

1   tablespoon plus 1 teaspoon vegetable oil
12 ounces turkey (or chicken) frankfurters, diced into 1/4-inch
       pieces
2   cups carrots, diced into 1/4-inch pieces
2   cups green pepper, diced into 1/4-inch pieces
3   tablespoons soy sauce
2   tablespoons water
3   tablespoons firmly-packed brown sugar (or sweetener
       equivalent to 9 teaspoons brown sugar)

Heat oil in a large nonstick skillet over medium heat.
Add frankfurters and cook, stirring, until lightly browned.
Stir in carrots. Cover and cook 2 minutes.
Add green pepper, soy sauce, and water. Cover and cook 3 minutes.
Stir in sweetener.
Spoon over rice to serve.

Each serving provides:

320 Calories*

3	Protein Servings	12 g	Protein
2	Vegetable Servings	21 g	Fat
1	Fat Serving	23 g	Carbohydrate
36	Additional Calories (if	1,660 mg	Sodium
	brown sugar is used as	73 mg	Cholesterol
	sweetener)		

*If brown sugar is used as sweetener

Herbed Turkey Roll

This rolled "roast" is simple enough for a family dinner, yet elegant enough for a fancy dinner party. And, if there's any left over, it makes great sandwiches.

Makes 12 to 14 servings

1   6-pound turkey breast, skin and bone removed
1/2   teaspoon dried rosemary, crumbled
1/2   teaspoon dried oregano
1/2   teaspoon dried thyme
1/4   teaspoon garlic powder
     Salt and pepper to taste

Preheat oven to 350°.

Using a sharp knife, make a lengthwise slit in the turkey breast, as if creating a pocket. Do not cut all the way through. Open at the pocket and lay flat.

Place turkey between 2 pieces of wax paper. Flatten with a mallet to about 1-1/2 inches thick.

Sprinkle spices evenly over turkey.

Starting at one end, roll turkey like a jelly roll. Tie with cord in 3 or 4 places.

Wrap turkey securely in aluminum foil and place in a shallow baking pan.

Bake 2 hours.

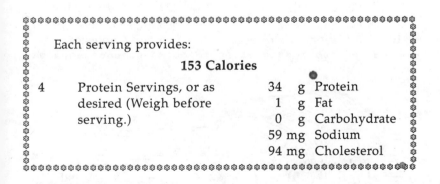

Each serving provides:

153 Calories

4	Protein Servings, or as desired (Weigh before serving.)	34	g	Protein
		1	g	Fat
		0	g	Carbohydrate
		59	mg	Sodium
		94	mg	Cholesterol

Grilled Turkey Sandwich

This sandwich is also delicious on a toasted bagel or English muffin. It's one of our after-Thanksgiving favorites, but can also be enjoyed at any time of the year.

Makes 1 serving

2	teaspoons reduced-calorie mayonnaise
1	slice white or whole wheat bread, lightly toasted
1	teaspoon imitation bacon bits
2	ounces sliced, cooked turkey
1/2	tomato, sliced
1	ounce lowfat Cheddar or lowfat Swiss cheese, sliced

Preheat oven to 375°.

Spread mayonnaise on toast.

Layer bacon bits, turkey, tomato, and cheese. Place sandwich on a baking sheet or piece of aluminum foil.

Bake 15 minutes, until sandwich is hot and cheese is melted.

Each serving provides:

280 Calories

3	Protein Servings	25	g	Protein
1	Bread Serving	11	g	Fat
1/2	Vegetable Serving	22	g	Carbohydrate
1	Fat Serving	375	mg	Sodium
10	Additional Calories	56	mg	Cholesterol

Red Meat

Hints for Red Meat

Red meats contain more saturated fat and cholesterol than most other protein sources. Therefore, most health professionals recommend that you limit the amount of red meat that you consume. However, when you do eat meat, here are some hints that will help you to choose leaner cuts and prepare them in more healthful ways.

- When buying meat, choose the cuts that are lower in fat content. Examples for beef are flank steak and round steak, and examples for pork are tenderloin and center loin.
- Be aware that generally the higher the grade of meat, the more fat it contains.
- Also note that, regardless of the grade or cut, the fat in red meat is mostly saturated fat. This is the fat that your body turns into cholesterol.
- Always trim all visible fat from meat *before* cooking.
- Instead of gravy, baste meats with broth, lemon juice, or wine.
- Tomato products make another delicious, low-fat alternative to gravy.
- In most marinades, you can remove 3/4 of the oil and replace it with fruit juice, wine, broth, or water.
- When a recipe calls for browning the meat in a frying pan, broil it instead.
- Always brown ground meat or stew meat under the broiler before adding it to a recipe. This will allow a lot of the fat to drip away.
- Cook meat and roasts on a rack. The preferred cooking methods are broiling, roasting, baking, and grilling.
- Reduce the size of the meat portions that you eat. Instead, eat larger servings of vegetables and grains.
- Replace bacon in a recipe with imitation bacon bits.
- Be aware that sausage and lunch meats are extremely high in saturated fat and also in sodium.

Sukiyaki

This recipe also works well with chicken or shrimp in place of the beef.

Makes 6 servings

1-1/2 pounds sirloin or round steak, sliced paper-thin
2   tablespoons vegetable oil
2   cups sliced onions
1   cup sliced celery
1/2   cup canned bamboo shoots, drained
2   cups bean sprouts, canned or fresh
1   cup sliced mushrooms
1/4   cup soy sauce
1/2   cup water
1   packet instant beef-flavored broth mix
2   teaspoons sherry extract
2   tablespoons sugar (or sweetener equivalent to 6 teaspoons)
1/4   teaspoon pepper
1   cup sliced green onions
3   cups raw spinach leaves, stems removed
3   ounces canned water chestnuts, sliced

Brown beef on a rack under the broiler, turning once. Heat oil in a large nonstick skillet, or a wok, over medium heat. Add onions, celery, bamboo shoots, bean sprouts, and mushrooms. Cook until vegetables are tender, stirring frequently.

In a small bowl, combine soy sauce, water, broth mix, sherry extract, sugar, and pepper. Pour over vegetables.

Add cooked meat, green onions, spinach, and water chestnuts, tossing to mix well. Cook, tossing frequently, until mixture is heated through and vegetables are done to desired crispness.

Each serving provides:

298 Calories*

3	Protein Servings	30	g	Protein
3-1/2	Vegetable Servings	13	g	Fat
1	Fat Serving	16	g	Carbohydrate
18	Additional Calories	976	mg	Sodium
	(plus 16 more calories if	76	mg	Cholesterol
	sugar is used as			
	sweetener)			

*If sugar is used as a sweetener.

Steak en Casserole

We've broiled the meat first to allow the fat to drip off, then added a wonderful combination of spices and flavors. The result is superb.

Makes 4 servings

4	beef top or bottom round steaks (4 ounces each)
1	1-pound can tomatoes, chopped, undrained
1	packet instant beef-flavored broth mix
1	tablespoon minced onion flakes
1	teaspoon dried oregano
1/8	teaspoon garlic powder
1	tablespoon wine vinegar
1	teaspoon sugar (or equivalent amount of sweetener)
	Salt and pepper to taste

Broil steaks on a rack until lightly browned on each side. Transfer to a casserole.

Preheat oven to 350°.

In a medium bowl, combine remaining ingredients. Pour over steak.

Bake, uncovered, 1 hour, until steaks are tender.

Each serving provides:

200 Calories

3	Protein Servings	28	g	Protein
1	Vegetable Serving	6	g	Fat
3	Additional Calories	7	g	Carbohydrate
	(plus 4 more calories if	492	mg	Sodium
	sugar is used as	72	mg	Cholesterol
	sweetener)			

Steak-Ka-Bobs

From summer cook-outs to elegant dinner parties, this one can't miss.

Makes 6 servings

1-1/2 pounds sirloin steak, cut into 1-inch cubes, fat removed
1/4   cup soy sauce
1   tablespoon vegetable oil
2   teaspoons sherry extract
1/2   teaspoon ground ginger
2   tablespoons firmly-packed brown sugar (or sweetener
          equivalent to 6 teaspoons brown sugar)
1   teaspoon onion powder
1/8   teaspoon garlic powder
1-1/2 cups canned pineapple chunks (unsweetened), drained
2   tablespoons juice from pineapple
2   teaspoons cornstarch

Place meat in a shallow pan.

In a small bowl, combine soy sauce, oil, sherry extract, ginger, brown sugar, onion powder, and garlic powder. Pour over meat and marinate several hours, turning meat occasionally. Drain, reserving marinade. Thread the meat and pineapple on 6 skewers. Place on a broiler rack or outdoor grill. Broil 3 inches from heat for about 10 minutes, or until done to taste, turning skewers to brown on both sides.

In a small saucepan, combine the reserved marinade with the pineapple juice and cornstarch. Stir to dissolve cornstarch. Cook over low heat, stirring, until mixture thickens and boils. Serve with the meat.

Each serving provides:

274 Calories*

3	Protein Servings	27	g	Protein
1/2	Fat Serving	10	g	Fat
1/2	Fruit Serving	17	g	Carbohydrate
3	Additional Calories	744	mg	Sodium
	(plus 16 more calories if	76	mg	Cholesterol
	brown sugar is used as			
	sweetener)			

*If brown sugar is used as sweetener

Lemon Marinated Steak

This tangy marinade is also great with chicken or seafood.

Makes 4 servings

1	pound boneless sirloin steak
1/2	teaspoon grated lemon peel
2	tablespoons lemon juice
1	tablespoon water
1	tablespoon dried chives
2	teaspoons honey
1	teaspoon Worcestershire sauce
1/2	teaspoon Dijon mustard
1/8	teaspoon pepper
2	teaspoons vegetable oil

Place beef in a shallow pan.

Combine remaining ingredients and pour over meat. Marinate in the refrigerator several hours or overnight, turning meat occasionally.

Preheat broiler or grill.

Place steak on a broiler pan or barbecue rack, reserving marinade. Broil, turning once and basting occasionally with reserved marinade, until done to taste.

Each serving provides:

214 Calories

3	Protein Servings	26	g	Protein
1/2	Fat Serving	10	g	Fat
10	Additional Calories	4	g	Carbohydrate
		90	mg	Sodium
		76	mg	Cholesterol

Oriental Burgers

We've added some Oriental flair to the traditional burger. For a delicious feast, serve these over cooked brown rice, with stir-fried vegetables.

Makes 4 servings

1	pound lean ground beef
1	egg white
1	tablespoon soy sauce
1/4	teaspoon garlic powder
1/4	teaspoon ground ginger
1	teaspoon grated lemon peel
1	tablespoon minced onion flakes
1/4	teaspoon pepper

In a large bowl, combine beef with remaining ingredients. Mix well.

Shape into 4 patties.

Place on a rack in a broiler pan or on a barbecue grill. Cook 3 inches from heat about 5 minutes per side, or until done to taste.

Each serving provides:

230 Calories

3	Protein Servings	21	g	Protein
5	Additional Calories	15	g	Fat
		2	g	Carbohydrate
		332	mg	Sodium
		70	mg	Cholesterol

Pepper Burgers

For a really pretty effect, use a combination of red and green peppers.

Makes 4 servings

1	pound lean ground beef
1	egg white
3/4	ounce wheat germ
1	cup finely chopped green or red peppers
1/4	cup tomato sauce
1/4	teaspoon garlic powder
1/4	teaspoon dry mustard
1	packet instant beef-flavored broth mix
	Pepper to taste

In a large bowl, combine beef with remaining ingredients. Mix well.

Shape into 4 patties.

Place on a rack in a broiler pan or on a barbecue grill. Cook 3 inches from heat about 5 minutes per side, or until done to taste.

Each serving provides:

259 Calories

3	Protein Servings	23	g	Protein
1/4	Bread Serving	16	g	Fat
3	Additional Calories	6	g	Carbohydrate
		423	mg	Sodium
		70	mg	Cholesterol

Curried Meat Loaf

Apples give this meat loaf an unusually sweet taste and moist texture. Who said meat loaf has to be dull?

Makes 4 servings

1	tablespoon plus 1 teaspoon reduced-calorie margarine
2	small, sweet apples, peeled, chopped
1/2	cup chopped onions
1	pound lean ground beef
2	teaspoons curry powder
1/8	teaspoon garlic powder
	Salt and pepper to taste
2	egg whites
3/4	ounce wheat germ
3/4	cup tomato sauce

Preheat oven to 350°.

Melt margarine in a small nonstick skillet over medium heat. Add apples and onions and cook until onion are lightly browned, about 15 minutes.

In a large bowl, combine onion mixture with remaining ingredients, using only 1/2 cup of the tomato sauce. Mix well.

Shape mixture into a loaf. Place on a rack in a shallow baking pan. Top with remaining tomato sauce.

Bake, uncovered, 1 hour.

Each serving provides:

317 Calories

3	Protein Servings	24	g	Protein
1/4	Bread Serving	18	g	Fat
1	Vegetable Serving	16	g	Carbohydrate
1/2	Fat Serving	405	mg	Sodium
1/2	Fruit Serving	70	mg	Cholesterol
10	Additional Calories			

Meat and Potato Loaf

The addition of potatoes and carrots to this juicy meat loaf makes it almost a meal-in-one. Just add a salad and some steamed broccoli and you're there!

Makes 4 servings

1	pound lean ground beef
2	egg whites
1/4	cup finely chopped onions
1/4	cup grated carrots
3	ounces grated potatoes, unpeeled
2	tablespoons ketchup
1/4	teaspoon dried thyme
	Salt and pepper to taste

Preheat oven to 350°.

In a large bowl, combine meat with remaining ingredients. Mix well.

Shape mixture into a loaf. Place on a rack in a shallow baking pan.

Bake, uncovered, 1 hour.

Each serving provides:

259 Calories

3	Protein Servings	22	g	Protein
1/4	Bread Serving	15	g	Fat
1/4	Vegetable Serving	7	g	Carbohydrate
18	Additional Calories	181	mg	Sodium
		70	mg	Cholesterol

French Meat Loaf

Sweet and spicy French dressing gives new life to this traditional dish. Add a baked potato and a cooked green vegetable and your meal is complete.

Makes 4 servings

1   pound lean ground beef
1/4   cup reduced-calorie sweet-and-spicy French dressing (16 calories per tablespoon)
3/4   ounce wheat germ
1/2   cup finely chopped onions
2   egg whites
1/8   teaspoon pepper
       Salt to taste

Preheat oven to 350°.

In a large bowl, combine beef with remaining ingredients. Mix well.

Shape mixture into a loaf. Place on a rack in a shallow baking pan.

Bake, uncovered, 1 hour.

Each serving provides:

270 Calories

3	Protein Servings	23	g	Protein
1/4	Bread Serving	15	g	Fat
1/4	Vegetable Serving	7	g	Carbohydrate
26	Additional Calories	213	mg	Sodium
		70	mg	Cholesterol

Rosemary Veal Loaf

This spicy meat loaf works well with ground turkey, too.

Makes 4 servings

1   pound lean ground veal
1   egg white
1/2   teaspoon dried rosemary, crumbled
1/4   teaspoon garlic powder
       Salt and pepper to taste

Preheat oven to 350°.

In a large bowl, combine veal with remaining ingredients. Mix well.

Shape into a loaf. Place on a rack in a shallow baking pan.

Bake, uncovered, 1 hour.

Each serving provides:

205 Calories

3	Protein Servings	25	g	Protein
5	Additional Calories	11	g	Fat
		0	g	Carbohydrate
		54	mg	Sodium
		86	mg	Cholesterol

Savory Veal Stew

The delicious sauce blends the flavors of garlic and white wine for spectacular results.

Makes 6 servings

1-1/2 pounds boneless veal cut into 1-inch cubes
2 tablespoons vegetable oil
1-1/2 cups sliced onions
2 cloves garlic, minced
1 cup carrot, cut into 1-inch pieces
3 cups mushrooms, cut in half
1-1/2 cups water
1 packet instant chicken- or beef-flavored broth mix
1 1-pound can tomatoes, chopped, undrained
9 ounces potato, unpeeled, cut into 1-inch cubes
1 teaspoon dried thyme
1 bay leaf
Salt and pepper to taste
1/4 cup dry white wine
1/4 cup water
2 tablespoons all-purpose flour

Place veal on a rack in a broiler pan. Broil until meat is lightly browned on all sides, turning several times.

Heat oil in a large saucepan. Add onion, garlic, carrots, and mushrooms. Cook, stirring frequently, until vegetables are slightly tender.

Add browned veal, water, broth mix, tomatoes, potato, and spices. Reduce heat to low; cover and simmer 45 minutes, until veal is tender.

In a small bowl, combine wine, water, and flour. Stir until smooth. Add to stew. Cook, stirring 5 minutes.

Each serving provides:

334 Calories

3	Protein Servings	27	g	Protein
1/2	Bread Serving	16	g	Fat
2-1/2	Vegetable Servings	20	g	Carbohydrate
1	Fat Serving	365	mg	Sodium
18	Additional Calories	86	mg	Cholesterol

Veal with Olives

Unusual and delicious, this dish tastes even better reheated. Serve it with rice or noodles for a real gourmet treat.

Makes 4 servings

1   pound thinly sliced veal
1   tablespoon plus 1 teaspoon olive oil
3   cups sliced onions
2   cloves garlic, minced
1   1-pound can tomatoes, chopped, drained
2   tablespoons lemon juice
1   tablespoon honey
1   teaspoon dried oregano
12 stuffed olives, sliced

Place veal on a rack in a broiler pan. Broil 3 inches from heat until browned, about 2 minutes per side.

Heat oil in a large nonstick skillet over medium heat. Add onions and garlic and cook until onions are tender, about 10 minutes.

Add cooked veal, covering each piece with onions.

Combine remaining ingredients and pour over veal and onions. Reduce heat to low; cover and cook 30 minutes.

Each serving provides:

323 Calories

3	Protein Servings	25	g	Protein
2-1/2	Vegetable Servings	17	g	Fat
1	Fat Serving	19	g	Carbohydrate
30	Additional Calories	519	mg	Sodium
		81	mg	Cholesterol

Shish Ka-Bob

Our Rice Pilaf on page 300 is a natural accompaniment to this very impressive dinner.

Makes 4 servings

1	pound boneless lamb, cut into 1-inch cubes
1	tablespoon lemon juice
1	tablespoon plus 1 teaspoon vegetable oil
1/4	cup dry white wine
1/4	teaspoon dried oregano
1/4	teaspoon pepper
1/8	teaspoon dried thyme
	Dash ground allspice
1	cup green pepper, cut into 1-inch squares
8	cherry tomatoes
8	small onions, peeled

Place meat cubes in a plastic bag and set bag in a large bowl. Combine lemon juice, oil, wine, and spices and pour over meat. Marinate in the refrigerator 1 to 2 hours, turning bag over several times.

Thread the meat, green pepper, tomatoes, and onions alternately on 4 skewers. Brush with marinade.

Grill 4 inches from heat, turning several times and basting with marinade, until done to taste.

Each serving provides:

236 Calories

3	Protein Servings	24	g	Protein
2	Vegetable Servings	13	g	Fat
1	Fat Serving	5	g	Carbohydrate
13	Additional Calories	61	mg	Sodium
		85	mg	Cholesterol

Marinated Lamb Roast

Since we discovered that a leg of lamb can be boned and grilled, our cookouts have become a lot more exciting. Put some potatoes on the grill, add a tossed salad, and what a feast!

Makes 10 servings

1	3- to 4-pound leg of lamb
3	tablespoons lemon juice
1/4	cup dry white wine
1	tablespoon plus 2 teaspoons vegetable oil
1/4	teaspoon dried thyme
1/4	teaspoon garlic powder
1/2	teaspoon dried rosemary, crumbled
1/4	teaspoon dried oregano

Have butcher remove bone from leg of lamb and open it length-wise so it can be spread on the grill.

Place meat in a large plastic bag and set in a large pan.

Combine remaining ingredients and pour over meat. Marinate in the refrigerator several hours or overnight, turning bag over several times.

Grill 4 to 5 inches from heat, turning every 15 minutes and basting with marinade, until done to taste. (Allow about 1 hour for medium.)

Each serving provides:

180 Calories

3	Protein Servings, or as desired (weigh before serving)	24	g	Protein
		8	g	Fat
		0	g	Carbohydrate
1/2	Fat Serving	61	mg	Sodium
5	Additional Calories	85	mg	Cholesterol

Roast Leg of Lamb

The unusual method of placing slivers of garlic into slits in the meat really gives this roast a wonderful flavor.

Makes 10 servings

1   3- to 4-pound leg of lamb
3   cloves garlic, slivered
    Salt and pepper to taste

Preheat oven to 325°.

Make small slits in all meat surfaces with the tip of a sharp knife. Insert slivers of garlic in each slit.

Place meat on a rack in a shallow roasting pan. Sprinkle with salt and pepper.

Roast, uncovered, 30 to 35 minutes per pound, or until a meat thermometer registers 175 degrees.

Each serving provides:

159 Calories

3	Protein Servings, or as desired (weigh before serving)	24 g	Protein
		6 g	Fat
		0 g	Carbohydrate
		60 mg	Sodium
		85 mg	Cholesterol

Dijon Pork Steaks

This unusual marinade combines soy sauce and Dijon mustard. The result is tangy and delicious. It's also a good marinade to use with chicken.

Makes 4 servings

1	pound boneless pork chops
3	tablespoons soy sauce
1/4	cup dry white wine
2	teaspoons sherry extract
1	tablespoon Dijon mustard
1/8	teaspoon garlic powder
2	teaspoons vegetable oil

Place pork chops in a shallow baking pan.

Combine remaining ingredients and pour over chops. Marinate, in the refrigerator, several hours or overnight, turning occasionally.

Preheat broiler or grill.

Place chops on a broiler pan or barbecue rack, reserving marinade. Broil, turning once and basting occasionally with reserved marinade, until done to taste.

Each serving provides:

237 Calories

3	Protein Servings	28	g	Protein
1/2	Fat Serving	11	g	Fat
13	Additional Calories	2	g	Carbohydrate
		950	mg	Sodium
		83	mg	Cholesterol

Orange Baked Pork Chops

Sweet sauces, like this one, seem to bring out the flavor of pork. For an elegant touch, serve these chops over cooked brown rice, garnished with fresh orange sections.

Makes 4 servings

4	pork loin chops, 5 ounces each
1/2	cup orange juice (unsweetened)
1	tablespoon soy sauce
1	tablespoon honey
1/8	teaspoon dried thyme
1/2	teaspoon grated orange peel
1/4	teaspoon dry mustard
2	teaspoons minced onion flakes

Broil chops on a rack in a preheated broiler, turning once, until lightly browned.

Place browned chops in a shallow baking pan.

Preheat oven to 350°.

Combine remaining ingredients and pour over chops. Cover and bake 1 hour.

Each serving provides:

232 Calories

3	Protein Servings	28	g	Protein
1/4	Fruit Serving	9	g	Fat
15	Additional Calories	9	g	Carbohydrate
		324	mg	Sodium
		83	mg	Cholesterol

Dill Roasted Pork

Roast pork is a simple and delicious favorite all over the country. We've added dill for a nice accent.

Makes 8 servings

1	3- to 4-pound pork loin roast
1/4	teaspoon garlic powder
1	teaspoon dill weed
	Salt and pepper to taste

Preheat oven to 325°.

Place roast on a rack in a shallow baking pan. Combine spices and rub over meat.

Bake 30 minutes per pound or until a meat thermometer registers 185 degrees.

Each serving provides:

205 Calories

3	Protein Servings, or as desired (weigh before serving)	24	g	Protein
		11	g	Fat
		0	g	Carbohydrate
		59	mg	Sodium
		77	mg	Cholesterol

Apricot Glazed Ham Steak

Slightly sweet and slightly tangy, this dish is one of our easiest favorites.

Makes 4 servings

1   12-ounce fully-cooked boneless ham steak
2   tablespoons reduced-calorie apricot jam (8 calories per
        teaspoon)
2   tablespoons white wine
1   teaspoon Dijon mustard

Score one side of ham steak in a crisscross pattern. Place in a
shallow baking pan.

In a small bowl, combine remaining ingredients. Spread evenly
over ham.

Broil 5 inches from heat until glaze is hot and bubbly, about 3
minutes.

Each serving provides:

137 Calories

3	Protein Servings	18	g	Protein
18	Additional Calories	5	g	Fat
		4	g	Carbohydrate
		1,061	mg	Sodium
		45	mg	Cholesterol

Legumes

Hints for Legumes

- Legumes are the fruit or seeds from pod-bearing plants. We know them as "beans" and "peas."
- Some familiar types of beans are kidney, pinto, navy, black, lima, garbanzo, and soy beans.
- Other legumes are split peas, black-eyed peas, and lentils.
- While peanuts are legumes, they have a higher fat content and are generally more expensive than most other legumes.
- Legumes contain high levels of complex carbohydrates and are a good source of dietary fiber.
- Legumes provide iron, B vitamins, zinc, calcium, potassium, magnesium, and phosphorus.
- Beans and peas are low in fat, and the fat they do contain is mostly unsaturated.
- Legumes contain no cholesterol.
- Most beans are very low in cost and, therefore, can provide very inexpensive meals.
- One cup of most dried beans weighs 6 ounces and will yield about 3 cups of cooked beans.
- Except for split peas and lentils, which need no soaking, legumes can be soaked in water overnight to reduce the cooking time. Use 2 to 3 times their volume of water. Discarding the soaking water will help eliminate digestive problems that the beans might otherwise cause.
- To cook legumes, use 3 to 4 cups of water for each cup of beans. Bring the pot of water and beans to a boil, reduce heat, cover, and simmer until tender. Use our cooking chart for times.
- When cooking beans or peas, always prepare extra for the freezer. Freeze in small containers or plastic bags, and the beans will always be handy for recipes.
- Canned beans can be used in recipes calling for cooked beans. However, they usually contain added sugar and salt.

Cooking Chart for Legumes*

Legume	Cooking Time
Black Beans	1-1/2 to 2 hours
Black-eyed Peas	30 to 45 minutes
Garbanzo Beans	2 to 3 hours
Great Northern Beans	1 to 1-1/2 hours
Kidney Beans	1-1/2 to 2 hours
Lentils	30 to 45 minutes
Lima Beans	1 to 1-1/2 hours
Navy Beans	1-1/2 to 2 hours
Pinto Beans	1-1/2 to 2 hours
Pink Beans	1 to 1-1/2 hours
Soybeans	2 to 3 hours
Split Peas	30 to 45 minutes

*Times given are for soaked beans, except for split peas and lentils. Cooking time will vary with the size, quality, and freshness of the beans, and the mineral content of the water being used.

Italian Beans and Cheese

For a complete meal, serve this hearty dish over cooked brown rice or a split baked potato.

· *Makes 6 servings*

2	tablespoons vegetable oil
1/2	cup chopped onions
1/2	cup chopped green pepper
1	1-pound can tomatoes, chopped and drained (Reserve liquid.)
16	ounces cooked kidney or pinto beans
1	teaspoon dry mustard
1/8	teaspoon garlic powder
1/2	teaspoon dried basil
1	teaspoon dried oregano
1/8	teaspoon dried thyme
2	ounces shredded lowfat Cheddar cheese
2	ounces shredded part-skim Mozzarella cheese

Heat oil in a large nonstick skillet over medium-high heat. Add onions and green pepper and sauté until golden.

Reduce heat to medium. Add tomatoes, beans, and spices. Cook, stirring frequently, until mixture is heated through. Add reserved tomato liquid as necessary to prevent drying.

Turn off heat, sprinkle cheese evenly over bean mixture, cover pan, and let cheese melt (about 5 minutes).

Each serving provides:

208 Calories

2	Protein Servings	12	g	Protein
1	Vegetable Serving	8	g	Fat
1	Fat Serving	24	g	Carbohydrate
		199	mg	Sodium
		8	mg	Cholesterol

"Fried" Beans

These beans are delicious on tacos or stuffed in a pita bread. Enjoy the beans alone or with lettuce and tomato.

Makes 4 servings

2   tablespoons vegetable oil
2   cloves garlic, minced
1   cup chopped onions
12   ounces cooked kidney or pinto beans
1/2   teaspoon dried oregano
1/2   teaspoon ground cumin

Heat oil in a large nonstick skillet over medium heat. Add garlic and onions and cook until tender, about 10 minutes. Reduce heat to low.

Mash beans, using fork or potato masher.

Add beans and remaining ingredients to onion mixture. Cook 5 minutes, stirring frequently.

Each serving provides:

186 Calories

1-1/2	Protein Servings	8 g	Protein
1/2	Vegetable Serving	7 g	Fat
1-1/2	Fat Servings	23 g	Carbohydrate
		3 mg	Sodium
		0 mg	Cholesterol

Easy Bean Bake

For a quick, easy high-protein entree, this dish can't be beat. To lower the cholesterol, use an egg substitute or egg whites in place of the eggs.

Makes 6 servings

3	eggs, beaten
2	tablespoons minced onion flakes
1	teaspoon poultry seasoning
1/4	teaspoon ground sage
	Salt and pepper to taste
2	tablespoons vegetable oil
3	slices whole wheat bread, crumbled
4	ounces shredded lowfat Cheddar cheese
16	ounces cooked kidney or pinto beans

Preheat oven to 350°.

In a large bowl, combine all ingredients, *except* kidney beans. Mix until blended.

Add beans. Mix well.

Place in a casserole dish that has been sprayed with a nonstick cooking spray.

Cover and bake 30 minutes.

Each serving provides:

255 Calories

2-1/2	Protein Servings	14	g	Protein
1/2	Bread Serving	11	g	Fat
1	Fat Serving	28	g	Carbohydrate
		155	mg	Sodium
		143	mg	Cholesterol

Barbecue Beans

Naturally good over cooked noodles or rice, this dish also makes a unique and delicious topping for scrambled eggs.

Makes 4 servings

2	tablespoons plus 2 teaspoons reduced-calorie margarine
1/2	cup chopped onions
1/2	cup chopped green pepper
1	clove garlic, minced
1	8-ounce can tomato sauce
1	teaspoon Worcestershire sauce
1	tablespoon molasses
1/2	teaspoon dry mustard
1	tablespoon sweet pickle relish
2	tablespoons water
8	ounces cooked kidney or pinto beans

Melt margarine in a large nonstick skillet over medium heat. Add onions, green pepper, and garlic. Sauté until tender, about 10 minutes.

Stir in remaining ingredients, adding beans last.

Reduce heat to low; cover and cook 10 minutes, stirring occasionally.

Each serving provides:

155 Calories

1	Protein Servings	6	g	Protein
1-1/2	Vegetable Servings	5	g	Fat
1	Fat Serving	25	g	Carbohydrate
23	Additional Calories	467	mg	Sodium
		0	mg	Cholesterol

Lentil Loaf

The leftovers make great sandwiches—hot or cold.

Makes 6 servings

12   ounces cooked lentils
2-1/4   ounces wheat germ
1/2   cup finely chopped onions
2   eggs, beaten
1/2   cup tomato sauce
2   ounces shredded lowfat Cheddar cheese
2   ounces shredded part-skim Mozzarella cheese
1/2   teaspoon dried oregano
1/4   teaspoon dried basil
1/4   teaspoon dried thyme
        Salt and pepper to taste

Preheat oven to 350°.

Place lentils in a large bowl and mash slightly, using a fork or potato masher.

Add remaining ingredients. Mix well.

Place mixture in a 4 x 8-inch loaf pan that has been sprayed with a nonstick cooking spray.

Bake 30 minutes, until firm.

Each serving provides:

192 Calories

2	Protein Servings	15	g	Protein
1/2	Bread Serving	6	g	Fat
1/2	Vegetable Serving	22	g	Carbohydrate
		221	mg	Sodium
		99	mg	Cholesterol

Lentil-Rice Stew

This stew is wonderful on a cold day. Just add a tossed salad and a piece of crusty whole grain bread, and your meal is complete.

Makes 4 servings

2	tablespoons plus 2 teaspoons reduced-calorie margarine
1	cup chopped onions
1	cup chopped celery
2	1-pound cans tomatoes, undrained, chopped
2	cups water
6	ounces lentils, uncooked
4	ounces brown rice, uncooked
1/2	teaspoon dried thyme
1/4	teaspoon garlic powder
	Salt and pepper to taste

Melt margarine in a large nonstick skillet over medium heat. Add onions and celery and cook until tender, about 10 minutes. Add water, if necessary, to prevent drying. Reduce heat to low.

Add remaining ingredients; cover and cook 40 minutes, stirring occasionally. Add small amounts of water while cooking if more liquid is desired.

Each serving provides:

344 Calories

2	Protein Servings	17	g	Protein
1	Bread Serving	6	g	Fat
3	Vegetable Servings	60	g	Carbohydrate
1	Fat Serving	484	mg	Sodium
		0	mg	Cholesterol

Hoppin' John

A New Year's tradition throughout the South, this dish is supposed to bring good luck in the coming year. We've lowered the fat in our delicious version.

Makes 4 servings

6	ounces dry black-eyed peas
1	tablespoon plus 1 teaspoon vegetable oil
1	cup chopped onions
2	cloves garlic, minced
1-1/2	cups water
1/2	teaspoon dried thyme
1	bay leaf
	Salt and pepper to taste
2	cups cooked brown rice

Place peas in a large bowl. Add 3 to 4 cups of water and soak overnight.

Heat oil in a large saucepan over medium heat. Add onions and garlic and sauté until onions are tender, about 10 minutes. Add small amounts of water, if necessary, to prevent drying. Reduce heat to low.

Rinse and drain peas. Add to saucepan.

Add 1-1/2 cups water and remaining ingredients, *except* rice. Cover and simmer 30 minutes, until peas are tender.

Add rice. Cook 10 minutes, stirring occasionally.

Remove and discard bay leaf before serving.

Each serving provides:

316 Calories

2	Protein Servings	13	g	Protein
1	Bread Serving	6	g	Fat
1/2	Vegetable Serving	54	g	Carbohydrate
1	Fat Serving	8	mg	Sodium
		0	mg	Cholesterol

Lima Loaf

This hearty dish is high in protein and very tasty. To lower the cholesterol, try using an egg substitute, or 4 egg whites, in place of the 2 eggs.

Makes 4 servings

2	eggs, beaten
2/3	cup nonfat dry milk
1/2	cup water
2	slices whole wheat bread, crumbled
2	ounces shredded lowfat Cheddar cheese
1	ounce grated Parmesan cheese
	Salt and pepper to taste
10	ounces cooked lima beans
1/2	cup finely chopped onions
1	4-ounce can mushroom pieces, drained

Preheat oven to 350°.

In a large bowl, combine eggs, dry milk, water, bread, cheeses, and salt and pepper. Mix well.

Add remaining ingredients. Mix until blended. Place mixture in a 5 x 9-inch loaf pan that has been sprayed with a nonstick cooking spray.

Bake 45 minutes, until set.

Each serving provides:

275 Calories

2-1/2	Protein Servings	19	g	Protein
1/2	Bread Serving	8	g	Fat
1/2	Vegetable Serving	33	g	Carbohydrate
1/2	Milk Serving	431	mg	Sodium
		149	mg	Cholesterol

Fiesta Beans and Peppers

The festive, colorful look of this side dish inspired the name. The wonderful, sweet taste of the peppers will inspire you to make it over and over again.

Makes 4 servings

1	tablespoon plus 1 teaspoon olive oil
2	cloves garlic, minced
1-1/2	cups sliced onions
1	large red pepper, sliced
1	large yellow pepper, sliced
2	tablespoons soy sauce
4	ounces cooked black beans

Heat oil in a large nonstick skillet over medium heat. Add garlic, onions, peppers, and soy sauce. Cook until onions and peppers are tender, about 10 minutes, stirring occasionally.

Add beans. Cook, stirring frequently, until onions and peppers are desired crispness.

Each serving provides:

117 Calories

1/2	Protein Serving	4 g	Protein
1-3/4	Vegetable Servings	5 g	Fat
1	Fat Serving	15 g	Carbohydrate
		518 mg	Sodium
		0 mg	Cholesterol

Black Beans and Rice

This wonderfully spiced entree works equally well with any type of bean. The portions are large and the meal just needs a salad and a vegetable to be complete.

Makes 4 servings

4	ounces shredded part-skim Mozzarella cheese
1	cup part-skim ricotta cheese
1	ounce grated Parmesan cheese
1/2	teaspoon dried thyme
1/2	teaspoon dried oregano
1/2	teaspoon dried basil
	Salt and pepper to taste
6	ounces cooked black beans
2	cups cooked brown rice

Preheat oven to 350°.

In a large bowl, combine Mozzarella cheese, ricotta cheese, and Parmesan cheese, reserving 1 tablespoon of the Parmesan cheese to sprinkle on top of the casserole.

Add spices. Mix well.

Add beans and rice. Stir to combine.

Place mixture in a casserole dish that has been sprayed with a nonstick cooking spray. Sprinkle with reserved Parmesan cheese.

Cover and bake 20 minutes.

Uncover and bake an additional 15 minutes.

Each serving provides:

363 Calories

3	Protein Servings	23	g	Protein
1	Bread Serving	12	g	Fat
		39	g	Carbohydrate
		342	mg	Sodium
		41	mg	Cholesterol

Black Beans and Corn Combo

Beans and corn make a colorful, high-protein combination that can be used either as an entree for 4 people or a side dish for 6.

Makes 4 servings

1	tablespoon plus 1 teaspoon vegetable oil
1	cup chopped onions
1	cup diced carrots
1	cup chopped celery
2	cloves garlic, minced
1/4	teaspoon dried thyme
1/2	teaspoon dried oregano
1	cup water
1	packet instant chicken-flavored broth mix
1	teaspoon Worcestershire sauce
1	10-ounce package frozen corn, thawed
12	ounces cooked black beans

Heat oil in a large nonstick skillet over medium heat. Add onions, carrots, celery, and garlic. Cook until vegetables are tender, adding small amounts of water, as necessary, to prevent drying. Reduce heat to low.

Add remaining ingredients, cover and cook until heated through, stirring occasionally.

Each serving provides:

257 Calories

1-1/2	Protein Servings	11	g	Protein
1	Bread Serving	6	g	Fat
1-1/2	Vegetable Servings	44	g	Carbohydrate
1	Fat Serving	335	mg	Sodium
2	Additional Calories	0	mg	Cholesterol

Butter Beans and Cheese Squares

The blend of onions, garlic, and Cheddar cheese make this a dish that your family and guests will love. Add steamed broccoli or green beans, and your meal is complete.

Makes 4 servings

12	ounces coarsely shredded, unpeeled baking potatoes
1/3	cup nonfat dry milk
8	ounces canned butter beans, drained
3	eggs, slightly beaten
2/3	cup lowfat cottage cheese
3	ounces lowfat Cheddar cheese
1	tablespoon minced onion flakes
1/8	teaspoon garlic powder
1	tablespoon all-purpose flour
1	tablespoon dried parsley flakes

Preheat oven to 350°.

Place potatoes in an 8-inch square baking pan that has been sprayed with a nonstick cooking spray. Press them lightly in place with the back of a spoon.

Sprinkle dry milk evenly over potatoes.

Top with beans.

In a medium bowl, combine remaining ingredients and mix well. (Mixture will be lumpy.) Pour over beans.

Bake 30 to 35 minutes, until set.

Cut into squares to serve.

Each serving provides:

273 Calories

3	Protein Servings	20	g	Protein
1	Bread Serving	8	g	Fat
1/4	Milk Serving	33	g	Carbohydrate
8	Additional Calories	486	mg	Sodium
		214	mg	Cholesterol

Soybean and Spinach Bake

The protein and vegetable are combined in this subtly spiced casserole. Toss some cooked noodles with a small amount of melted margarine as a perfect accompaniment.

Makes 4 servings

6	ounces cooked soybeans
2	eggs
1	ounce grated Parmesan cheese
1/2	cup water
1	tablespoon plus 1 teaspoon vegetable oil
1	teaspoon baking powder
1/8	teaspoon garlic powder
1	tablespoon minced onion flakes
1	teaspoon Dijon mustard
1	10-ounce package frozen, chopped spinach, thawed and drained

Preheat oven to 350°.

In a blender container, combine all ingredients, *except* spinach. Blend until smooth.

Stir in spinach.

Place mixture in a 1-quart baking dish that has been sprayed with a nonstick cooking spray.

Bake, uncovered, 40 minutes, until set.

Each serving provides:

208 Calories

1-1/2	Protein Servings	15	g	Protein
1	Vegetable Serving	14	g	Fat
1	Fat Serving	9	g	Carbohydrate
		363	mg	Sodium
		143	mg	Cholesterol

Soybean Croquettes

Our favorite way to serve these delicious croquettes is with cooked pasta, topped with tomato sauce.

Makes 2 servings

2	teaspoons margarine
1/2	cup chopped onions
1/2	cup chopped green pepper
1	egg
6	ounces cooked soybeans
1/2	cup water
1/8	teaspoon garlic powder
1	tablespoon minced onion flakes
1/2	teaspoon poultry seasoning
1	packet instant chicken-flavored broth mix

Preheat oven to 350°.

Melt margarine in a small nonstick skillet over medium heat. Add onions and green pepper. Sauté until golden, adding small amounts of water, if necessary, to prevent drying.

In a blender container, combine remaining ingredients. Blend until smooth. Stir in onion mixture.

Divide mixture evenly into 4 muffin tins that have been sprayed with a nonstick cooking spray.

Bake 20 minutes.

Invert onto a serving plate.

Each serving provides:

256 Calories

2	Protein Servings	19	g	Protein
1/2	Vegetable Serving	15	g	Fat
1	Fat Serving	15	g	Carbohydrate
5	Additional Calories	640	mg	Sodium
		137	mg	Cholesterol

Bean Gravy

What a wonderful idea—a gravy that is made from protein instead of fat. We like to serve it over rice, pasta, steamed vegetables, or omelets. It's so versatile.

Makes 4 servings

10   ounces cooked kidney or pinto beans
1   packet instant chicken or beef-flavored broth mix
1   teaspoon minced onion flakes
1/2   cup water
      Pepper to taste

Combine all ingredients in a blender container. Blend until smooth.

Place mixture in a small saucepan over medium-low heat. Heat, stirring, and adding water until gravy is desired consistency.

Each serving provides:

95 Calories

1-1/4	Protein Servings	6	g	Protein
3	Additional Calories	1	g	Fat
		17	g	Carbohydrate
		280	mg	Sodium
		0	mg	Cholesterol

Chick Pea Spread

The sesame oil gives this spread a delicate flavor. Try it on crackers or in a pita bread with lettuce and sliced onions.

Makes 4 servings

8	ounces cooked chick peas (garbanzo beans)
1	clove garlic, minced
2	tablespoons lemon juice
1/8	teaspoon pepper
2	tablespoons toasted sesame seeds
3	tablespoons water
1	packet instant chicken-flavored broth mix
1	teaspoon sesame oil

Combine all ingredients in a blender container. Blend until smooth.

Chill to blend flavors.

Each serving provides:

133 Calories

1	Protein Serving	6	g	Protein
1/4	Fat Serving	5	g	Fat
33	Additional Calories	18	g	Carbohydrate
		286	mg	Sodium
		0	mg	Cholesterol

Bean Stuffed Peppers

These peppers make an attractive and delicious buffet dish. For a real flair, try using a combination of green, red, and yellow peppers.

Makes 6 servings

6	medium green peppers
12	ounces cooked chick peas (garbanzo beans)
1/4	cup finely minced onions
1/2	cup finely minced celery
1/2	cup finely shredded carrots
1/8	teaspoon garlic powder
1/4	teaspoon ground cumin
1/2	teaspoon dried oregano
1/2	cup tomato sauce
	Salt and pepper to taste
3	tablespoons dry bread crumbs
2	tablespoons reduced-calorie margarine

Preheat oven to 350°.

Slice off the top of each pepper. Finely chop the slice and remove the seeds from the peppers.

Place peppers in a pot of boiling water. Boil 5 minutes. Remove peppers from water and drain, upside-down, on paper towels.

Mash beans, using a fork or potato masher. Add the chopped pepper slices, onions, celery, carrots, spices, and tomato sauce. Mix well.

Fill green peppers with bean mixture. Sprinkle evenly with bread crumbs. Dot with margarine.

Place peppers in a shallow baking pan that has been sprayed with a nonstick cooking spray.

Bake, uncovered, 30 minutes.

Each serving provides:

155 Calories

1	Protein Servings	7	g	Protein
2-3/4	Vegetable Servings	4	g	Fat
1/2	Fat Serving	25	g	Carbohydrate
15	Additional Calories	204	mg	Sodium
		0	mg	Cholesterol

Peanut Butter-Bean Spread

This spread may sound strange, but it's sooooo good. We love it on rice cakes for lunch.

Makes 2 servings

4   ounces cooked kidney or pinto beans
2   tablespoons peanut butter
1/4   teaspoon ground cinnamon
1/2   teaspoon vanilla extract
1   teaspoon honey

In a small bowl, mash beans, using a fork or potato masher. Add remaining ingredients. Mix well.

Enjoy!

Each serving provides:

182 Calories

2	Protein Servings	10	g	Protein
1	Fat Serving	9	g	Fat
10	Additional Calories	19	g	Carbohydrate
		77	mg	Sodium
		0	mg	Cholesterol

Tofu

Hints for Tofu

Tofu. The name sounds strange, almost mysterious. Many people have seen tofu in supermarkets or health food stores, but are afraid to try it because they don't know what to do with it. Following are some interesting facts about this unusual food, along with some cooking hints that will help you to discover the wonderful versatility of tofu.

- Tofu isn't new. It has been a mainstay of the Japanese and Chinese diets for thousands of years.

- Japanese doctors have been known to prescribe tofu for anyone suffering from diabetes, heart disease, or hardening of the arteries. And, because the Japanese have one of the world's lowest rates of heart and circulatory diseases, tofu is believed to provide long life.

- Tofu is made from soy milk in much the same way that cheese is made from animal milk.

- Another name for tofu is soybean curd.

- Nutritionally, tofu has much to offer. It is high in protein, low in saturated fat, low in sodium, and contains no cholesterol.

- One 3-1/2 ounce serving of tofu provides only 75 calories.

- Also provided in one 3-1/2 ounce serving is 128 mg. of calcium.

- The flavor of tofu is so bland that it takes on the flavor of whatever it is mixed with.

- It provides a wonderful "invisible" way to extend dishes, such as meat loaves, mashed potatoes, and cheese dishes, while adding a considerable amount of protein.

- Another advantage of tofu is that it is very inexpensive.

- Tofu is usually found in the produce section of most supermarkets and is most often sold in 1-pound blocks.

- Be sure to store tofu in water, in a covered container, in the refrigerator. Change the water daily to keep the tofu fresh for one week.

- In many areas tofu is available as soft or firm, referring to the texture. In most recipes any type can be used. However, firm tofu contains almost twice as many calories as soft tofu.

Tofu Macaroni and Cheese

Whoever said that meatless meals aren't filling? This hearty dish serves 4 for dinner or 6 to 8 for lunch, and can be made even more nutritious by using whole wheat macaroni.

Makes 8 servings

12	ounces tofu, sliced, drained well between paper towels
1/2	cup part-skim ricotta cheese
6	ounces shredded lowfat Cheddar cheese
2	ounces grated Parmesan cheese
1/8	teaspoon garlic powder
2	teaspoons minced onion flakes
1	tablespoon plus 1 teaspoon vegetable oil
1/2	teaspoon Worcestershire sauce
1/4	teaspoon dried thyme, crushed slightly
1/4	teaspoon paprika
2	cups cooked macaroni

Preheat oven to 350°.

In a large bowl, combine all ingredients, *except* macaroni. Mash with a fork or potato masher until well blended.

Place half of the mixture in an 8-inch square baking dish that has been sprayed with a nonstick cooking spray. Top with macaroni, then the remaining cheese mixture.

Bake, uncovered, 35 minutes.

Each serving provides:

200 Calories

1-3/4	Protein Servings	13	g	Protein
1/2	Bread Serving	11	g	Fat
1/2	Fat Serving	15	g	Carbohydrate
		224	mg	Sodium
		16	mg	Cholesterol

Chili Con Tofu

For chili lovers, this dish has all the flavor in a meatless dish. Served over a baked potato, with steamed broccoli on the side, it's delicious, nutritious, and very filling.

Makes 4 servings

6	ounces tofu, sliced, drained well between paper towels
2	ounces shredded lowfat Cheddar cheese
1	ounce shredded part-skim Mozzarella cheese
1/2	cup tomato sauce
1/8	teaspoon garlic powder
1/2	teaspoon chili powder
3/4	teaspoon ground cumin
1	tablespoon minced onion flakes
1/2	teaspoon poultry seasoning
1/8	teaspoon ground sage
2	teaspoons vegetable oil
1	4-ounce can mushroom pieces, drained
6	ounces cooked kidney beans, drained

(handwritten: 15 m can) *(handwritten: 1 1/3 C)*

Preheat oven to 350°.

In a large bowl, combine all ingredients, *except* mushrooms and kidney beans. Mash with a fork until well blended.

Stir in mushrooms and beans.

Place mixture in a 1-quart casserole that has been sprayed with a nonstick cooking spray.

Bake, uncovered, 25 minutes.

Each serving provides: *(handwritten: 260)*

180 Calories

2	Protein Servings	12	g	Protein
1	Vegetable Serving	8	g	Fat
1/2	Fat Serving	17	g	Carbohydrate
		354	mg	Sodium
		8	mg	Cholesterol

(handwritten: 1 Starch)

(handwritten left margin: 140, 25, 20, 25, 260)

Tofu Double Cheese Patties

These patties are at home with any meal. Try them for brunch with our delicious Bran Muffins on page 341. And, if you wish to reduce the cholesterol, you can use an egg substitute, or replace some of the eggs with egg whites. (Two egg whites will work in place of 1 egg in most recipes.)

Makes 4 servings

12	ounces tofu, sliced, drained well between paper towels
4	eggs, beaten
2	ounces shredded lowfat Cheddar cheese
2	ounces shredded part-skim Mozzarella cheese
1	teaspoon baking powder
3	tablespoons minced onion flakes
1/4	teaspoon garlic powder
1/2	teaspoon dry mustard
1/4	cup plus 2 tablespoons dry bread crumbs

Place tofu in a large bowl and mash with a fork.

Add remaining ingredients. Mix well.

Drop mixture onto a preheated nonstick skillet over medium heat, making 8 patties. (Use about 1/3 cup for each patty.)

When edges are dry and bottoms are lightly browned, turn patties and brown the other side.

Each serving provides:

263 Calories

3	Protein Servings	20	g	Protein
1/2	Bread Serving	14	g	Fat
		15	g	Carbohydrate
		361	mg	Sodium
		287	mg	Cholesterol

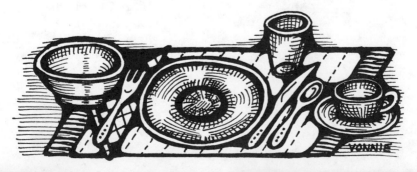

Sweet and Spicy Tofu and Vegetables

Serve this superb dish over rice or noodles for an easy and inexpensive dinner.

Makes 4 servings

2   tablespoons plus 1 teaspoon reduced-calorie sweet and
       spicy French dressing
1   tablespoon plus 1 teaspoon vegetable oil
1/8   teaspoon garlic powder
1   tablespoon soy sauce
2   teaspoons lemon juice
1   tablespoon water
12   ounces firm tofu, sliced, drained well between paper towels
1   cup thinly sliced zucchini, unpeeled
1   cup broccoli, cut into small flowerets
1   medium onion, sliced 1/4-inch thick, separated into rings
1   cup sliced mushrooms

In a small bowl, combine dressing, oil, garlic powder, soy sauce, lemon juice, and water.

Pour about 2 tablespoons of dressing mixture into a large non-stick skillet that has been preheated over medium heat. Add tofu and brown on both sides, turning carefully with a spatula. Remove tofu from pan and cover with aluminum foil to keep warm.

Add remaining dressing mixture to skillet. Stir in vegetables. Cover and cook for 15 minutes, stirring occasionally. Add water, if necessary, to prevent drying.

Reduce heat to low, add tofu, and cook for 5 minutes.

Each serving provides:

198 Calories

1	Protein Serving	15	g	Protein
2	Vegetable Servings	12	g	Fat
1	Fat Serving	10	g	Carbohydrate
9	Additional Calories	351	mg	Sodium
		0	mg	Cholesterol

Tofu-Tuna Florentine

The portions are large and hearty, and the flavor is reminiscent of our favorite tuna casserole. Add a tossed salad and dinner is complete. (Or use to serve 6 or 8 for lunch.)

Makes 4 servings

12	ounces tofu, sliced, drained well between paper towels
4	ounces drained, water-packed tuna, flaked
1/4	cup finely chopped onions
4	ounces shredded part-skim Mozzarella cheese
1	10-ounce package frozen chopped spinach, thawed and drained
1/2	cup finely chopped green pepper
2	teaspoons Dijon mustard
2	tablespoons reduced-calorie Italian dressing
2	tablespoons plus 2 teaspoons reduced-calorie mayonnaise
1/8	teaspoon pepper
1/8	teaspoon garlic powder

Preheat oven to 350°.

Place tofu in a large bowl and mash with a fork.

Add remaining ingredients. Mix well.

Place mixture in an 8-inch square baking pan that has been sprayed with a nonstick cooking spray. Press down gently with the back of a spoon.

Bake, uncovered, 40 minutes.

Each serving provides:

231 Calories

3	Protein Servings	25	g	Protein
1-1/4	Vegetable Servings	12	g	Fat
1	Fat Serving	8	g	Carbohydrate
15	Additional Calories	552	mg	Sodium
		32	mg	Cholesterol

Oriental Rice Patties with Sweet and Sour Sauce

This Oriental delight just needs a vegetable with it and the meal is complete.

Makes 2 servings

6	ounces tofu, sliced, drained well between paper towels
2	eggs, beaten
1	tablespoon soy sauce
1/8	teaspoon *each* garlic powder and ground ginger
1	tablespoon all-purpose flour
1	teaspoon baking powder
1	cup cooked brown rice

Sauce

1	tablespoon cornstarch
1/2	cup water
2	teaspoons vinegar
2	tablespoons reduced-calorie apricot preserves (8 calories per teaspoon)
1	packet instant chicken-flavored broth mix
1	teaspoon sherry extract

Combine all patty ingredients, *except* rice, in a large bowl. Mash with a fork or potato masher until well blended. Stir in rice.

Drop mixture onto a nonstick skillet or griddle that has been preheated over medium heat and sprayed with a nonstick cooking spray. Use about 1/3 cup of mixture for each patty. When bottoms are lightly browned, turn patties and brown the other side.

While patties are cooking, dissolve cornstarch in water in a small saucepan. Add remaining ingredients and bring to a boil over medium heat, stirring constantly. Boil 1 minute, stirring. Spoon over patties to serve.

Each serving provides:

336 Calories

2	Protein Servings	17	g	Protein
1	Bread Serving	11	g	Fat
58	Additional Calories	42	g	Carbohydrate
		1,360	mg	Sodium
		274	mg	Cholesterol

Tofu and Spinach Casserole

This casserole makes a wonderful luncheon dish. Add a tossed salad and a light, fruity dessert and watch them rave! (Or use to serve 4 for a hearty dinner.)

Makes 6 servings

1	10-ounce package frozen chopped spinach, thawed and drained well
1-1/2	cups cooked noodles
12	ounces tofu, sliced, drained well between paper towels
5	eggs
3	ounces grated Parmesan cheese
1/2	teaspoon dried rosemary
1	packet instant chicken-flavored broth mix
2	tablespoons minced onion flakes
1/2	teaspoon Worcestershire sauce
3	tablespoons reduced-calorie margarine

Preheat oven to 350°.

In a large bowl, combine spinach and noodles. Toss to combine. Place in an 8-inch square baking pan that has been sprayed with a nonstick cooking spray.

In a blender container, combine remaining ingredients. Blend until smooth. Pour evenly over spinach mixture.

Bake, uncovered, 35 minutes, until set.

Cool 5 minutes. Cut into squares to serve.

Each serving provides:

267 Calories

2	Protein Servings	19	g	Protein
1/2	Bread Serving	15	g	Fat
2/3	Vegetable Serving	15	g	Carbohydrate
3/4	Fat Serving	612	mg	Sodium
2	Additional Calories	252	mg	Cholesterol

Tofu-Broccoli Patties

The elegant flavor of rosemary enhances these deliciously herbed patties. A salad and a potato make the meal complete.

Makes 4 servings

12	ounces tofu, sliced, drained well between paper towels
4	eggs, slightly beaten
1/2	teaspoon dried rosemary, crushed
1	packet instant chicken-flavored broth mix
2	tablespoons minced onion flakes
1	tablespoon all-purpose flour
1	teaspoon baking powder
1	cup cooked, chopped broccoli

In a large bowl, combine tofu with remaining ingredients, except broccoli. Mash with a fork until well blended.

Stir in broccoli.

Using 1/4 cup for each patty, drop mixture onto a nonstick skillet or griddle that has been preheated over medium heat and sprayed with a nonstick cooking spray. Turn patties carefully to brown both sides. (Makes 8 patties.)

Each serving provides:

173 Calories

2	Protein Servings	15	g	Protein
1/2	Vegetable Serving	10	g	Fat
10	Additional Calories	8	g	Carbohydrate
		465	mg	Sodium
		274	mg	Cholesterol

Italian Tofu Squares

This is our very favorite tofu recipe. You can lower the cholesterol count by using an egg substitute or 8 egg whites in place of the eggs.

Makes 4 servings

12 ounces tofu, sliced, drained well between paper towels
4 eggs
1 cup lowfat cottage cheese
1 ounce grated Parmesan cheese, divided in half
2 tablespoons minced onion flakes
1 tablespoon all-purpose flour
1 teaspoon dried oregano
1/4 teaspoon *each* pepper and garlic powder
1 tablespoon dried parsley flakes
3 tablespoons dry bread crumbs
1 tablespoon plus 1 teaspoon margarine
Sauce
1 8-ounce can tomato sauce
1/4 teaspoon *each* dried oregano and basil
1/8 teaspoon garlic powder

Preheat oven to 350°.

In a blender container, combine tofu, eggs, cottage cheese, *half* of the Parmesan cheese, onion flakes, flour, oregano, pepper, garlic powder, and parsley flakes. Blend until smooth.

Pour mixture into an 8-inch square baking dish that has been sprayed with a nonstick cooking spray.

Combine bread crumbs with remaining Parmesan cheese and sprinkle evenly over the top. Dot with margarine.

Bake 35 minutes, until set and lightly browned.

Cut into squares to serve.

While tofu is baking, combine sauce ingredients in a small saucepan and heat until bubbly. Serve over tofu squares.

Each serving provides:

302 Calories

3	Protein Servings	25	g	Protein
1/4	Bread Serving	16	g	Fat
1	Vegetable Serving	15	g	Carbohydrate
1	Fat Serving	859	mg	Sodium
7	Additional Calories	282	mg	Cholesterol

Tofu Creole

Over a mound of steaming brown rice, this makes an unforgettable lunch or dinner. And, the use of a whole grain adds lots of fiber.

Makes 4 servings

1	cup chopped green pepper
1	8-ounce can tomato sauce
1/2	teaspoon dried oregano
1/4	teaspoon dried basil
1/8	teaspoon garlic powder
12	ounces firm tofu, cut into 1/2-inch cubes, drained well between paper towels
1	tablespoon grated Parmesan cheese

In a large nonstick skillet, combine green pepper, tomato sauce, oregano, basil, and garlic powder. Cover and cook over medium heat until green pepper is tender, about 10 to 15 minutes, stirring occasionally.

Reduce heat to low and gently stir in tofu. Heat through.

Transfer mixture to a serving bowl and sprinkle with Parmesan cheese.

Each serving provides:

153 Calories

1	Protein Serving	15	g	Protein
1-1/2	Vegetable Servings	8	g	Fat
8	Additional Calories	9	g	Carbohydrate
		379	mg	Sodium
		1	mg	Cholesterol

Tofu "Stuffing"

This is a wonderful, high-protein dish that tastes just like the holiday favorite. Try it as a side dish the next time you serve roast chicken or turkey.

Makes 4 servings

12	ounces tofu, sliced, drained well between paper towels
2	tablespoons minced onion flakes
1	teaspoon poultry seasoning
1/4	teaspoon ground sage
1	tablespoon plus 1 teaspoon vegetable oil
4	ounces shredded lowfat Cheddar cheese
	Dash garlic powder
	Salt and pepper to taste

Preheat oven to 350°.

Place tofu in a bowl and mash with a fork. Add remaining ingredients and stir until well blended.

Place mixture in a 1-quart casserole that has been sprayed with a nonstick cooking spray.

Cover and bake 30 minutes.

Each serving provides:

182 Calories

2	Protein Servings	12	g	Protein
1	Fat Serving	13	g	Fat
		9	g	Carbohydrate
		94	mg	Sodium
		8	mg	Cholesterol

Tofu Raisin and Rice Patties

These sweet little patties make a great high-protein brunch dish. They taste a lot like rice pudding, and the leftovers are delicious cold.

Makes 4 servings

6	ounces tofu, sliced, drained well between paper towels
2	eggs, beaten
1	tablespoon all-purpose flour
1	teaspoon baking powder
2	tablespoons sugar (or sweetener equivalent to 6 teaspoons sugar)
2	teaspoons vanilla extract
1/4	teaspoon lemon extract
3/4	teaspoon ground cinnamon
1/4	cup raisins
1	cup cooked brown rice

Sauce

1	tablespoon cornstarch
1/2	cup water
2	tablespoons reduced-calorie peach or apricot preserves (8 calories per teaspoon)
1	tablespoon sugar (or sweetener equivalent to 3 teaspoons sugar)

Combine all ingredients, *except* raisins and rice, in a large bowl. Mash with a fork or potato masher until well blended. Stir in raisins and rice.

Drop mixture onto a nonstick skillet or griddle that has been preheated over medium heat and sprayed with a nonstick cooking spray. Use about 2 tablespoons of mixture for each patty. When edges are dry and bottoms are lightly browned, turn patties and brown the other side. (Makes 12 small patties.)

While patties are cooking, prepare sauce:

Dissolve cornstarch and water in a small saucepan. Add remaining ingredients and bring to a boil over medium heat, stirring constantly. Boil 1 minute, stirring.

Spoon over patties to serve.

Each serving provides:

230 Calories*

1	Protein Serving	8	g	Protein
1/2	Bread Serving	5	g	Fat
1/2	Fruit Serving	37	g	Carbohydrate
27	Additional Calories	145	mg	Sodium
	(plus 36 more calories if	137	mg	Cholesterol
	sugar is used as			
	sweetener)			

*If sugar is used as a sweetener

Tofu Stuffed Potatoes

Simple and nutritious! They reheat beautifully and are even good cold.

Makes 4 servings

2	6-ounce potatoes, baked
6	ounces tofu, sliced, drained well between paper towels
2	ounces shredded lowfat Cheddar cheese
1	tablespoon minced onion flakes
1	tablespoon plus 1 teaspoon reduced-calorie margarine
1	teaspoon Dijon mustard
1/8	teaspoon garlic powder
2	tablespoons skim milk
	Salt and pepper to taste
	Paprika

Preheat oven to 375°.

Cut potatoes in half lengthwise. Carefully scoop out the pulp with a spoon, leaving a 1/4-inch shell.

In a large bowl, combine potato pulp with remaining ingredients, *except* paprika. Mash with a fork or potato masher until well blended.

Divide mixture evenly and fill the potato shells, smoothing the top with the back of a spoon.

Sprinkle with paprika.

Place potatoes in a shallow baking pan that has been sprayed with a nonstick cooking spray.

Bake 30 minutes, until lightly browned.

Each serving provides:

154 Calories

1	Protein Serving	8	g	Protein
1	Bread Serving	6	g	Fat
1/2	Fat Serving	19	g	Carbohydrate
3	Additional Calories	134	mg	Sodium
		4	mg	Cholesterol

Tofu Cinnamon Cheese Pudding

The mellow blending of vanilla, almond, and cinnamon makes this a remarkable brunch dish or dessert.

Makes 4 servings

6	ounces tofu, sliced, drained well between paper towels
2	eggs
2/3	cup lowfat cottage cheese
1	teaspoon vanilla butternut flavor
1	teaspoon almond extract
1	teaspoon ground cinnamon
1/4	cup sugar (or sweetener equivalent to 12 teaspoons sugar)

Preheat oven to 350°.

In a blender container, combine tofu with remaining ingredients. Blend until smooth.

Pour mixture into a 4 x 8-inch nonstick loaf pan or one that has been sprayed with a nonstick cooking spray.

Bake 35 to 40 minutes, until set.

Cool slightly. Then chill.

Cut into squares to serve.

Each serving provides:

158 Calories*

1-1/2	Protein Servings	11	g	Protein
48	Additional Calories (if	5	g	Fat
	sugar is used as	16	g	Carbohydrate
	sweetener)	191	mg	Sodium
		139	mg	Cholesterol

*If sugar is used as sweetener

Tofu Raspberry Mousse

This is a dessert you can actually encourage your family to eat. It's high in protein and tastes delicious. Try other flavors of gelatin, too, but still use the lemon extract.

Makes 4 servings

1	package raspberry-flavored gelatin (sugar-free)
3/4	cup boiling water
2/3	cup nonfat dry milk
6	ounces tofu, sliced, drained well between paper towels
1	teaspoon honey
1/2	teaspoon lemon extract
1-1/2	cups ice cubes

Dissolve gelatin in boiling water, stirring until completely dissolved. Pour into a blender container.

Add remaining ingredients and blend until ice cubes are completely dissolved. Pour mixture into 1 large bowl or 4 individual serving bowls.

Chill.

Each serving provides:

89 Calories

1/2	Protein Serving	8	g	Protein
1/2	Milk Serving	2	g	Fat
13	Additional Calories	8	g	Carbohydrate
		126	mg	Sodium
		2	mg	Cholesterol

Tropical Tofu Fritters

What a delicious breakfast! Everyone loves pancakes, and in these the protein, fruit, and milk are all rolled into one.

Makes 2 servings

3   ounces tofu, sliced, drained well between paper towels
1/3   cup nonfat dry milk
1   egg
3   tablespoons all-purpose flour
1/2   teaspoon baking powder
1   teaspoon vanilla extract
1/4   teaspoon coconut extract
2   teaspoons vegetable oil
1   tablespoon plus 1 teaspoon sugar (or sweetener equivalent
            to 4 teaspoons sugar)
1/2   medium, ripe banana
1/2   cup canned crushed pineapple (unsweetened), drained

In a blender container, combine all ingredients, *except* pineapple. Blend until smooth. Pour mixture into a small bowl and stir in pineapple.

Preheat a nonstick skillet or griddle over medium heat. Drop batter onto skillet, using about 2 tablespoons of batter for each fritter. Turn fritters, browning evenly on both sides. (Makes 10 4-inch fritters.)

Each serving provides:

299 Calories*

1	Protein Serving	12	g	Protein
1/2	Bread Serving	10	g	Fat
1	Fat Serving	42	g	Carbohydrate
1	Fruit Serving	206	mg	Sodium
1/2	Milk Serving	139	mg	Cholesterol
32	Additional Calories (if sugar is used as sweetener)			

*If sugar is used as sweetener

Vegetables

Hints for Vegetables

- For the best flavor and nutritional value, cook vegetables just until tender-crisp.
- Try steaming fresh or frozen vegetables (in a rack over boiling water) so the flavor won't be lost in the cooking water.
- Be aware that canned vegetables usually contain added salt.
- For added fiber, leave the skin on vegetables whenever possible.
- Use spices to enhance the flavor of your vegetables.
- When experimenting with new spices, use them sparingly.
- When oil is needed in a recipe, choose a polyunsaturated oil, such as safflower, sunflower, corn, or soybean oil.
- Use margarine in place of butter. The calories are the same, but butter is high in saturated fat and cholesterol.
- Reduced-calorie tub-style margarines have a high water content, but will usually work well with vegetables.
- When sautéing vegetables, start with a small amount of oil or margarine in a nonstick skillet; then add water or broth as needed to prevent vegetables from drying.
- When a recipe calls for a cream sauce, use evaporated skim milk in place of the cream.
- When a recipe calls for a cheese sauce, use a lowfat cheese.
- A small amount of soy sauce on cooked vegetables adds a flavorful touch. It's a lowfat topping but go easy because it's high in sodium.
- Try onion powder on cooked green vegetables.
- Add a small amount of imitation butter flavor to any vegetable for a buttery taste.
- See our Spice Up Your Life section for lots of hints for adding flavor to vegetables.

Asparagus Sesame

(Shown on Cover)

The Parmesan cheese really enhances the flavor of the asparagus. This dish goes well with any entree.

Makes 6 servings

2   10-ounce packages frozen asparagus
1   4-ounce can mushroom pieces, drained
2   tablespoons margarine
2   teaspoons lemon juice
1   tablespoon grated Parmesan cheese
1   tablespoon toasted sesame seeds
     Salt and pepper to taste

Cook asparagus according to package directions. Drain slightly.

Add mushrooms, margarine, and lemon juice. Cook until heated through. Place in a serving bowl.

Sprinkle with Parmesan cheese, sesame seeds, and salt and pepper.

Each serving provides:

72 Calories

1	Vegetable Serving	4	g	Protein
1	Fat Serving	5	g	Fat
15	Additional Calories	4	g	Carbohydrate
		125	mg	Sodium
		1	mg	Cholesterol

Mushroom Pâté

This pâté is a wonderful party-starter. Try the leftovers for lunch.

Makes 12 servings

3	tablespoons margarine
1/2	cup finely chopped onions
1/3	cup lowfat cottage cheese
2	eggs
2	teaspoons lemon juice
1/8	teaspoon garlic powder
1/4	teaspoon *each* dried basil and oregano
1/4	teaspoon dried oregano
1/4	teaspoon dried rosemary
1	pound mushrooms, cut into quarters
1/2	cup plus 1 tablespoon dry bread crumbs

Melt margarine in a small nonstick skillet over medium heat. Add onions and cook until tender, about 5 minutes.

Preheat oven to 375°.

In a blender container, combine cottage cheese, eggs, lemon juice, and spices. Blend until smooth. Add onions and mushrooms. Blend for a few seconds, until mushrooms are chopped fine, but not puréed. Pour mixture into a bowl.

Stir in bread crumbs.

Line a 4 x 8-inch nonstick loaf pan with wax paper, leaving edges of paper long enough to fold loosely over the top. Spray the wax paper with a nonstick cooking spray.

Pour mushroom mixture into pan. Cover loosely with edges of the wax paper.

Bake 1 hour.

Cool slightly. Then chill until firm. Remove from pan and peel off wax paper. Serve cold with crackers.

Each serving provides:

74 Calories

1/4	Protein Serving	3	g	Protein
1/4	Bread Serving	4	g	Fat
3/4	Vegetable Serving	6	g	Carbohydrate
3/4	Fat Serving	106	mg	Sodium
		46	mg	Cholesterol

Broccoli Muenster Bake

This mild and flavorful cheese sauce proves that broccoli and cheese are a perfect match. Serve this dish with eggs for a perfect brunch menu, or just add a baked potato for a nice, light lunch or dinner.

Makes 4 servings

1   10-ounce package frozen cut broccoli
4   ounces Muenster cheese, cut into cubes
1   tablespoon plus 1 teaspoon reduced-calorie mayonnaise
1   tablespoon minced onion flakes   *add ham*
1   teaspoon Worcestershire sauce
1   teaspoon Dijon mustard
1   tablespoon skim milk

Cook broccoli according to package directions, cooking until just tender-crisp. Drain.

Preheat oven to 350°.

While broccoli is cooking, combine remaining ingredients in a large bowl. Gently stir in cooked broccoli.

Place mixture in a 1-quart baking dish that has been sprayed with a nonstick cooking spray.

Bake, covered, 20 minutes.

Each serving provides:

143 Calories

1	Protein Serving	9 g	Protein
1	Vegetable Serving	10 g	Fat
1/2	Fat Serving	5 g	Carbohydrate
2	Additional Calories	286 mg	Sodium
		29 mg	Cholesterol

3 pts

Sesame Broccoli and Cauliflower

This wonderfully tasty side dish can also be prepared in a wok. It takes only minutes to prepare and is a perfect accompaniment to your favorite broiled seafood.

Makes 4 servings

2   teaspoons vegetable oil
2   teaspoons sesame oil
1   tablespoon plus 1 teaspoon soy sauce
2   cups broccoli, cut into small flowerets
2   cups cauliflower, cut into small flowerets
2   teaspoons toasted sesame seeds

Heat oil and soy sauce in a large nonstick saucepan over medium-high heat.

Add broccoli and cauliflower. Cook, stirring, 5 minutes.

Sprinkle with sesame seeds.

Each serving provides:

75 Calories

2	Vegetable Servings	3	g	Protein
1	Fat Serving	5	g	Fat
10	Additional Calories	6	g	Carbohydrate
		362	mg	Sodium
		0	mg	Cholesterol

Nacho Vegetable Medley

To make this into a complete meal, sprinkle a few ounces each of shredded part-skim Mozzarella cheese and lowfat Cheddar cheese over the cooked vegetables. Cover and let stand for a few minutes, until the cheese melts.

Makes 4 servings

2	teaspoons vegetable oil
2	cups shredded cabbage
1	cup thinly sliced green pepper
1	cup chopped onions
1	cup sliced mushrooms
1/8	teaspoon garlic powder
3/4	teaspoon ground cumin
1/4	cup tomato paste
2	tablespoons water

In a large nonstick skillet, combine all ingredients. Cover and cook over medium heat, stirring frequently, until vegetables are tender-crisp, about 15 minutes.

Each serving provides:

68 Calories

3	Vegetable Servings	2 g	Protein
1/2	Fat Serving	3 g	Fat
		10 g	Carbohydrate
		139 mg	Sodium
		0 mg	Cholesterol

Oriental Cabbage

The wonderful, aromatic sesame oil makes this dish a perfect companion for rice and your favorite Oriental entree.

Makes 6 servings

1	tablespoon sesame oil
1	cup sliced onions
6	cups cabbage, shredded 1/4-inch thick
1	tablespoon soy sauce
1/8	teaspoon garlic powder
1/4	ground ginger
1	packet instant beef-flavored broth mix
2	tablespoons water

Heat oil in a large nonstick skillet over medium heat. Add onions and cook until tender, about 5 minutes. Reduce heat to low.

Add cabbage.

In a small bowl, combine remaining ingredients. Pour over cabbage.

Cook, covered, until cabbage is tender, about 20 minutes. Stir occasionally while cooking.

Each serving provides:

50 Calories

2-1/3	Vegetable Servings	1	g	Protein
1/2	Fat Serving	3	g	Fat
2	Additional Calories	6	g	Carbohydrate
		354	mg	Sodium
		0	mg	Cholesterol

Baked Carrots

This carrot dish tastes just like Mom's chicken soup. It seems to taste best when served with baked chicken on a cold winter night.

Makes 4 servings

2   tablespoons plus 2 teaspoons reduced-calorie margarine
1/2   cup chopped onions
3   cups finely shredded carrots
1   packet instant chicken-flavored broth mix
1/8   teaspoon dill weed

Preheat oven to 350°.

Melt margarine in a small nonstick skillet over medium heat. Add onions and cook until tender, about 5 minutes. Remove from heat.

Stir in remaining ingredients. Place in a 1-quart baking dish. Bake, covered, 30 minutes.

Each serving provides:

78 Calories

1-3/4	Vegetable Servings	1	g	Protein
1	Fat Serving	4	g	Fat
3	Additional Calories	10	g	Carbohydrate
		388	mg	Sodium
		0	mg	Cholesterol

Herbed Cauliflower Bake

The ground sage, often called rubbed sage, adds the flavor that will remind you of stuffing. Served with sliced turkey, this dish seems right at home.

Makes 6 servings

2	10-ounce packages frozen cauliflower
1/4	cup reduced-calorie margarine
1/2	cup chopped onions
1/2	cup chopped celery
2	packets instant chicken-flavored broth mix
1	teaspoon poultry seasoning
1/2	teaspoon ground sage
1	4-ounce can mushroom pieces, drained
	Salt and pepper to taste

Cook cauliflower according to package directions. Drain. Place in a large bowl.

Melt margarine in a medium nonstick skillet. Add onions and celery and cook until tender, about 10 minutes. Remove from heat. Stir in broth mix, poultry seasoning, and sage.

Preheat oven to 350°.

Using 2 sharp knives, cut cauliflower into 1/4 inch pieces. Add onion mixture, mushrooms, and salt and pepper. Mix well.

Place mixture in a baking dish that has been sprayed with a non-stick cooking spray.

Bake, uncovered, 20 minutes.

Each serving provides:

72 Calories

2	Vegetable Servings	3	g	Protein
2	Fat Servings	5	g	Fat
4	Additional Calories	6	g	Carbohydrate
		540	mg	Sodium
		0	mg	Cholesterol

Stuffed Mushrooms

You'll get rave reviews when you serve these tasty morsels as a vegetable or as an appetizer.

Makes 4 servings

16   large mushrooms
1   tablespoon plus 1 teaspoon reduced-calorie margarine
1/4   cup finely chopped onions
2   ounces grated Parmesan cheese
1/8   teaspoon garlic powder
1/4   teaspoon imitation butter flavor

Remove stems from mushrooms. Chop stems.

Melt margarine in a medium nonstick skillet over medium heat. Add chopped stems and onions. Cook until onions are tender and all liquid cooks out of pan, about 10 to 15 minutes. Remove from heat.

Stir in remaining ingredients.

Preheat oven to 375°.

Pile mixture into mushroom caps. Place in a shallow baking pan that has been sprayed with a nonstick cooking spray.

Bake 20 minutes.

Each serving provides:

116 Calories

1/2	Protein Serving	9 g	Protein
2-1/2	Vegetable Servings	7 g	Fat
1/2	Fat Serving	7 g	Carbohydrate
		309 mg	Sodium
		11 mg	Cholesterol

Sautéed Mushrooms in White Wine

Quick and simple to prepare, this dish is the perfect companion for your favorite broiled seafood.

Makes 4 servings

2   tablespoons plus 2 teaspoons reduced-calorie margarine
4   cups sliced mushrooms
1/8 teaspoon garlic powder
     Salt and pepper to taste
1/4 cup dry white wine

Melt margarine in a large nonstick skillet over medium heat. Add mushrooms. Sprinkle with garlic powder and salt and pepper.

Cook, stirring occasionally, until mushrooms are tender, about 5 minutes.

Add wine. Cook, stirring, until heated through.

Each serving provides:

52 Calories

2	Vegetable Servings	1	g	Protein
1	Fat Serving	4	g	Fat
13	Additional Calories	3	g	Carbohydrate
		84	mg	Sodium
		0	mg	Cholesterol

Spanish Green Beans

This dish is colorful, as well as delicious. Stir in leftover chunks of chicken and it becomes a meal unto itself.

Makes 6 servings

2   10-ounce packages frozen cut green beans
2   tablespoons vegetable oil
1/4 cup chopped onions
1/2 cup chopped green pepper
2   medium tomatoes, peeled and chopped
1/2 teaspoon dried basil
1/4 teaspoon dried rosemary, crumbled
    Salt and pepper to taste

Cook beans according to package directions.

While beans are cooking, heat oil in a large saucepan over medium heat. Add onions and green pepper. Cook until tender, about 10 minutes.

Add tomatoes and spices to onion mixture.

Drain beans. Add to saucepan. Heat through.

Each serving provides:

84 Calories

2	Vegetable Servings	2 g	Protein
1	Fat Serving	5 g	Fat
		10 g	Carbohydrate
		7 mg	Sodium
		0 mg	Cholesterol

Pennsylvania Dutch Green Beans

The unique combination of flavors gives these beans a real lift. They're mildly tangy and slightly sweet.

Makes 6 servings

2   10-ounce packages frozen cut green beans
2   tablespoons margarine
1/2   cup chopped onions
1/2   teaspoon dry mustard
1   tablespoon vinegar
2   teaspoons imitation bacon bits
2   teaspoons firmly-packed brown sugar (or equivalent
         amount of sweetener)
       Salt and pepper to taste

Cook beans according to package directions, cooking until just tender-crisp. Drain.

Melt margarine in a large nonstick skillet over medium heat. Add onions and cook until tender, about 10 minutes. Reduce heat to low.

Add beans and remaining ingredients to saucepan. Heat, stirring, until hot.

Each serving provides:

80 Calories

1-1/2	Vegetable Servings	2	g	Protein
1	Fat Serving	4	g	Fat
4	Additional Calories	10	g	Carbohydrate
		63	mg	Sodium
		0	mg	Cholesterol

Sweet and Pungent Beets

Top a tossed salad with these beets for added color and flavor.

Makes 4 servings

2   cups cooked, sliced beets
1   tablespoon plus 1 teaspoon honey
2   tablespoons cider vinegar
     Salt to taste

In a small saucepan, combine all ingredients. Cook over medium-low heat until heated through.

Serve hot or refrigerate and serve cold.

Each serving provides:

49 Calories

1	Vegetable Serving	1	g	Protein
20	Additional Calories	0	g	Fat
		12	g	Carbohydrate
		42	mg	Sodium
		0	mg	Cholesterol

Spicy Squash Pudding

Serve this all-time favorite dish hot as a vegetable or cold as a dessert. (Yes, dessert!) Either way it's spicy, sweet, and just plain delicious. You can lower the cholesterol count by using 4 egg whites in place of the 2 eggs.

Makes 4 servings

3   cups zucchini or yellow summer squash, unpeeled, cut
       into chunks
2   eggs
1-1/2 teaspoons pumpkin pie spice
1-1/3 cups nonfat dry milk
1   teaspoon vanilla extract
1   teaspoon baking powder
1   tablespoon all-purpose flour
2   tablespoons plus 2 teaspoons sugar (or sweetener
       equivalent to 8 teaspoons sugar)

Preheat oven to 350°.
In a blender container, combine all ingredients. Blend until smooth.
Pour mixture into a 9-inch round cake or pie pan that has been sprayed with a nonstick cooking spray.
Bake 30 minutes, until set.

Each serving provides:

180 Calories*

1/2	Protein Serving	12	g	Protein
1-1/2	Vegetable Servings	3	g	Fat
1	Milk Serving	26	g	Carbohydrate
8	Additional Calories	269	mg	Sodium
	(plus 32 more calories if	141	mg	Cholesterol
	sugar is used as			
	sweetener)			

*If sugar is used as sweetener

Yellow Squash and Cheddar

The savory flavor of onions and Cheddar makes this one of our family favorites. It's a good accompaniment to almost any entree.

Makes 4 servings

4   cups yellow summer squash, unpeeled, cut into cubes
2   egg whites
1   tablespoon plus 1 teaspoon reduced-calorie margarine
2   tablespoons minced onion flakes
1/2   teaspoon dried basil
1   tablespoon all-purpose flour
1   teaspoon baking powder
1   teaspoon imitation butter flavor
2   ounces lowfat Cheddar cheese, shredded
      Salt and pepper to taste

Cook squash in a small amount of boiling water until just tender-crisp, about 10 minutes. Drain.

Preheat oven to 375°.

In a blender container, combine squash with remaining ingredients. Blend for a few seconds, until thoroughly mixed.

Pour mixture into a 1-quart casserole that has been sprayed with a nonstick cooking spray.

Bake 35 minutes.

Each serving provides:

100 Calories

1/2	Protein Serving	6	g	Protein
2	Vegetable Servings	4	g	Fat
1/2	Fat Serving	12	g	Carbohydrate
18	Additional Calories	219	mg	Sodium
		4	mg	Cholesterol

2 point per serving

Zucchini Pesto

The idea for this dish came from the ever-popular Italian favorite, Pasta Pesto. Try it to add a spark to your next broiled seafood dinner.

Makes 4 servings

2   cups zucchini, unpeeled, cut into thin julienne strips about
            2 inches long
2   tablespoons olive oil
1-1/4 teaspoons dried basil
2   tablespoons grated Parmesan cheese
        Salt and pepper to taste

Stir-fry zucchini in 1 tablespoon of the oil in a large nonstick skillet over medium heat. Cook until just tender-crisp, about 5 minutes. Stir in remaining ingredients.

Remove from heat and serve.

Each serving provides:

91 Calories

2	Vegetable Servings	3	g	Protein
1-1/2	Fat Servings	8	g	Fat
15	Additional Calories	4	g	Carbohydrate
		51	mg	Sodium
		2	mg	Cholesterol

Broiled Zucchini

This also works well on a barbecue grill and makes a perfect addition to any summer dinner.

Makes 2 servings

2   medium zucchini
1   tablespoon vegetable oil
1   tablespoon plus 1 teaspoon grated Parmesan cheese
     Salt and pepper to taste

Cut zucchini in half lengthwise. Place cut-side down on a broiler pan. Broil 5 inches from heat for 3 minutes.

Turn zucchini. Spread oil over cut sides. Sprinkle evenly with Parmesan cheese and salt and pepper. Broil 3 minutes, until cheese starts to brown.

Each serving provides:

99 Calories

2	Vegetable Servings	3	g	Protein
1-1/2	Fat Servings	8	g	Fat
20	Additional Calories	5	g	Carbohydrate
		67	mg	Sodium
		3	mg	Cholesterol

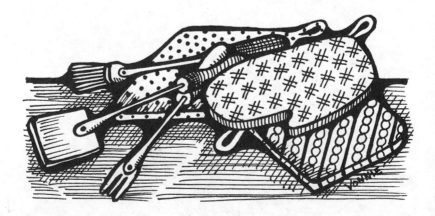

Zucchini and Peppers

This is delicious over rice or as a topper for a baked potato. You can even add leftover cooked chicken or any type of cooked beans and your meal is complete.

Makes 4 servings

2	tablespoons olive oil
1	cup chopped onions
1	cup chopped green pepper
2	cups zucchini, unpeeled, cut into small cubes
1/2	teaspoon dried oregano
1/8	teaspoon garlic powder
	Salt and pepper to taste
1/2	cup tomato paste

Heat oil in a large nonstick skillet over medium heat. Add onions and green pepper. Cook 5 minutes, stirring frequently.

Add zucchini. Cook 5 minutes. Add a small amount of water, if necessary, to prevent drying.

Reduce heat to low. Stir in remaining ingredients. Heat through.

Each serving provides:

117 Calories

2-1/2	Vegetable Servings	3 g	Protein
1-1/2	Fat Servings	7 g	Fat
		12 g	Carbohydrate
		262 mg	Sodium
		0 mg	Cholesterol

Broiled Tomatoes

This quick way to dress up tomatoes is a reminder that this favorite salad vegetable is very versatile. It's even great with eggs for a unique brunch addition.

Makes 4 servings

2   large tomatoes, sliced 1-inch thick
2   teaspoons minced onion flakes
1   teaspoon dried oregano
1   tablespoon plus 1 teaspoon grated Parmesan cheese
2   teaspoons vegetable oil

Place tomato slices in a single layer in a shallow pan that has been sprayed with a nonstick cooking spray.

Sprinkle with onion flakes, oregano, and Parmesan cheese. Drizzle with oil.

Broil 3 inches from heat for 3 to 5 minutes, until cheese is browned.

Each serving provides:

45 Calories

1	Vegetable Serving	1	g	Protein
1/2	Fat Serving	3	g	Fat
10	Additional Calories	4	g	Carbohydrate
		37	mg	Sodium
		1	mg	Cholesterol

Italian Spaghetti Squash Fritters

Wonderful as a side dish for dinner or a main course for lunch, these fritters are sure to be a hit.

Makes 4 servings

2	eggs
1/2	cup part-skim ricotta cheese
1	ounce grated Parmesan cheese
3	tablespoons all-purpose flour
1/2	teaspoon baking powder
2	teaspoons vegetable oil
1/8	teaspoon garlic powder
1/2	teaspoon dried oregano
1/4	teaspoon dried basil
1	tablespoon minced onion flakes
2	cups cooked spaghetti squash

Sauce

1	8-ounce can tomato sauce
1/4	teaspoon dried oregano
1/4	teaspoon dried basil
1/8	teaspoon garlic powder

In a blender container, combine all ingredients, *except* spaghetti squash. Blend until smooth. Pour mixture into a bowl.

Stir in squash.

Drop mixture onto a preheated nonstick skillet or griddle that has been sprayed with a nonstick cooking spray. Cook over medium heat until brown on both sides, turning carefully.

To prepare sauce, combine all ingredients in a small saucepan. Heat until hot and bubbly. Serve over fritters.

Each serving provides:

200 Calories

1-1/4	Protein Servings	11	g	Protein
1/4	Bread Serving	10	g	Fat
2	Vegetable Servings	17	g	Carbohydrate
1/2	Fat Serving	615	mg	Sodium
		152	mg	Cholesterol

Spaghetti Squash Alfredo

This is a wonderful way to turn a versatile vegetable into a delicious entree. A salad and a piece of garlic bread make the meal complete.

Makes 2 servings

1	tablespoon plus 1 teaspoon reduced-calorie margarine
1	cup part-skim ricotta cheese
2	ounces grated Parmesan cheese
1/8	teaspoon garlic powder
1	tablespoon dried parsley flakes
	Salt and pepper to taste
2	cups cooked spaghetti squash

Melt margarine in a medium nonstick skillet over medium-low heat.

Add remaining ingredients, *except* squash. Heat through, stirring to blend well.

Add spaghetti squash. Continue to heat, stirring gently, until squash is hot.

Each serving provides:

379 Calories

3	Protein Servings	27	g	Protein
2	Vegetable Servings	23	g	Fat
1	Fat Serving	18	g	Carbohydrate
		790	mg	Sodium
		61	mg	Cholesterol

Spaghetti Squash Verde

This unique combination of vegetables will add a new dimension to your next dinner party or buffet.

Makes 4 servings

1	10-ounce package frozen chopped spinach, thawed and drained
2	cups cooked spaghetti squash
1/4	teaspoon garlic powder
1/8	teaspoon pepper
2	ounces grated Parmesan cheese
1	tablespoon plus 1 teaspoon margarine, melted

Preheat oven to 350°.

Combine all ingredients in a large bowl. Toss until well blended.

Place mixture in a 1-quart baking dish that has been sprayed with a nonstick cooking spray.

Bake, covered, 25 minutes, until hot.

Each serving provides:

139 Calories

1/2	Protein Serving	9	g	Protein
2	Vegetable Servings	8	g	Fat
1	Fat Serving	9	g	Carbohydrate
		375	mg	Sodium
		11	mg	Cholesterol

Chinese Spinach

The soy sauce and garlic add an Oriental flair to this version of Popeye's favorite food. To dress it up for a party, sprinkle the top with slivered almonds.

Makes 4 servings

1   10-ounce package frozen chopped spinach, thawed and
        drained
1   4-ounce can mushroom pieces, drained
1   tablespoon plus 1 teaspoon reduced-calorie margarine
1/2   packet instant chicken-flavored broth mix
2   tablespoons soy sauce
1/8   teaspoon garlic powder
2   tablespoons chopped green onion (green part only)
1/2   teaspoon sugar (or equivalent amount of sweetener)
        Dash ground ginger

Combine all ingredients in a large nonstick skillet. Heat, stirring frequently, until hot.

Each serving provides:

49 Calories*

1-1/2	Vegetable Servings	3	g	Protein
1/2	Fat Serving	2	g	Fat
2	Additional Calories	4	g	Carbohydrate
	(plus 2 more calories if	831	mg	Sodium
	sugar is used as	0	mg	Cholesterol
	sweetener)			

*If sugar is used as sweetener

Grilled Onions

This summertime favorite can also be made under the broiler all year round. It makes a nice extra vegetable to serve with almost any entree.

Makes 4 servings

2   large onions, sliced 1-inch thick
     Soy sauce

Sprinkle onions with soy sauce and marinate for several hours or overnight.

Grill until tender-crisp and brown on both sides, turning carefully with a spatula.

Each serving provides:

19 Calories

1	Vegetable Serving	1	g	Protein
		0	g	Fat
		4	g	Carbohydrate
		1	mg	Sodium
		0	mg	Cholesterol

Pepper and Onion Kuchen

This versatile bread also works well with other vegetable combinations, such as mushrooms and peppers or broccoli and onions.

Makes 8 servings

Crust
4   slices whole wheat bread
1/3   cup nonfat dry milk
2   tablespoons plus 2 teaspoons reduced-calorie margarine
1   teaspoon baking powder
Filling
1   tablespoon plus 1 teaspoon reduced-calorie margarine
2   cups chopped onions
1   cup chopped green pepper
1   packet instant chicken-flavored broth mix
Topping
3   eggs
1/2   cup plain lowfat yogurt
1   ounce grated Parmesan cheese

Preheat oven to 350°. Combine crust ingredients in a medium bowl. Mix with a fork until mixture resembles coarse crumbs. Press into the bottom of an 8-inch square baking pan that has been sprayed with a nonstick cooking spray.

Bake 10 minutes. Melt margarine in a medium nonstick skillet over medium heat. Add onions, green pepper, and broth mix. Cook until onions are tender and golden, about 15 minutes. Add a small amount of water, if necessary, to prevent drying.

Spread onion mixture evenly over crust.

In a small bowl, beat eggs with a fork or wire whisk. Beat in yogurt and Parmesan cheese. Pour mixture evenly over onions.

Bake 30 to 35 minutes, until set. Cut into squares to serve.

Each serving provides:

137 Calories

1/2	Protein Serving	7 g	Protein
1/2	Bread Serving	7 g	Fat
3/4	Vegetable Serving	12 g	Carbohydrate
3/4	Fat Serving	432 mg	Sodium
1/4	Milk Serving	107 mg	Cholesterol
2	Additional Calories		

Vegetable Chili

This chili is so delicious, you won't even miss the meat. Try it over a baked potato or with a big crusty piece of whole grain bread.

Makes 4 servings

1   tablespoon plus 1 teaspoon vegetable oil
1/2   cup chopped onions
3   cups eggplant, peeled, finely chopped
3-1/2 cups finely chopped mushrooms
1   tablespoon all-purpose flour
12   ounces cooked kidney beans
1/2   clove garlic, minced
1   1-pound can tomatoes, undrained, chopped
1 to 2 tablespoons chili powder (or to taste)
1/2   cup tomato sauce
1   tablespoon vinegar
1   teaspoon sugar (or equivalent amount of sweetener)
         Salt and pepper to taste

Heat oil in a large nonstick skillet over medium heat. Add onions and eggplant and cook until onions are tender, about 10 minutes. Stir frequently. Reduce heat to low.

Stir in mushrooms and flour.

Add remaining ingredients. Simmer, covered, 30 minutes, stirring frequently.

Each serving provides:

239 Calories*

1-1/2	Protein Servings	12 g	Protein
5	Vegetable Servings	6 g	Fat
1	Fat Serving	39 g	Carbohydrate
8	Additional Calories (if sugar is used as sweetener)	405 mg	Sodium
		0 mg	Cholesterol

*If sugar is used as sweetener

Four-Veggie Bake

For a wonderful brunch treat, spoon a serving of this delicious casserole over scrambled eggs and fold in half for a veggie omelet that can't be beat.

Makes 4 servings

1	10-ounce package frozen chopped spinach, thawed and drained
1	4-ounce can mushroom pieces, drained
1/4	cup finely chopped onions
1	cup finely shredded carrots
2	egg whites
3	tablespoons dry bread crumbs
2	tablespoons plus 2 teaspoons reduce-calorie margarine
	Salt and pepper to taste

Preheat oven to 350°.

In a large bowl, combine all ingredients. Mix well.

Place in a 1-quart baking dish that has been sprayed with a nonstick cooking spray.

Bake, covered, 20 minutes.

Uncover and bake 20 more minutes.

Each serving provides:

97 Calories

1/4	Bread Serving	5	g	Protein
2	Vegetable Servings	4	g	Fat
1	Fat Serving	10	g	Carbohydrate
10	Additional Calories	287	mg	Sodium
		0	mg	Cholesterol

Veggie Packets

A great summer favorite, these packets of fresh vegetables are cooked on the grill. They're easy to do and won't make a mess.

Makes 6 servings

3   cups fresh tomatoes, cut into chunks
2   cups eggplant, peeled, cut into 1-inch chunks
1   cup red or green pepper, cut into 1-inch chunks
2   cups zucchini, cut into 1/2-inch slices
1/2   teaspoon garlic powder
1-1/2 teaspoons dried oregano
       Salt and pepper to taste
3   tablespoons vegetable oil

Cut 6 pieces of heavy duty foil about 12-inches square. Divide vegetables evenly in center of each piece.

Sprinkle with spices. Drizzle with oil.

Wrap vegetables in their foil packets, folding edges to seal.

Place on preheated grill and cook for about 30 minutes, turning occasionally.

Each serving provides:

97 Calories

2-2/3 Vegetable Servings	2 g	Protein
1-1/2 Fat Servings	7 g	Fat
	8 g	Carbohydrate
	10 mg	Sodium
	0 mg	Cholesterol

Mixed Vegetable Sauté

Shredded vegetables cook so quickly that you can whip this up in no time.

Makes 4 servings

2   tablespoons plus 2 teaspoons reduced-calorie margarine
1/2   cup chopped onions
2   cups coarsely shredded carrots
1   cup coarsely shredded zucchini, unpeeled
1   cup coarsely shredded yellow summer squash, unpeeled
2   tablespoons soy sauce

Melt margarine in a large nonstick skillet over medium-high heat. Add onions and cook until tender, about 5 minutes.

Add remaining ingredients. Cook 5 minutes, until vegetables are tender-crisp, stirring frequently.

Each serving provides:

79 Calories

2-1/4 Vegetable Servings   2   g Protein
1   Fat Serving   4   g Fat
                                  10 g Carbohydrate
                                  616 mg Sodium
                                  0   mg Cholesterol

Vegetables and Fettucini

Hot or cold, this is really a party-like way to dress up vegetables. Serve it as a side dish along with your favorite chicken or fish, or as a colorful and tasty entree for lunch.

Makes 6 servings

2   tablespoons olive oil
3   cups broccoli, cut into flowerets
3   cups zucchini, unpeeled, sliced 1/2-inch thick
3   cups cooked fettucini noodles
1/4   cup grated Parmesan cheese
1   teaspoon dried basil
1/8   teaspoon pepper

Heat oil in a large nonstick skillet over medium heat. Add broccoli and cook until bright green, about 5 minutes.

Add zucchini. Cover and cook 5 minutes, stirring once. Remove from heat.

Add noodles. Toss.

Add remaining ingredients. Toss gently.

Serve hot or chill and serve cold.

Each serving provides:

177 Calories

1	Bread Serving	7	g	Protein
2	Vegetable Servings	7	g	Fat
1	Fat Serving	23	g	Carbohydrate
20	Additional Calories	78	mg	Sodium
		27	mg	Cholesterol

Japanese Vegetables

Add some leftover cooked chicken or fish, serve over rice or noodles, and your dinner is done.

Makes 6 servings

2   tablespoons vegetables oil
1   cup sliced onions, broken into rings
1   cup broccoli, cut into flowerets
1   cup sliced mushrooms
1/4   cup water
1   10-ounce package frozen French-style green beans
1/4   cup soy sauce
1/4   teaspoon ground ginger
1/16   teaspoon garlic powder
2   tablespoons cornstarch

Heat oil in a large nonstick skillet over medium heat. Add onions. Cook until slightly tender, about 5 minutes. Add broccoli and mushrooms, cover, and cook 5 minutes. Add a small amount of water, if necessary, to prevent drying.

Add water and frozen beans. Cover and cook 10 to 15 minutes, until beans are tender-crisp, stirring occasionally.

In a small bowl, combine remaining ingredients. Stir to dissolve cornstarch. Add to hot vegetables. Cook 5 minutes, stirring frequently.

Each serving provides:

88 Calories

1-2/3	Vegetable Servings	2	g	Protein
1	Fat Serving	5	g	Fat
10	Additional Calories	10	g	Carbohydrate
		692	mg	Sodium
		0	mg	Cholesterol

Starchy Vegetables

Hints for Starchy Vegetables

This category of vegetables includes white potatoes, sweet potatoes, yams, corn, peas, and all varieties of winter squash.

- These vegetables are higher in carbohydrates, protein, and calories than other vegetables.
- Many weight-reduction organizations consider one serving of a starchy vegetable to be equivalent to one serving of bread.
- The skin of potatoes, sweet potatoes, and yams contains a lot of nutrients and fiber, and should be left on and eaten whenever possible.
- All potatoes should be stored in a cool, dark place with good ventilation. Higher temperatures cause sprouting and refrigeration turns some of the starch to sugar.
- When baking potatoes, be sure to make several holes with a fork or knife. This will let the steam escape and prevent the potatoes from "exploding" in the oven.
- The versatile potato goes well with so many spices. For starters, sprinkle cooked potatoes with dried chives, oregano, dill weed, or basil.
- Top a baked potato with dried chives, imitation bacon bits, or any lowfat cheese.
- Try cooked potatoes topped with your favorite pasta sauce.
- Yams are a variety of sweet potatoes with a reddish skin and orange flesh. They are very sweet and moist.
- Sweet potatoes taste great when sprinkled with, or mashed with, ground cinnamon, nutmeg, cloves, ginger, or allspice.
- Sweet potatoes also blend well with fruits such as apples, pineapple, and oranges.
- Although they can be peeled before cooking, winter squash are much easier to peel after they are cooked.
- When ready to cook, cut squash in half and remove seeds and stringy portions.
- Squash halves make an attractive "basket" for many fillings, such as meat, bread stuffings, fruits, or other vegetables.
- To bake squash: Place halves, cut-side down, in a shallow baking pan. Cover with foil and bake in a 400 degree oven 30 to 45 minutes, until tender.

- Squash can also be cut into cubes and cooked in 1 inch of boiling water until tender. This takes about 15 minutes.

- Winter squash goes well with the flavors of cinnamon, nutmeg, cloves, ginger, or allspice.

- When buying fresh peas, choose full, bright green pods. Store peas unshelled in the refrigerator.

- Cook fresh peas, covered, in 1 inch of boiling water with 2 or 3 empty pods 8 to 10 minutes, until tender.

- The flavor of peas blends well with basil, thyme, rosemary, sage, marjoram, and mint.

- Adding onions to peas while cooking is another flavor-enhancer.

- The flavor of corn can be enhanced by so many different spices. Among them are curry, chili powder, nutmeg, or rosemary.

- Corn also mixes well with other vegetables, such as onions, green and red peppers, and chopped pimiento.

- "Cream" sauces made with evaporated skim milk or cheese sauces made with lowfat cheeses are delicious toppers for cooked corn.

Potato Flapjack

This large flapjack will be the star of any meal it accompanies. From breakfast through dinner, it adds a "homey" touch you're sure to love.

Makes 4 servings

12   ounces potatoes, unpeeled, coarsely shredded
1/2   cup finely minced onions
2   tablespoons plus 2 teaspoons reduced-calorie margarine
      Salt and pepper to taste
      Paprika

Combine potatoes and onions, mixing well.

Melt *half* of the margarine in an 8-inch nonstick skillet over medium heat.

Add potato mixture, pressing it into the shape of a pancake, 1/2-inch thick. Sprinkle with salt, pepper, and paprika. Cook until brown on the bottom, about 8 to 10 minutes.

Loosen pancake with a spatula. Dot with remaining margarine. Invert pancake onto a large plate and then slide back into skillet so that brown side is up. Sprinkle again with salt, pepper, and paprika.

Cook 8 to 10 minutes, until bottom is brown.

Each serving provides:

103 Calories

1	Bread Serving	2 g	Protein
1/4	Vegetable Serving	4 g	Fat
1	Fat Serving	16 g	Carbohydrate
		86 mg	Sodium
		0 mg	Cholesterol

Sautéed Potatoes and Peppers

For a real festive confetti-like appearance, try making this easy side dish with a combination of red, green, and yellow peppers.

Makes 4 servings

2   tablespoons plus 2 teaspoons reduced-calorie margarine
1   cup finely chopped onions
1/2 cup finely chopped green or red peppers
12 ounces potatoes, unpeeled, coarsely shredded
     Salt and pepper to taste

Melt margarine in a large nonstick skillet over medium heat. Add onions and peppers and cook 5 minutes, stirring frequently.

Add potatoes. Sprinkle with salt and pepper. Cook, stirring frequently, until onions and peppers are lightly browned and potatoes are tender, about 5 minutes.

Each serving provides:

113 Calories

1	Bread Serving	2	g	Protein
3/4	Vegetable Serving	4	g	Fat
1	Fat Serving	18	g	Carbohydrate
		87	mg	Sodium
		0	mg	Cholesterol

Easy Potato Casserole

Leaving the skin on the potatoes adds vitamins and fiber to this tasty casserole, and shredding the potatoes makes the dish cook quickly.

Makes 4 servings

12	ounces potatoes, unpeeled, coarsely shredded
1/2	cup coarsely grated onions
2/3	cup nonfat dry milk
1/8	teaspoon garlic powder
1/4	teaspoon salt
1/8	teaspoon pepper
2	tablespoons water
1	tablespoon all-purpose flour

Preheat oven to 375°.

In a large bowl, combine all ingredients, mixing well. Place in a 9-inch pie pan that has been sprayed with a nonstick cooking spray. Press mixture down gently with the back of a spoon.

Bake, uncovered, 30 minutes, until lightly browned.

Each serving provides:

118 Calories

1	Bread Serving	6	g	Protein
1/4	Vegetable Serving	0	g	Fat
1/2	Milk Serving	23	g	Carbohydrate
8	Additional Calories	204	mg	Sodium
		2	mg	Cholesterol

Mustard Potato Salad

The coarse, grainy mustard gives this old favorite a new and tangy twist.

Makes 4 servings

12	ounces cooked potatoes, unpeeled, cut into 1-inch chunks
1	tablespoon red wine vinegar
2	teaspoons coarse, grainy mustard
1	tablespoon plus 1 teaspoon reduced-calorie mayonnaise
2	teaspoons dried chives
2	teaspoons dried parsley
1/8	teaspoon pepper
	Salt to taste

Place potatoes in a large bowl.

In a small bowl, combine remaining ingredients, mixing well. Add to potatoes. Toss until well blended.

Chill.

Each serving provides:

90 Calories

1	Bread Serving	2	g	Protein
1/2	Fat Serving	2	g	Fat
		18	g	Carbohydrate
		67	mg	Sodium
		2	mg	Cholesterol

Parmesan Potatoes

In this recipe we've taken an old high-calorie favorite and greatly reduced the amount of cheese. For a unique serving idea, try a mound of these delicious potatoes as a "bed" for steamed or stir-fried vegetables.

Makes 4 servings

12   ounces peeled, hot cooked potatoes
2   tablespoons plus 2 teaspoons reduced-calorie margarine
1/8   teaspoon garlic powder
        Pepper to taste
1   ounce grated Parmesan cheese

In a large bowl, combine all ingredients. Mash with a potato masher until smooth. Serve hot.

Each serving provides:

139 Calories

1/4	Protein Serving	4	g	Protein
1	Bread Serving	6	g	Fat
1	Fat Serving	17	g	Carbohydrate
		216	mg	Sodium
		6	mg	Cholesterol

Potatoes Italiano

This recipe makes an easy one-dish entree, or serve it without the cheese as a classy side dish.

Makes 6 servings

1	tablespoon olive oil
18	ounces potatoes, unpeeled, sliced 1/8-inch thick
1/2	cup green or red pepper, thinly sliced
1/2	cup onions, thinly sliced
1	clove garlic, minced
1	8-ounce can tomato sauce
1/2	teaspoon dried oregano
1/4	teaspoon dried basil
	Salt and pepper to taste
3	ounces part-skim Mozzarella cheese, shredded

Heat oil in a large nonstick skillet over medium heat. Add potatoes, green pepper, onions, and garlic. Cook, stirring frequently, until vegetables are slightly tender, about 5 minutes. Reduce heat to low.

Add tomato sauce and spices, cover, and cook 30 minutes, until vegetables are tender. Stir occasionally while cooking.

Remove from heat. Sprinkle with cheese, cover, and let stand about 3 minutes until cheese is melted.

Each serving provides:

138 Calories

1/2	Protein Serving	6	g	Protein
1	Bread Serving	5	g	Fat
1	Vegetable Serving	19	g	Carbohydrate
1/2	Fat Serving	301	mg	Sodium
		8	mg	Cholesterol

Potatoes in Dill Sauce

The creamy dill sauce really makes this an elegant side dish.

Makes 4 servings

2   cups potatoes, unpeeled, cubed
1   tablespoon plus 1 teaspoon margarine
1/4   cup sliced green onions (green part only)
1/2   cup plain lowfat yogurt
2   tablespoons skim milk
        Salt and pepper to taste
1/2   teaspoon dill weed

Cook potatoes in boiling water, in a covered saucepan, until tender, about 15 minutes. Drain. Set aside in a covered serving dish to keep warm.

Melt margarine in a small nonstick skillet over medium heat. Add onions and cook until tender, about 5 minutes. Reduce heat to low. Stir in remaining ingredients. Cook, stirring, until mixture is hot. Do not boil.

Spoon sauce over potatoes to serve.

Each serving provides:

112 Calories

1	Bread Serving	4	g	Protein
1/8	Vegetable Serving	4	g	Fat
1	Fat Serving	15	g	Carbohydrate
1/4	Milk Serving	74	mg	Sodium
3	Additional Calories	2	mg	Cholesterol

Brown Sugared Sweets

We've used a little brown sugar to bring out the already sweet flavor of the potatoes.

Makes 4 servings

2 tablespoons plus 2 teaspoons reduced-calorie margarine
1 tablespoon firmly-packed brown sugar (or sweetener
    equivalent to 3 teaspoons brown sugar)
12 ounces peeled, cooked sweet potatoes, sliced 1/2-inch thick
    Ground cinnamon

Melt margarine in a large nonstick skillet over low heat. Stir in brown sugar.

Add sweet potatoes. Sprinkle with cinnamon.

Cook, turning potatoes occasionally, until hot.

Each serving provides:

135 Calories

1	Bread Serving	1	g	Protein
1	Fat Serving	4	g	Fat
12	Additional Calories (if	24	g	Carbohydrate
	brown sugar is used as	92	mg	Sodium
	sweetener	0	mg	Cholesterol

Mashed Sweet Potatoes and Apples

This started out as a holiday side-dish, but it became so popular that we now make it all year round. Sweet potatoes and apples are a "natural" together.

Makes 6 servings

18   ounces sweet potatoes
3   small, sweet apples
2   teaspoons firmly-packed brown sugar (or equivalent
        amount of sweetener)
1/2   teaspoon ground cinnamon
1/8   teaspoon ground nutmeg
      Dash ground cloves

Preheat oven to 400°.

Place sweet potatoes and apples on a nonstick baking sheet. Using a fork or sharp knife, make several holes in each potato to let the steam escape while cooking.

Bake 20 minutes, until apples are slightly tender. Remove apples from oven. Continue to bake sweet potatoes 20 more minutes, until tender.

Peel potatoes and apples and place in a large bowl. Add remaining ingredients. Mash with a fork, making mixture as chunky or as smooth as you like.

Serve hot.

Each serving provides:

126 Calories*

1	Bread Serving	1	g	Protein
1/2	Fruit Serving	0	g	Fat
15	Additional Calories (if	30	g	Carbohydrate
	brown sugar is used as	12	mg	Sodium
	sweetener)	0	mg	Cholesterol

*If brown sugar is used as sweetener

Sweet Potato Pancakes

These moist little pancakes can be served as a side dish or as an unusual breakfast. We love them topped with applesauce and a dash of cinnamon.

Makes 4 servings

12	ounces cooked sweet potatoes
2	eggs, beaten
1	tablespoon all-purpose flour
1	teaspoon baking powder
1/4	teaspoon ground nutmeg
1/2	teaspoon ground cinnamon
2	tablespoons firmly-packed brown sugar (or sweetener equivalent to 6 teaspoons brown sugar)
1	teaspoon vanilla extract
1/4	teaspoon maple extract
2	teaspoons vegetable oil

Place potatoes in a large bowl. Mash well, using a fork or potato masher.

Add remaining ingredients. Mix well.

Preheat a nonstick griddle or skillet over medium heat. Spray with a nonstick cooking spray. Drop mixture onto griddle, making 8 pancakes, using 2 tablespoons of batter for each pancake.

Turn carefully when edges become dry and bottoms are lightly browned. Cook until brown on both sides.

Note: To make turning pancakes easier, spray both sides of your spatula with a nonstick cooking spray.

Each serving provides:

188 Calories*

1/2	Protein Serving	5	g	Protein
1	Bread Serving	5	g	Fat
1/2	Fat Serving	30	g	Carbohydrate
8	Additional Calories	154	mg	Sodium
	(plus 24 more calories if brown sugar is used as sweetener)	137	mg	Cholesterol

*If brown sugar is used as sweetener

Sweet Potato and Orange Bake

You'll love the leftovers cold. That is, if there are any leftovers!

Makes 4 servings

12	ounces peeled sweet potatoes, sliced 1/4-inch thick
2	small oranges, peeled, sectioned
1/4	cup orange juice (unsweetened)
1	tablespoon honey
3/4	ounce wheat germ
1/4	teaspoon ground cinnamon
4	teaspoons margarine

Preheat oven to 375°.

Place half the sweet potato slices in the bottom of a 1-quart baking dish that has been sprayed with a nonstick cooking spray. Top with half of the orange sections.

Top with remaining sweet potatoes and then remaining oranges.

In a small bowl, combine orange juice and honey. Pour over casserole. Sprinkle with wheat germ and cinnamon. Dot with margarine.

Bake, covered, 30 minutes, until sweet potatoes are tender. Uncover and bake 10 more minutes.

Each serving provides:

196 Calories

1-1/4	Bread Servings	4	g	Protein
1	Fat Serving	5	g	Fat
2/3	Fruit Serving	37	g	Carbohydrate
15	Additional Calories	56	mg	Sodium
		0	mg	Cholesterol

Sweet Potato Pudding

Raisins and nuts enhance the flavor of this luscious casserole. It's definitely a "go" for any party and the recipe can easily be doubled or tripled.

Makes 4 servings

12	ounces peeled raw sweet potatoes, grated
1	cup carrots, grated
1	small, sweet apple, grated
1	teaspoon vanilla extract
1	teaspoon ground cinnamon
1/2	cup orange juice (unsweetened)
1	tablespoon plus 1 teaspoon maple syrup
1/4	cup raisins
1/2	ounce chopped walnuts

Preheat oven to 350°.

In a large bowl, combine all ingredients. Mix well. Place in a 1-quart casserole that has been sprayed with a nonstick cooking spray.

Bake, uncovered, 50 minutes.

Each serving provides:

202 Calories

1	Bread Serving	3	g	Protein
1/2	Vegetable Serving	3	g	Fat
1	Fruit Serving	44	g	Carbohydrate
44	Additional Calories	23	mg	Sodium
		0	mg	Cholesterol

Corn and Squash Casserole

This casserole makes a nice lunch dish or an interesting side dish. To lower the
cholesterol, use an egg substitute or 2 egg whites in place of the egg.

Makes 6 servings

4	cups yellow summer squash, sliced
1/2	cup chopped onions
1	cup canned corn, drained
1	egg, slightly beaten
	Pepper to taste
1	teaspoon grated Parmesan cheese
3/4	ounce wheat germ

Steam squash and onions over boiling water until tender, about
10 minutes. Drain. Place in a blender container or food processor
and process a few seconds, just until chopped.

Set aside 1 teaspoon each of the Parmesan cheese and the wheat
germ to use as topping.

In a large bowl, combine squash mixture with remaining ingredients. Mix well. Pour into a 1-quart baking dish that has been
sprayed with a nonstick cooking spray.

Sprinkle with reserved topping.

Bake, uncovered, 35 minutes, until firm.

Each serving provides:

74 Calories

1/2	Bread Serving	4	g	Protein
1-1/2	Vegetable Servings	2	g	Fat
13	Additional Calories	11	g	Carbohydrate
		29	mg	Sodium
		46	mg	Cholesterol

Corn Fritters

These delicate little pancakes are a delicious treat with any chicken or fish dinner. Remember to use an egg substitute or 4 egg whites if you are watching your cholesterol.

Makes 4 servings

1   cup canned cream-style corn
2   eggs, beaten
1/2   teaspoon baking powder
1-1/2 ounces yellow cornmeal
1   tablespoon all-purpose flour
        Salt and pepper to taste

Combine all ingredients and mix well with a fork or wire whisk.

Preheat a nonstick griddle or skillet over medium heat. Spray with a nonstick cooking spray.

Drop corn mixture by tablespoonfuls onto skillet, making 16 small pancakes. Brown on both sides, turning carefully when edges appear dry.

Note: To make turning easier, spray both sides of spatula with a nonstick cooking spray.

Each serving provides:

132 Calories

1/2	Protein Serving	5	g	Protein
1	Bread Serving	3	g	Fat
8	Additional Calories	22	g	Carbohydrate
		270	mg	Sodium
		137	g	Carbohydrate

Roasted Corn on the Cob

What a summertime favorite!

Makes 6 servings

6   small ears of corn, in husks
1/4   cup reduced-calorie margarine
1   teaspoon dill weed (or any other favorite spice)
       Salt and pepper to taste

Without removing husks, loosen them and remove silk. Soak corn in cold water 30 minutes. Drain well.

In a small bowl, combine margarine, dill weed, and salt and pepper. Spread evenly over corn. Close husks and wrap each ear in a piece of foil.

Place on grill and cook 25 minutes, turning every 5 minutes. Remove husks to serve.

Each serving provides:

111 Calories

1	Bread Serving	3 g	Protein
1	Fat Serving	5 g	Fat
		17 g	Carbohydrate
		94 mg	Sodium
		0 mg	Cholesterol

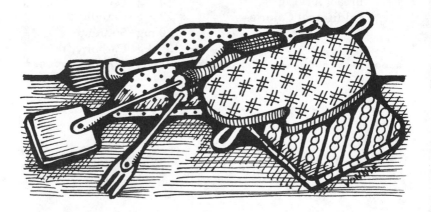

Corn Pudding

Nutmeg gives this traditional dish a new spark. It can be made with eggs or an egg substitute, and goes well with roasted chicken or turkey.

Makes 4 servings

2	eggs, beaten
1	tablespoon all-purpose flour
1/2	teaspoon baking powder
1	tablespoon minced onion flakes
1/8	teaspoon ground nutmeg
	Salt and pepper to taste
1	cup evaporated skim milk
2	cups canned corn, drained
1	tablespoon plus 1 teaspoon margarine, melted

Preheat oven to 325°.

Place eggs in a large bowl. Add flour, baking powder, onion flakes, nutmeg, and salt and pepper. Beat with a fork or wire whisk until blended. Whisk in milk, then corn, and then margarine.

Place mixture in a 1-quart baking dish that has been sprayed with a nonstick cooking spray.

Bake, uncovered, 1 hour, until golden.

Each serving provides:

200 Calories

1/2	Protein Serving	10	g	Protein
1	Bread Serving	8	g	Fat
1	Fat Serving	25	g	Carbohydrate
1/2	Milk Serving	206	mg	Sodium
8	Additional Calories	140	mg	Cholesterol

Butternut Soufflé

Although we've used butternut squash, any winter squash will do. For ease in preparation, we prefer to bake the squash first and then peel it.

Makes 4 servings

2	cups cooked butternut squash, peeled, mashed
2	tablespoons reduced-calorie margarine
1	tablespoon plus 1 teaspoon firmly-packed brown sugar (or sweetener equivalent to 4 teaspoons brown sugar)
1/4	teaspoon grated orange peel
1/8	teaspoon ground nutmeg
1/8	teaspoon ground cinnamon
2	eggs, separated
1/4	teaspoon cream of tartar

Preheat oven to 350°.

In a large bowl, combine squash, margarine, brown sugar, orange peel, nutmeg, and cinnamon. Beat on medium speed of an electric mixer until fluffy.

Add egg yolks and beat well.

In a medium, deep bowl, beat egg whites and cream of tartar on medium speed until stiff. (Be sure to wash beaters and dry them thoroughly before beating egg whites.)

Fold squash mixture into egg whites, gently but thoroughly. Place mixture in a 1-quart soufflé dish or casserole that has been sprayed with a nonstick cooking spray.

Bake 50 minutes, until set. Serve right away.

Each serving provides:

123 Calories*

1/2	Protein Serving	4	g	Protein
1	Bread Serving	6	g	Fat
3/4	Fat Serving	16	g	Carbohydrate
16	Additional Calories (if	100	mg	Sodium
	brown sugar is used as	137	mg	Cholesterol
	sweetener)			

*If brown sugar is used as sweetener

Butternut Squash in Marmalade Sauce

Any winter squash can be substituted in this luscious dish. The flavor of the orange marmalade blends so well with the flavor and texture of the squash.

Makes 4 servings

2   cups butternut squash, unpeeled, cubed
1   tablespoon cornstarch
1/2   cup water
2   tablespoons reduced-calorie orange marmalade (8 calories
           per teaspoon)
1/8   teaspoon ground cinnamon

Cook squash in a small amount of boiling water, in a covered saucepan, until tender, about 15 minutes. Drain and peel squash. Set aside in a covered serving dish to keep warm.

In a small saucepan, combine remaining ingredients, stirring to dissolve cornstarch. Bring to a boil over medium heat, stirring constantly. Boil 1 minute, stirring. Add more water if a thinner sauce is desired.

Spoon sauce over squash to serve.

Each serving provides:

51 Calories

1	Bread Serving	0 g	Protein
20	Additional Calories	0 g	Fat
		13 g	Carbohydrate
		3 mg	Sodium
		0 mg	Cholesterol

Buttery Pecan Squash

This absolutely delicious casserole is a great buffet dish, and it complements almost any entree.

Makes 6 servings

4-1/2 cups butternut or hubbard squash, cut into cubes
2   tablespoons reduced-calorie margarine
1   tablespoon firmly-packed brown sugar (or sweetener
         equivalent to 3 teaspoons brown sugar)
1/4   teaspoon maple extract
1   teaspoon imitation butter flavor
1/2   ounce chopped pecans
1   tablespoon maple syrup

Preheat oven to 400°.

Cook squash in a small amount of boiling water, in a covered saucepan, until tender, about 15 minutes. Drain and peel squash.

In a large bowl, combine squash with margarine, brown sugar, and extracts. Mash with a fork or potato masher until puréed. Place mixture in a casserole that has been sprayed with a nonstick cooking spray. Sprinkle with pecans. Drizzle with maple syrup.

Bake, uncovered, 20 minutes.

Each serving provides:

98 Calories*

1-1/2	Bread Servings	1	g	Protein
1/2	Fat Serving	4	g	Fat
25	Additional Calories	17	g	Carbohydrate
	(plus 8 more calories if	45	mg	Sodium
	brown sugar is used as	0	mg	Cholesterol
	sweetener)			

*If brown sugar is used as sweetener

Applesauce Acorn Squash

Acorn squash has a natural sweetness that is really complemented by the applesauce, making this one of our favorite side dishes.

Makes 4 servings

2	acorn squash, 10 ounces each
1	teaspoon lemon juice
1	cup applesauce (unsweetened)
2	tablespoons raisins
1	tablespoon sugar (or sweetener equivalent to 3 teaspoons sugar)
1/2	teaspoon maple extract
2	teaspoons margarine

Preheat oven to 375°.

Cut squash in half, lengthwise, and remove seeds.

In a small bowl, combine remaining ingredients, *except* margarine. Fill squash halves. Top each with 1/2 teaspoon of the margarine.

Place squash in a shallow baking pan. Pour hot water around squash to a depth of 1/2 inch.

Cover and bake 30 minutes.

Uncover and bake 30 more minutes.

Each serving provides:

113 Calories*

1	Bread Serving	1	g	Protein
1/2	Fat Serving	2	g	Fat
3/4	Fruit Serving	25	g	Carbohydrate
12	Additional Calories (if sugar is used as sweetener)	28	mg	Sodium
		0	mg	Cholesterol

*If sugar is used as sweetener

Stuffed Acorn Squash

Apples, onions, and herbs make a slightly sweet, savory stuffing that can be used in any variety of winter squash.

Makes 4 servings

2	acorn squash, 10 ounces each
1	tablespoon plus 1 teaspoon reduced-calorie margarine
1/4	cup chopped onions
1/4	cup chopped celery
1	small, sweet apple, peeled, chopped
1	slice whole wheat bread, crumbled
1/8	teaspoon dried thyme
1/8	teaspoon ground sage
	Salt and pepper to taste

Preheat oven to 375°.

Cut squash in half, lengthwise. Remove seeds.

Melt margarine in a small nonstick skillet over medium heat. Add onions, celery, and apple. Cook until tender, about 5 minutes.

In a small bowl, combine onion mixture with remaining ingredients. Add water in small amounts until all ingredients are moistened. Spoon mixture into squash halves, mounding if necessary.

Place squash in a shallow baking pan. Pour hot water around squash to a depth of 1/2 inch.

Cover and bake 45 minutes, until squash is tender.

Each serving provides:

93 Calories

1-1/4	Bread Servings	2	g	Protein
1/4	Vegetable Serving	2	g	Fat
1/2	Fat Serving	19	g	Carbohydrate
1/4	Fruit Serving	80	mg	Sodium
		0	mg	Cholesterol

Baked Italian Peas

Baked peas in tomato sauce makes a very colorful side dish. For a main dish, after peas are cooked, top with part-skim Mozzarella cheese and place under the broiler until cheese is hot and bubbly.

Makes 4 servings

1	10-ounce package frozen peas
1	8-ounce can tomato sauce
1	packet instant chicken-flavored broth mix
1	tablespoon minced onion flakes
1/8	teaspoon garlic powder
1/2	teaspoon dried oregano
1	ounce grated Parmesan cheese

Preheat oven to 400°.

Place peas in a colander and rinse under cool water to thaw. Drain.

In a large bowl, combine peas with remaining ingredients, *except* Parmesan cheese. Place in a 1-1/2 quart baking dish that has been sprayed with a nonstick cooking spray. Top with Parmesan cheese.

Bake, uncovered, 30 minutes.

Each serving provides:

112 Calories

1/4	Protein Serving	8	g	Protein
1	Bread Serving	3	g	Fat
1	Vegetable Serving	15	g	Carbohydrate
3	Additional Calories	833	mg	Sodium
		6	mg	Cholesterol

Peas and Mushrooms

The delicate flavor of the mushrooms blends nicely with the taste of the peas, making this one of our favorite side dishes. For a lunch treat, reheat the leftovers after topping with a slice of Muenster cheese.

Makes 4 servings

2	teaspoons margarine
1	cup sliced mushrooms
1	10-ounce package frozen peas, thawed
1/8	teaspoon garlic powder
1/8	teaspoon dried thyme
1/4	cup water

Melt margarine in a small saucepan over medium heat. Add mushrooms and cook, stirring, 2 minutes.

Add peas, spices, and water. Cover and cook 10 to 12 minutes, until tender.

Each serving provides:

76 Calories

1	Bread Serving	4	g	Protein
1/2	Vegetable Serving	2	g	Fat
1/2	Fat Serving	11	g	Carbohydrate
		102	mg	Sodium
		0	mg	Cholesterol

Minted Peas

In the summer, when fresh mint is available, we make this all the time. After you taste it you will, too.

Makes 4 servings

2	tablespoons plus 2 teaspoons reduced-calorie margarine
1/4	cup chopped onions
1/4	cup chopped celery
1	10-ounce package frozen peas
2	teaspoons finely minced fresh mint leaves, or 1/2 teaspoon dried leaves
1/4	teaspoon dried rosemary, crushed
3	tablespoons water

Melt margarine in a small saucepan over medium heat. Add onions and celery and cook until tender, about 5 minutes.

Add remaining ingredients. Cover and cook 10 minutes, until peas are tender.

Each serving provides:

93 Calories

1	Bread Serving	4	g	Protein
1/4	Vegetable Serving	4	g	Fat
1	Fat Serving	11	g	Carbohydrate
		166	mg	Sodium
		0	mg	Cholesterol

Grains and Pasta

Hints for Grains and Pasta

- The food value of whole grains is considerably higher than that of refined grains.
- When grains are refined, the outer layers are removed. These outer layers contain the wholesome "germ" of the grain. The germ contains vitamins, minerals, and fiber.
- Examples of refined grains are white rice and white flour.
- Many breakfast cereals are made from refined grains, such as corn, wheat, and oats. Unfortunately, many of the nutrients have been lost during the refining process.
- Examples of whole grains are whole wheat, barley, millet, brown rice, bulgur and corn meal.
- Whole wheat flour has slightly fewer calories than white flour and is higher in protein, calcium, potassium, iron, vitamin B and fiber.
- Brown rice is higher in protein, calcium, iron, and potassium than white rice. Converted rice has fewer nutrients than brown rice, but more than white rice.
- For added flavor, grains can be cooked in water with broth mix, soy sauce, fruit juice, or spices added.
- Cooked grains freeze well. To defrost, simply place grains in a strainer and pour boiling water over them.
- For added nutrition, try replacing half the white flour in a recipe with whole wheat flour.
- As a general rule of thumb: To replace all of the white flour in a recipe, for each cup of white flour, use 1 cup minus 2 tablespoons of whole wheat flour. Or, use the same amount of whole wheat flour and add more liquid to the recipe.
- Whole wheat macaroni and noodles can be substituted in any pasta or noodle recipe.
- Cooked grains make an excellent low-fat filler for meat loaves and casseroles.
- Try cooked grains for breakfast. Either hot or cold, with milk and cinnamon, they are delicious and nutritious.

Herbed Rice Toss

The wonderful blend of spices will make this a favorite side dish. It goes especially well with baked chicken or fish.

Makes 4 servings

2   tablespoons plus 2 teaspoons reduced-calorie margarine
1/2 cup chopped onions
1   clove garlic, minced
1   cup chopped celery
2   cups chopped mushrooms
1/2 teaspoon poultry seasoning
1/2 teaspoon ground sage
1/2 teaspoon dried thyme
1   packet instant chicken-flavored broth mix
2   cups cooked brown rice

Melt margarine in a large nonstick skillet over medium heat.

Add onions, garlic, and celery. Sauté until tender, about 10 minutes.

Add mushrooms, spices, and broth mix. Cook, stirring occasionally, 10 more minutes, until mushrooms are tender. Add small amounts of water, if necessary, to prevent drying.

Add rice. Toss until heated through.

Each serving provides:

176 Calories

1	Bread Serving	4 g	Protein
1-3/4	Vegetable Servings	5 g	Fat
1	Fat Serving	30 g	Carbohydrate
3	Additional Calories	387 mg	Sodium
		0 mg	Cholesterol

Chinese Fried Rice

This Oriental favorite is a wonderful accompaniment to our Oriental Fish with Almonds on page 110. Add steamed broccoli and what a feast!

Makes 4 servings

1	tablespoon plus 1 teaspoon vegetable oil
1	tablespoon soy sauce
2	cups cooked brown rice
2	eggs, beaten
1/8	teaspoon garlic powder
1/8	teaspoon ground ginger
1/4	cup chopped green onions (green part only)

Heat oil and soy sauce in a medium nonstick skillet over medium-high heat.

In a small bowl, combine remaining ingredients, mixing well. Add to skillet.

Cook, stirring, until eggs are cooked and rice is hot.

Each serving provides:

200 Calories

1/2	Protein Serving	6	g	Protein
1	Bread Serving	8	g	Fat
1/8	Vegetable Serving	26	g	Carbohydrate
1	Fat Serving	292	mg	Sodium
		137	mg	Cholesterol

Rice Pilaf

There are so many versions of this versatile side dish. We prefer using brown rice because of its nutritional value, and raisins for a slightly sweet touch. To lower the sodium count in this recipe, use low-sodium broth mix.

Makes 6 servings

2-1/2 cups water
2   packets instant chicken-flavored broth mix
1   tablespoon lemon juice
1   tablespoon margarine
1   small bay leaf
1/4   cup plus 2 tablespoons raisins
6   ounces uncooked brown rice (1 cup)

In a large saucepan, combine all ingredients, *except* rice. Bring to a boil over medium-high heat.

Stir in rice, reduce heat to low, cover, and simmer until all liquid is absorbed, about 40 to 50 minutes.

Check after 30 minutes. Add boiling water, if necessary, if rice seems too dry.

Remove and discard bay leaf before serving.

Each serving provides:

152 Calories

1	Bread Serving	3 g	Protein
1/2	Fat Serving	3 g	Fat
1/2	Fruit Serving	30 g	Carbohydrate
3	Additional Calories	398 mg	Sodium
		0 mg	Cholesterol

Curried Rice and Spinach

Curry lovers may want to increase the amount of curry powder in this elegant but easy side dish.

Makes 6 servings

1	10-ounce package frozen, chopped spinach, thawed and drained well
1/4	cup finely chopped onions
1/8	teaspoon garlic powder
1	teaspoon curry powder
	Salt and pepper to taste
1/2	cup skim milk
1	egg, beaten
3	cups cooked brown rice.

Preheat oven to 350°.

In a large bowl, combine all ingredients, mixing well.

Spoon mixture into a casserole dish that has been sprayed with a nonstick cooking spray.

Bake, uncovered, 30 minutes, until set.

Each serving provides:

151 Calories

1	Bread Serving	6	g	Protein
3/4	Vegetable Serving	2	g	Fat
17	Additional Calories	29	g	Carbohydrate
		57	mg	Sodium
		46	mg	Cholesterol

Couscous Sauté

Couscous is a grain dish that is available in the gourmet section of most supermarkets. One of the beauties of it is that it cooks in only 5 minutes. Look for the low-salt variety of soy sauce if you wish to lower the sodium count of this recipe.

Makes 4 servings

1	tablespoon plus 1 teaspoon vegetable oil
3	tablespoons soy sauce
1/4	teaspoon ground ginger
2	cups finely chopped green pepper
1	cup finely chopped carrots
2	tablespoons firmly-packed brown sugar (or sweetener equivalent to 6 teaspoons brown sugar)
2/3	cup boiling water
3	ounces uncooked couscous (1/2 cup)

Combine oil, soy sauce, and ginger in a large nonstick skillet over medium heat.

Add green pepper and carrots. Cover and cook until tender, about 10 minutes. Add small amounts of water, if necessary, to prevent drying.

Stir in remaining ingredients, cover, and remove from heat. Let stand 5 minutes.

Each serving provides:

172 Calories*

1	Bread Serving	4	g	Protein
1-1/2	Vegetable Servings	5	g	Fat
1	Fat Serving	24	g	Carbohydrate
29	Additional Calories (if	785	mg	Sodium
	brown sugar is used as	0	mg	Cholesterol
	sweetener)			

*If brown sugar is used as sweetener

Breakfast Couscous

This is a delicious change from oatmeal, and so quick to prepare.

Makes 2 servings

1/2	cup skim milk
1	teaspoon vanilla extract
2	teaspoons maple syrup
2	tablespoons raisins
1-1/2	ounces uncooked couscous (1/4 cup)
	Ground cinnamon

In a small saucepan, combine milk, vanilla, maple syrup, and raisins. Heat, stirring constantly, until hot and steamy. Do not boil.
Stir in couscous, cover, and remove from heat.
Let stand 5 minutes.
Sprinkle with cinnamon.

Each serving provides:

147 Calories

1	Bread Serving	5	g	Protein
1/2	Fruit Serving	0	g	Fat
1/4	Milk Serving	31	g	Carbohydrate
20	Additional Calories	34	mg	Sodium
		1	mg	Cholesterol

Herbed Bulgur

Bulgur (cracked wheat) is a nutritious grain that cooks in only 15 minutes. For variations, try it with other combinations of spices.

Makes 6 servings

6	ounces uncooked bulgur (1 cup)
2	cups water
2	tablespoons margarine
1	tablespoon dried parsley flakes
2	tablespoons minced onion flakes
1/8	teaspoon garlic powder
1/2	teaspoon ground sage
1/2	teaspoon ground savory
	Salt and pepper to taste

In a medium saucepan, combine all ingredients. Cover and bring to a boil over medium heat.

Reduce heat to low and simmer 15 minutes, until liquid is absorbed.

Each serving provides:

140 Calories

1	Bread Serving	3	g	Protein
1	Fat Serving	4	g	Fat
		24	g	Carbohydrate
		46	mg	Sodium
		0	mg	Cholesterol

Date and Nut Breakfast Treat

The taste of this unique cereal is reminiscent of a moist date and nut bread.
Who said breakfast has to be boring?

Makes 4 servings

2	ounces uncooked bulgur
3/4	ounce uncooked rolled oats
3/4	ounce wheat germ
1	teaspoon ground cinnamon
1/8	teaspoon ground nutmeg
2	cups water
2	tablespoon molasses
1	teaspoon vanilla extract
1	tablespoon chopped walnuts
2	tablespoons raisins
2	dates, chopped

In a medium saucepan, combine bulgur, oats, wheat germ, cinnamon, and nutmeg. Mix well.

Add remaining ingredients and bring to a boil over medium heat, stirring frequently.

Reduce heat to low and cook 15 minutes, until water is absorbed, stirring occasionally.

Each serving provides:

145 Calories

1	Bread Serving	4	g	Protein
1/2	Fruit Serving	2	g	Fat
28	Additional Calories	28	g	Carbohydrate
		7	mg	Sodium
		0	mg	Cholesterol

Kasha and Bow Ties

We've taken this traditional Jewish side dish and lowered the calories so it can be enjoyed all the time, alongside any of your favorite entrees. It uses the uniquely flavored buckwheat groats, commonly known as kasha.

Makes 6 servings

1   tablespoon vegetable oil
1/2   cup finely chopped onions
3   ounces buckwheat groats (1/2 cup)
1   egg white
1   cup boiling water
1   packet instant chicken-flavored broth mix
3   cups cooked bow tie-shaped noodles
2   tablespoons reduced-calorie margarine
        Pepper to taste

Heat oil in a large nonstick skillet over medium heat. Add onions and cook until lightly browned. Add small amounts of water, if necessary, to prevent drying. Place onions in a small bowl and set aside.

Place kasha and egg white in pan and cook, stirring, until egg white is dry and set. Add boiling water and broth mix. Cover, reduce heat to low, and simmer 10 minutes.

Add onions, noodles, margarine, and pepper. Toss until heated through.

Each serving provides:

172 Calories

1-1/2	Bread Servings	5	g	Protein
1/6	Vegetable Serving	5	g	Fat
1	Fat Serving	28	g	Carbohydrate
5	Additional Calories	235	mg	Sodium
		0	mg	Cholesterol

Buckwheat Pancakes

Buckwheat flour is available in many large supermarkets and in most health food stores. We like to serve these nutritious pancakes topped with cooked apples or blueberries. What a delicious brunch!

Makes 8 servings
(2 pancakes each serving)

1   cup buckwheat flour
1/2   cup all-purpose flour
3-1/2 teaspoons baking powder
1/8   teaspoon salt
1   teaspoon ground cinnamon
2   tablespoons plus 2 teaspoons sugar
1   egg
2   cups skim milk
2   tablespoons plus 2 teaspoons vegetable oil

Sift both flours, baking powder, salt, and cinnamon.

In a large bowl, combine remaining ingredients. Beat with a wire whisk until blended.

Add dry ingredients to liquids. Whisk until blended.

Drop batter by 1/4-cupfuls onto a preheated nonstick griddle that has been sprayed lightly with a nonstick cooking spray.

Turn pancakes when edges appear dry, and brown lightly on both sides.

Each serving provides:

160 Calories

1	Bread Serving	4	g	Protein
1	Fat Serving	6	g	Fat
1/4	Milk Serving	23	g	Carbohydrate
24	Additional Calories	262	mg	Sodium
		35	mg	Cholesterol

Corn Bread Stuffing

For this hearty stuffing we've used our Double Corn Bread on page 335, but it will work with other corn breads as well. If you have a favorite one, simply use 6 one-ounce servings and proceed with the rest of the recipe. (You may have to adjust the liquid a little.)

Makes 6 servings

1	recipe of Double Corn Bread
2	tablespoons margarine
1	cup chopped onions
1	cup chopped celery
2	cups sliced mushrooms
1/4	teaspoon ground sage
1/4	teaspoon dried thyme
1/4	teaspoon ground savory
1/4	teaspoon garlic powder
	Salt and pepper to taste
1	packet instant chicken-flavored broth mix
1	cup water

Divide corn bread into 8 servings. Crumble 6 servings into a bowl and reserve remaining pieces for another use.

Melt margarine in a large nonstick skillet over medium heat. Add onions, celery, and mushrooms and cook until onions are tender, about 15 minutes. Add small amounts of water, if necessary, to prevent drying. Remove from heat and stir in spices.

Add corn bread and toss gently to combine.

Preheat oven to 350°.

Add water gradually, tossing gently. (Use more or less water, until desired moistness is reached.)

Place in a casserole dish that has been sprayed with a nonstick cooking spray. Bake, covered, 30 minutes, until heated through.

Each serving provides:

244 Calories

1-1/4	Bread Servings	7	g	Protein
1-1/3	Vegetable Servings	8	g	Fat
1-1/2	Fat Servings	36	g	Carbohydrate
42	Additional Calories	586	mg	Sodium
		47	mg	Cholesterol

Rice 'n Grain Balls

For a unique and tasty alternative to meatballs, try these grain balls in spaghetti sauce the next time you serve pasta or spaghetti squash. They're also delicious made into burgers and served on a bun.

Makes 8 servings

3	ounces yellow corn meal (1/2 cup)
1/2	cup whole wheat flour
1/3	cup nonfat dry milk
1/4	teaspoon garlic powder
1	teaspoon dried oregano
	Salt and pepper to taste
1	cup cooked brown rice
1/2	cup tomato sauce
1/2	cup water
2	tablespoons finely minced onions
1	tablespoon plus 1 teaspoon vegetable oil

Preheat oven to 375°.

In a large bowl, combine corn meal, flour, dry milk, garlic powder, oregano, and salt and pepper. Mix well.

Stir in rice.

In a small bowl, combine remaining ingredients. Add to dry mixture, mixing until all ingredients are moistened.

Wetting hands slightly as you work, form mixture into 24 walnut-size balls. Place on a cookie sheet that has been sprayed with a nonstick cooking spray.

Bake 20 minutes, until lightly browned.

Each serving provides:

129 Calories

1	Bread Serving	4	g	Protein
1/4	Vegetable Serving	3	g	Fat
1/2	Fat Serving	23	g	Carbohydrate
20	Additional Calories	108	mg	Sodium
		1	mg	Cholesterol

Millet and Raisin Pudding

Millet is a grain that has been used in India and Egypt as far back as history can record. It has a pleasant flavor, similar to brown rice, and is usually found in health food stores or in the health food section of large supermarkets. It's definitely worth seeking out. Try this for breakfast or as a dessert.

Makes 6 servings

1	cup nonfat dry milk
2	cups water
1/4	teaspoon ground cinnamon
1	tablespoon cornstarch
3	tablespoons sugar (or sweetener equivalent to 9 teaspoons sugar)
2	teaspoons vanilla extract
1/4	teaspoon almond extract
2	cups cooked millet
1/4	cup plus 2 tablespoons raisins
	Ground cinnamon

In a medium saucepan, combine dry milk, water, cinnamon, cornstarch, sugar, and extracts. Stir to dissolve cornstarch.

Add millet. Cook over medium heat, stirring constantly, until mixture comes to a boil. Continue to cook, stirring, 1 minute. Remove from heat.

Stir in raisins.

Pour mixture into a shallow bowl.

Sprinkle generously with cinnamon.

Chill. (Mixture will thicken as it cools.)

Each serving provides:

172 Calories*

1	Bread Serving	6	g	Protein
1/2	Fruit Serving	1	g	Fat
1/2	Milk Serving	37	g	Carbohydrate
5	Additional Calories	64	mg	Sodium
	(plus 24 more calories if	2	mg	Cholesterol
	sugar is used as			
	sweetener)			

*If sugar is used as sweetener

Tropical Millet Pudding

This milk-free pudding is a snap to make. For a special occasion, spoon it into sherbet glasses and sprinkle with a little bit of shredded coconut and slivered almonds.

Makes 6 servings

2	cups hot, cooked millet
1	cup canned crushed pineapple (unsweetened), drained
1	medium, ripe banana
1/2	teaspoon coconut extract
1	teaspoon vanilla extract
1/4	teaspoon almond extract
1/4	cup raisins
	Ground cinnamon *or* nutmeg

In a blender container, combine millet, pineapple, banana, and extracts. Blend until smooth. (Stop blender several times to scrape sides.) Stir in raisins.

Spoon into a shallow serving dish and sprinkle lightly with cinnamon or nutmeg.

Chill.

Each serving provides:

134 Calories

1	Bread Serving	3	g	Protein
1	Fruit Serving	1	g	Fat
		32	g	Carbohydrate
		2	mg	Sodium
		0	mg	Cholesterol

Italian Barley

A tasty side dish for almost any entree, this filling grain also reheats nicely in the microwave.

Makes 4 servings

1	tablespoon plus 1 teaspoon olive oil
1/2	cup chopped onions
1/2	cup chopped green pepper
1	clove garlic, minced
1	1-pound can tomatoes, undrained, cut into chunks
1/2	teaspoon dried oregano
1/2	teaspoon dried basil
2	cups water

5-1/4 ounces uncooked barley (3/4 cup)

Heat oil in a medium saucepan over medium heat. Add onions, green pepper, and garlic and cook until lightly browned. Add small amounts of water, if necessary, to prevent drying.

Add tomatoes, spices, and water. Bring to a boil.

Stir in barley, reduce heat to low, cover, and simmer 50 minutes, until barley is tender and water is absorbed. Stir occasionally while cooking and add more water if necessary.

Each serving provides:

207 Calories

1-1/3	Bread Servings	6	g	Protein
1-1/4	Vegetable Servings	5	g	Fat
1	Fat Serving	36	g	Carbohydrate
		189	mg	Sodium
		0	mg	Cholesterol

Barley Mushroom Casserole

Add your favorite spice to this casserole, if you wish. Try 1/2 teaspoon of either curry powder, basil, oregano, dill, or thyme, or enjoy it as is, with the delicious, subtle flavor of mushrooms.

Makes 4 servings

2   tablespoons plus 2 teaspoons reduced-calorie margarine
1   cup chopped onions
2   cups sliced mushrooms
2   . packets instant chicken- *or* beef-flavored broth mix
2-1/2 cups water
     Salt and pepper to taste
5-1/4 ounces uncooked barley (3/4 cup)

Melt margarine in a medium saucepan over medium heat. Add onions and mushrooms and cook until tender, about 10 minutes. Add small amounts of water, if necessary, to prevent drying.

Add broth mix, water, and salt and pepper and bring to a boil.

Stir in barley, reduce heat to low, cover, and simmer 50 minutes, until barley is tender and liquid is absorbed. Stir occasionally while cooking and add more water if necessary.

Each serving provides:

196 Calories

1-1/3	Bread Servings	6 g	Protein
1-1/2	Vegetable Servings	5 g	Fat
1	Fat Serving	33 g	Carbohydrate
5	Additional Calories	643 mg	Sodium
		0 mg	Cholesterol

Party Pasta Primavera

This salad is pretty enough for a party, but don't wait to have guests to try it. For an added touch, we like to serve it on a bed of lettuce, garnished with sliced tomatoes and radish "flowers."

Makes 8 servings

2   cups carrots, cut into 1/2-inch chunks
2   cups broccoli, cut into small flowerets
1   cup zucchini, unpeeled, cut into 1/2-inch chunks
4   cups cooked macaroni
1/2   cup finely minced onions
1/4   cup reduced-calorie mayonnaise
1/2   cup plain lowfat yogurt
1   ounce grated Parmesan cheese
2   tablespoons olive oil
1/8   teaspoon pepper
1/2   teaspoon dried basil
1/2   teaspoon dried oregano
       Dash garlic powder

Steam vegetables until just tender-crisp, about 5 minutes for carrots and broccoli and 3 minutes for zucchini. Place in a large bowl.

Add macaroni and onions and toss gently.

In a small bowl, combine remaining ingredients. Mix well. Add to vegetable mixture. Toss gently until well mixed.

Chill.

For best flavor, bring to room temperature to serve.

Each serving provides:

181 Calories

1	Bread Serving	6	g	Protein
1-1/3	Vegetable Servings	7	g	Fat
1-1/2	Fat Servings	24	g	Carbohydrate
19	Additional Calories	152	mg	Sodium
		6	mg	Cholesterol

Italian Macaroni Salad

Perfect for a summer barbecue, but delicious all year round, this salad is colorful and easy.

Makes 6 servings

1	10-ounce package frozen cut green beans
3	cups cooked macaroni
1	cup coarsely shredded carrots
1	cup sliced celery
1/4	cup sliced green onions (green part only)
1/2	cup reduced-calorie Italian dressing (16 calories per tablespoon)
1/4	teaspoon dried oregano

Cook green beans according to package directions, cooking until tender-crisp. Drain.

In a large bowl, combine green beans, macaroni, carrots, celery, and onions. Toss until blended.

Add remaining ingredients and mix well.

Chill to blend flavors. Stir occasionally while chilling.

Each serving provides:

115 Calories

1	Bread Serving	4	g	Protein
1-1/2	Vegetable Servings	1	g	Fat
21	Additional Calories	23	g	Carbohydrate
		320	mg	Sodium
		0	mg	Cholesterol

Macaroni and Mushrooms

Mushrooms and garlic with the spark of Parmesan cheese make this pasta dish a gourmet's delight.

Makes 4 servings

1	tablespoon plus 1 teaspoon vegetable oil
2	cloves garlic, minced
4	cups sliced mushrooms
2	cups cooked macaroni
2	ounces grated Parmesan cheese
	Pepper to taste

Heat oil in a large nonstick skillet over medium heat. Add garlic and cook until lightly browned.

Add mushrooms. Cook, stirring frequently, until mushrooms are just slightly tender. Remove from heat.

Stir in macaroni, Parmesan cheese, and pepper.

Each serving provides:

202 Calories

1/2	Protein Serving	10	g	Protein
1	Bread Serving	9	g	Fat
2	Vegetable Servings	20	g	Carbohydrate
1	Fat Serving	268	mg	Sodium
		11	mg	Cholesterol

Pasta and Broccoli

This is an unusual blend of pasta, garlic, and broccoli. It makes a wonderful side dish or, topped with cheese, an unbeatable entree.

Makes 6 servings

3 cups broccoli, cut into flowerets
2 tablespoons vegetable oil
2 cloves garlic, minced
1 1-pound can tomatoes, drained slightly, chopped
3 cups cooked pasta spirals

Steam broccoli until tender-crisp, about 8 minutes.

Heat oil in a large nonstick skillet over medium heat. Add garlic and cook until lightly browned.

Add tomatoes. Cook, stirring frequently, until heated through. Add broccoli. Cook until heated.

Add pasta. Toss gently until mixture is well blended and hot.

Each serving provides:

147 Calories

1	Bread Serving	4	g	Protein
1-2/3	Vegetable Servings	5	g	Fat
1	Fat Serving	22	g	Carbohydrate
		136	mg	Sodium
		0	mg	Cholesterol

Eggplant Tomato Sauce for Pasta

Serve this chunky sauce over any type of cooked pasta for a zesty Italian dinner. It freezes well, so you'll want to make plenty.

Makes 4 servings

1	cup eggplant, peeled, cut into 1/4-inch pieces
1	1-pound can tomatoes, undrained, cut into chunks
1	8-ounce can tomato sauce
1/2	cup chopped onions
1/2	cup chopped green pepper
1	teaspoon dried oregano
1	teaspoon dried basil
1/8	teaspoon garlic powder
	Salt and pepper to taste
1	teaspoon sugar (or equivalent amount of sweetener)

In a large saucepan, combine all ingredients. Bring to a boil over medium heat. Reduce heat to low.

Simmer, uncovered, 1 hour, until thickened. Stir occasionally while cooking.

Each serving provides:

61 Calories*

3	Vegetable Servings	2	g	Protein
4	Additional Calories (if	1	g	Fat
	sugar is used as	14	g	Carbohydrate
	sweetener)	530	mg	Sodium
		0	mg	Cholesterol

*If sugar is used as sweetener

Spaghetti Sauce Italiano

This recipe makes a big pot of sauce, but you'll be glad you have it. Not only is it good over pasta, but also over burgers or baked chicken or fish.

Makes 12 servings

2   tablespoons olive oil
1   cup chopped onions
1   cup chopped green pepper
1   cup sliced mushrooms
3   cloves garlic, minced
3   8-ounce cans tomato sauce
1   6-ounce can tomato paste
1   1-pound can tomatoes, drained and chopped
2   teaspoons dried oregano
1   teaspoon dried basil
1   bay leaf
    Salt and pepper to taste

Heat oil in a large saucepan. Add onions, green pepper, mushrooms, and garlic. Cook until onions and green pepper are tender. Stir occasionally and add small amounts of water, if necessary, to prevent drying.

Add tomato sauce, tomato paste, tomatoes, and spices. Reduce heat to low, cover, and simmer 1 hour, stirring occasionally.

Remove and discard bay leaf before serving.

Each serving provides:

56 Calories

1-1/2 Vegetable Servings	2 g	Protein
1/2 Fat Serving	3 g	Fat
	8 g	Carbohydrate
	289 mg	Sodium
	0 mg	Cholesterol

Italian Noodles

Top with cheese, add a green vegetable, and your dinner is complete.

Makes 6 servings

2	tablespoons olive oil
1	cup chopped onions
1	cup chopped green pepper
2	cloves garlic, minced
1	4-ounce can mushroom pieces, drained
1	1-pound can tomatoes, drained slightly, chopped
1/2	teaspoon dried basil
1/4	teaspoon dried oregano
	Pepper to taste
3	cups cooked noodles

Heat oil in a large nonstick skillet over medium heat. Add onions, green pepper, and garlic. Cook until lightly browned. Add small amounts of water, if necessary, to prevent drying.

Add tomatoes, mushrooms, and spices. When mixture is hot, stir in noodles. Toss until heated through.

Each serving provides:

174 Calories

1	Bread Serving	5	g	Protein
1-2/3	Vegetable Servings	6	g	Fat
1	Fat Serving	25	g	Carbohydrate
		183	mg	Sodium
		25	mg	Cholesterol

Garlic Noodles

If you like garlic, you'll like these noodles. If you love garlic, add a little more!

Makes 6 servings

3   cups cooked noodles
2   tablespoons olive oil
2   large cloves garlic, minced

Cook noodles just before using. Place in a large bowl and cover to keep warm.

Heat oil in a small nonstick skillet over medium heat. Add garlic and cook until lightly browned.

Pour oil and garlic over noodles. Toss until blended.

Each serving provides:

142 Calories

1	Bread Serving	3	g	Protein
1	Fat Serving	6	g	Fat
		19	g	Carbohydrate
		2	mg	Sodium
		25	mg	Cholesterol

Noodles with Peanut Sauce

Inspired by a love of Oriental food and a love of peanut butter, this dish is a favorite in our house. It can be used to serve 4 people as a side dish or 2 as an entree. Try it with whole wheat noodles for its best flavor.

Makes 4 servings

2   cups cooked noodles
2   tablespoons peanut butter
1   tablespoon soy sauce
1   tablespoon water
    Dash ground ginger
    Dash garlic powder

Have noodles at room temperature. Place in a medium bowl.

In a small bowl, combine remaining ingredients. Mix well, until blended. (Different brands of peanut butter vary in thickness, and you may need to add more water for a smooth, thick texture.)

Spoon over noodles to serve.

Each serving provides:

150 Calories

1/2	Protein Serving	6 g	Protein
1	Bread Serving	5 g	Fat
1/2	Fat Serving	20 g	Carbohydrate
		297 mg	Sodium
		25 mg	Cholesterol

Eggless Noodle Pudding

Unlike the traditional noodle puddings that contain lots of eggs, this one is especially good if you are watching your cholesterol. It can be served as a side dish, a dessert, or a wholesome and filling breakfast.

Makes 4 servings

2	cups skim milk
1	tablespoon plus 1 teaspoon cornstarch
1/4	teaspoon ground cinnamon
1	teaspoon vanilla butternut flavor
1/4	teaspoon lemon extract
2	tablespoons plus 2 teaspoons sugar (or sweetener equivalent to 8 teaspoons sugar)
2	cups cooked noodles
1/4	cup raisins

Have noodles at room temperature or warmer.

In a medium saucepan, combine milk, cornstarch, cinnamon, extracts, and sugar. Stir to dissolve cornstarch.

Heat over medium heat, stirring constantly, until mixture just starts to boil.

Stir in noodles and raisins. Cook, stirring, until mixture boils again. Continue to cook and stir 1 minute.

Pour into a 1-quart shallow bowl. Press noodles down into liquid with the back of a spoon.

Cool slightly; then cover and chill.

Each serving provides:

217 Calories*

1	Bread Serving	8	g	Protein
1/2	Fruit Serving	1	g	Fat
1/2	Milk Serving	43	g	Carbohydrate
10	Additional Calories	67	mg	Sodium
	(plus 32 more calories if	27	mg	Cholesterol
	sugar is used as			
	sweetener)			

*If sugar is used as a sweetener

Pineapple Noodle Pudding

Most noodle puddings are made with milk. However, this sweet version is made with fruit juice instead. The cholesterol can be lowered by using an egg substitute. Try it with whole wheat noodles for a slightly nutty flavor.

Makes 8 servings

4	cups cooked noodles
1-1/2	cups canned crushed pineapple (unsweetened), undrained
1/2	cup orange juice
2	eggs, beaten
3	tablespoons sugar (or sweetener equivalent to 9 teaspoons sugar)
1	teaspoon vanilla extract
1-1/2	ounces bran cereal flakes, crushed
	Ground cinnamon
2	tablespoons plus 2 teaspoons reduced-calorie margarine

Preheat oven to 350°.

In large bowl, combine all ingredients, *except* cereal and margarine. Mix well. Pour into an 8-inch square baking pan that has been sprayed with a nonstick cooking spray. Press noodles down into liquid with the back of a spoon.

Sprinkle with cereal and cinnamon.

Dot with margarine.

Bake 40 minutes, until set.

Serve hot or cold.

Each serving provides:

209 Calories*

1/4	Protein Serving	6	g	Protein
1-1/4	Bread Servings	5	g	Fat
1/2	Fat Serving	37	g	Carbohydrate
1/2	Fruit Serving	109	mg	Sodium
18	Additional Calories (if sugar is used as sweetener)	93	mg	Cholesterol

*If sugar is used as sweetener

Breads and Muffins

Hints for Breads and Muffins

- In most muffin and bread recipes, you can use half the amount of sugar called for without affecting the texture of the finished product, and you'll be amazed at how little the flavor is altered. (In our recipes we have already reduced the amount of sugar.)
- Artificial sweeteners can alter the texture of breads and muffins. We suggest using half sugar and half sweetener, rather than all sweetener. All of our bread and muffin recipes were tested in this manner, as well as with all sugar, and we found that the taste and texture were consistently better than when we used all sweetener.
- When reducing the amount of sugar, increase the amount of vanilla extract called for in a recipe. If there is no vanilla extract, add some. This gives a perceived sweetness to baked goods and makes things taste sweeter than they are.
- Most bread and muffin recipes will work with an egg substitute in place of the eggs.
- Using 2 egg whites in place of one egg will also lower the cholesterol, and usually will not affect the outcome of the recipe.
- When vegetable oil is called for, choose a polyunsaturated oil, such as safflower, sunflower, corn, or soybean oil.
- Use margarine in place of butter. The calories are the same, but butter is high in saturated fat and cholesterol.
- Be careful when using a tub-style margarine. If it is a reduced-calorie margarine that has a high water content (read the label), it may add too much water to the recipe.
- When a recipe calls for canned fruit, always choose the variety packed in water or fruit juice.
- To add fiber to a recipe, replace half of the flour called for with whole wheat flour. If you substitute more than half, you may need to add a little more liquid to the recipe.
- Instead of greasing the bread or muffin pan, use a nonstick cooking spray.
- When a recipe calls for nuts or coconut, try using one half or one quarter of the amount called for. Both of these ingredients are very high in calories and fat.

Whole Wheat Zucchini Bread

When zucchini is plentiful, make lots of these moist, delicious breads to freeze.

Makes 8 servings

3/4   cup whole wheat flour
3/4   cup all-purpose flour
1-1/2 teaspoons baking powder
1/2   teaspoon baking soda
1   teaspoon ground cinnamon
1/2   teaspoon ground nutmeg
1   egg
1/4   cup sugar (or sweetener equivalent to 12 teaspoons sugar)
1   teaspoon vanilla extract
2   tablespoons plus 2 teaspoons margarine, melted
1-1/2 cups finely shredded, unpeeled zucchini
1/2   cup raisins

Preheat oven to 350°. In a large bowl, combine both flours, baking powder, baking soda, and spices.

In a medium bowl, combine egg, sugar, vanilla, and margarine. Beat with a fork or wire whisk until blended. Add zucchini.

Stir zucchini mixture and raisins into dry ingredients, stirring until all ingredients are moistened.

Place batter in a 4 x 8-inch nonstick loaf pan or one that has been sprayed with a nonstick cooking spray.

Bake 50 minutes, or until a toothpick inserted in the center comes out clean.

Cool in pan 10 minutes; then invert onto a rack to finish cooling.

Each serving provides:

183 Calories*

1	Bread Serving	4	g	Protein
1/3	Vegetable Serving	5	g	Fat
1	Fat Serving	32	g	Carbohydrate
1/2	Fruit Serving	187	mg	Sodium
9	Additional Calories	34	mg	Cholesterol
	(plus 24 more calories if sugar is used as sweetener)			

*If sugar is used as sweetener

Anise Raisin Bread

The taste and aroma of anise make this bread a real treat. Try it plain or toast some slices in the oven until crisp.

Makes 10 servings

2   cups minus 2 tablespoons all-purpose flour
2-1/2 teaspoons baking powder
3   tablespoons plus 1 teaspoon reduced-calorie margarine
1/2   cup skim milk
1/4   cup sugar (or sweetener equivalent to 12 teaspoons sugar)
1   tablespoon anise seeds, crushed
1/4   teaspoon anise extract
1/2   teaspoon lemon extract
1   egg
1/4   cup plus 1 tablespoon raisins

Preheat oven to 350°.

In a large bowl, combine flour and baking powder. Add margarine and blend with a fork until mixture resembles coarse crumbs.

In a medium bowl, combine remaining ingredients, *except* raisins. Beat with a fork or wire whisk until blended.

Add this mixture and raisins to dry ingredients, stirring until all ingredients are moistened.

Place in a 4 x 8-inch nonstick loaf pan or one that has been sprayed with a nonstick cooking spray. Pat dough down gently with slightly wet fingertips.

Bake 30 minutes, until a toothpick inserted in the center comes out clean.

Cool in pan 10 minutes; then invert onto a rack to finish cooling.

Each serving provides:

151 Calories*

1	Bread Serving	4	g	Protein
1/2	Fat Serving	3	g	Fat
1/2	Fruit Serving	28	g	Carbohydrate
12	Additional Calories	161	mg	Sodium
	(plus 19 more calories if	28	mg	Cholesterol
	sugar is used as			
	sweetener)			

*If sugar is used as sweetener

Cranberry Nut Bread

(Shown on Cover)

Everyone who tastes this bread wants the recipe!

Makes 10 servings

3/4	cup whole wheat flour
1/2	cup plus 1 tablespoon all-purpose flour
2	teaspoons baking powder
1/2	teaspoon baking soda
2-1/4	ounces wheat germ
1	teaspoon ground cinnamon
1	egg
1	cup buttermilk
1	tablespoon plus 2 teaspoons vegetable oil
1	teaspoon vanilla extract
1/4	teaspoon orange extract
3	tablespoons honey
1	cup cranberries
1/2	cup raisins
1	ounce chopped walnuts

Preheat oven to 350°. In a large bowl, combine dry ingredients.

In a medium bowl, combine egg, buttermilk, oil, extracts, and honey. Beat with a fork or wire whisk until blended.

Place cranberries and raisins in a blender or food processor. Turn on and off a few times so fruit is chopped, but not puréed.

Add cranberry mixture and nuts to buttermilk mixture. Stir in dry ingredients, stirring until all ingredients are moistened.

Place batter in a 4 x 8-inch nonstick loaf pan or one that has been sprayed with a nonstick cooking spray.

Bake 35 minutes, until nicely browned.

Cool 5 minutes; then invert onto a rack to finish cooling.

Each serving provides:

186 Calories*

1	Bread Serving	6	g	Protein
1/2	Fat Serving	6	g	Fat
1/2	Fruit Serving	29	g	Carbohydrate
55	Additional Calories	161	mg	Sodium
		28	mg	Cholesterol

Coconut Bread

Different and delicious, this bread is a great brunch accompaniment or a not-too-sweet dessert.

Makes 10 servings

2   cups minus 2 tablespoons all-purpose flour
2-1/2 teaspoons baking powder
2   tablespoons shredded coconut (unsweetened)
3   tablespoons plus 1 teaspoon reduced-calorie margarine
1/2   cup skim milk
1-1/2 teaspoons coconut extract
1   teaspoon vanilla extract
1   egg
1/4   cup sugar (or sweetener equivalent to 12 teaspoons sugar)

Preheat oven to 350°.

In a large bowl, combine flour, baking powder, and coconut. Add margarine and blend with a fork until mixture resembles coarse crumbs.

In a medium bowl, combine remaining ingredients. Beat with a fork or wire whisk until blended. Add to dry mixture, stirring until all ingredients are moistened.

Place batter in a 4 x 8-inch nonstick loaf pan or one that has been sprayed with a nonstick cooking spray.

Pat dough down gently with slightly wet fingertips.

Bake 30 minutes, or until a toothpick inserted in the center comes out clean.

Cool in pan 10 minutes; then invert onto a rack to finish cooling.

Each serving provides:

142 Calories*

1	Bread Serving	4 g	Protein
1/2	Fat Serving	3 g	Fat
16	Additional Calories	24 g	Carbohydrate
	(plus 19 more calories if	161 mg	Sodium
	sugar is used as	28 mg	Cholesterol
	sweetener)		

*If sugar is used as sweetener

Oatmeal Bread

This slightly sweet bread has a wonderful texture. Try it with peanut butter for a taste treat you'll love.

Makes 8 servings

2-1/4 ounces quick-cooking oats, uncooked
1   cup minus 1 tablespoon all-purpose flour
1   teaspoon baking soda
2   teaspoons baking powder
1   teaspoon ground cinnamon
2   eggs
3   tablespoons honey
1   cup plain lowfat yogurt
2   tablespoons plus 2 teaspoons vegetable oil
2   teaspoons vanilla extract

Preheat oven to 350°.

In a medium bowl, combine oats, flour, baking soda, baking powder, and cinnamon.

In a large bowl, combine remaining ingredients. Beat on low speed of an electric mixer until blended. Beat in dry mixture, adding half at a time. Continue to beat just until all ingredients are moistened.

Place batter in a 4 x 8-inch nonstick loaf pan or one that has been sprayed with a nonstick cooking spray.

Bake 30 to 35 minutes, until golden brown.

Cool in pan 10 minutes; then invert onto a rack to finish cooling.

Each serving provides:

191 Calories

1/4	Protein Serving	6	g	Protein
1	Bread Serving	7	g	Fat
1	Fat Serving	26	g	Carbohydrate
1/4	Milk Serving	248	mg	Sodium
23	Additional Calories	70	mg	Cholesterol

Zucchini and Cheese Bread

This moist, cheesy bread goes well with any pasta meal.

Makes 8 servings

1-1/2 cups coarsely shredded, unpeeled zucchini
1   tablespoon minced onion flakes
1   tablespoon dried parsley flakes
1   ounce grated Parmesan cheese
1/8   teaspoon garlic powder
2   tablespoons plus 2 teaspoons vegetable oil
2   eggs, beaten
3/4   cup all-purpose flour
1   teaspoon baking powder
1   ounce shredded lowfat Cheddar or Swiss cheese

Preheat oven to 350°.

In a large bowl, combine zucchini, onion flakes, parsley, Parmesan cheese, garlic powder, oil, and eggs. Mix with a fork or wire whisk.

Combine flour and baking powder. Stir into zucchini mixture, mixing well.

Place mixture in a 9-inch round nonstick cake pan or one that has been sprayed with a nonstick cooking spray. Sprinkle evenly with Cheddar or Swiss cheese.

Bake 40 minutes, until a toothpick inserted in the center comes out clean.

Serve warm for best flavor.

Each serving provides:

133 Calories

1/2	Protein Serving	5	g	Protein
1/2	Bread Serving	8	g	Fat
1/3	Vegetable Serving	11	g	Carbohydrate
1	Fat Serving	149	mg	Sodium
		72	mg	Cholesterol

Molasses Brown Bread

This bread will definitely become a favorite! And for a homemade holiday or housewarming gift, it can't be beat.

Makes 12 servings

1-1/2 cups plus 3 tablespoons whole wheat flour
2-1/4 ounces wheat germ
1   teaspoon baking soda
1   teaspoon ground cinnamon
1/3   cup nonfat dry milk
1   cup plain lowfat yogurt
1   egg, slightly beaten
1/4   cup water
1   teaspoon vanilla extract
1/4   cup plus 2 tablespoons molasses
2   tablespoons vegetable oil
1/4   cup plus 2 tablespoons raisins

Preheat oven to 350°.

In a large bowl, combine flour, wheat germ, baking soda, cinnamon, and dry milk. Mix well.

In a medium bowl, combine remaining ingredients, *except* raisins. Beat with a fork or wire whisk until blended. Add to dry mixture, along with raisins. Stir until all ingredients are moistened.

Place in a 5 x 9-inch nonstick loaf pan or one that has been sprayed with a nonstick cooking spray.

Bake 40 minutes, until a toothpick inserted in the center comes out clean.

Cool in pan 10 minutes; then invert onto a rack to finish cooling.

Each serving provides:

159 Calories

1	Bread Serving	6	g	Protein
1/2	Fat Serving	4	g	Fat
1/4	Fruit Serving	26	g	Carbohydrate
1/4	Milk Serving	109	mg	Sodium
34	Additional Calories	24	mg	Cholesterol

Cinnamon Custard Corn Bread

This unique bread settles into 2 layers when cooked—a custard layer on the bottom and a corn bread layer on the top. It's so moist and delicious that we often eat it for dessert.

Makes 12 servings

5-1/4 ounces yellow corn meal
1/2   cup all-purpose flour
1/2   cup minus 1 tablespoon whole wheat flour
1   teaspoon ground cinnamon
2   teaspoons baking powder
1   egg, slightly beaten
1-1/2 teaspoons vanilla extract
1/4   cup margarine, melted
1/4   cup brown sugar (or sweetener equivalent to 12 teaspoons
         brown sugar)
3   cups skim milk

Preheat oven to 350°.

In a large bowl, combine corn meal, both flours, cinnamon, and baking powder. Mix well.

In another bowl, combine remaining ingredients. Mix with a wire whisk until blended. Add to dry mixture. Beat with whisk until lumps are gone.

Pour into an 8-inch square glass baking pan that has been sprayed with a nonstick cooking spray.

Bake 45 minutes, until firm.

Cool in pan.

Each serving provides:

161 Calories*

1	Bread Serving	5 g	Protein
1	Fat Serving	5 g	Fat
1/4	Milk Serving	25 g	Carbohydrate
4	Additional Calories	155 mg	Sodium
	(plus 16 more calories if	24 mg	Cholesterol
	brown sugar is used as		
	sweetener)		

*If brown sugar is used as sweetener

Double Corn Bread

We've used both corn and corn meal for a double impact in this bread that goes well with any meal.

Makes 8 servings

1	tablespoon plus 1 teaspoon margarine
6	ounces yellow corn meal (1 cup)
1	teaspoon baking soda
1/2	teaspoon baking powder
1/4	teaspoon salt
1-1/2	cups sour milk (Add 4 teaspoons of lemon juice to 1-1/2 cups of skim milk.)
2	tablespoons honey
1	teaspoon vanilla extract
1	egg
1	cup drained canned corn
2	teaspoons all-purpose flour

Preheat oven to 425°.

Place margarine in an 8-inch square baking pan and set aside.

In a large bowl, combine corn meal, baking soda, baking powder, and salt.

In a blender container, combine milk, honey, vanilla, and egg. Blend until smooth.

Place pan in oven to preheat for 3 minutes.

Stir liquid mixture into dry ingredients.

Toss corn with flour and stir into batter.

Place batter in preheated pan and bake 20 to 22 minutes, until firm and lightly browned.

Each serving provides:

158 Calories

1-1/4	Bread Servings	5	g	Protein
1/2	Fat Serving	3	g	Fat
40	Additional Calories	28	g	Carbohydrate
		253	mg	Sodium
		35	mg	Cholesterol

Fruity Oat and Bran Bread

This high-fiber bread is delicious plain, but toasting really brings out the flavor.

Makes 8 servings

1/2	cup minus 1 tablespoon all-purpose flour
1/2	cup whole wheat flour
1-1/2	ounces bran
3/4	ounce quick-cooking oats, uncooked
1	teaspoon baking soda
1/2	teaspoon ground cinnamon
2	tablespoons plus 2 teaspoons margarine, melted
3	tablespoons firmly-packed brown sugar (or sweetener equivalent to 9 teaspoons brown sugar)
1/4	cup skim milk
1	teaspoon vanilla extract
1	egg, slightly beaten
1	cup applesauce (unsweetened)
1	teaspoon freshly grated orange peel
1/4	cup raisins

Preheat oven to 350°. In a large bowl, combine both flours, bran, oats, baking soda, and cinnamon. Mix well.

In a medium bowl, combine remaining ingredients, *except* raisins. Beat with a wire whisk until blended. Add to dry mixture with raisins. Stir until all ingredients are moistened.

Place in a 4 x 8-inch nonstick loaf pan.

Bake 40 minutes, until a toothpick inserted in the center comes out clean.

Cool in pan 10 minutes; then invert onto a rack to finish cooling.

Each serving provides:

171 Calories*

1	Bread Serving	4	g	Protein
1	Fat Serving	5	g	Fat
1/2	Fruit Serving	28	g	Carbohydrate
9	Additional Calories	163	mg	Sodium
	(plus 18 more calories if	34	mg	Cholesterol
	brown sugar is used as			
	sweetener)			

*If brown sugar is used as sweetener

Banana Bean Bread

This unusual recipe combines the flavor and moistness of bananas with the high protein of beans for a bread you're sure to love.

Makes 8 servings

3/4	cup all-purpose flour
1	teaspoon baking powder
1/2	teaspoon baking soda
1/4	teaspoon ground cinnamon
2	medium, ripe bananas, cut into chunks
6	ounces cooked kidney or pinto beans
1	egg
1	tablespoon plus 1 teaspoon vegetable oil
2/3	cup nonfat dry milk
3	tablespoons sugar (or sweetener equivalent to 9 teaspoons sugar)
1	teaspoon vanilla butternut flavor
1/4	teaspoon banana extract

Preheat oven to 350°. Sift flour, baking powder, baking soda, and cinnamon. Set aside.

In a blender container, combine remaining ingredients. Blend until smooth. Pour into a large bowl.

Add dry ingredients. Mix until all ingredients are moistened.

Place in a 4 x 8-inch nonstick loaf pan or one that has been sprayed with a nonstick cooking spray.

Bake 45 minutes, until firm and golden.

Cool in pan 10 minutes; then invert onto a rack to finish cooling.

Each serving provides:

167 Calories*

1/2	Protein Serving	6	g	Protein
1/2	Bread Serving	3	g	Fat
1/2	Fat Serving	28	g	Carbohydrate
1/4	Milk Serving	145	mg	Sodium
18	Additional Calories (if sugar is used as sweetener)	35	mg	Cholesterol

*If sugar is used as sweetener

Blueberry Muffins

We've lowered the fat and sugar in these moist, tender muffins and increased the extracts. The result is almost too good to be true.

Makes 8 servings

1-1/2 cups all-purpose flour
1-1/2 teaspoons baking powder
1   egg
1/4   cup sugar (or sweetener equivalent to 12 teaspoons sugar)
2   tablespoons plus 2 teaspoons margarine, melted
3/4   cup skim milk
2   teaspoons vanilla extract
1/4   teaspoon lemon extract
1   cup fresh or frozen blueberries (unsweetened). (If using
       frozen berries, thaw and drain them well.)

Preheat oven to 375°.

In a medium bowl, combine flour and baking powder.

In a large bowl, combine remaining ingredients, *except* blueberries. Beat on low speed of an electric mixer until smooth.

Stir dry ingredients into wet mixture, stirring until all ingredients are moistened.

Stir in blueberries.

Divide mixture evenly into 8 nonstick muffin cups or ones that have been sprayed with a nonstick cooking spray.

Bake 20 minutes, until firm and lightly browned.

Cool in pan 5 minutes; then transfer to a rack to finish cooling.

Each serving provides:

176 Calories*

1	Bread Serving	4 g	Protein
1	Fat Serving	5 g	Fat
1/2	Fruit Serving	28 g	Carbohydrate
16	Additional Calories	147 mg	Sodium
	(plus 24 more calories if	35 mg	Cholesterol
	sugar is used as		
	sweetener)		

*If sugar is used as sweetener

Banana Oat Muffins

These muffins, filled with peanut butter and jelly, will become a favorite lunch box treat—for the adults, as well as the children in your family.

Makes 8 servings

3/4	cup all-purpose flour
1-1/2	teaspoons baking powder
3	ounces quick-cooking oats, uncooked
1	egg
1/2	teaspoon vanilla butternut flavor
1/2	teaspoon almond extract
3	tablespoons plus 1 teaspoon sugar (or sweetener equivalent to 10 teaspoons sugar)
1/4	cup skim milk
2	tablespoons plus 2 teaspoons vegetable oil
2	medium, ripe bananas, mashed

Preheat oven to 400°.

In a small bowl, combine flour, baking powder, and oats.

In a large bowl, combine remaining ingredients. Beat with a fork or wire whisk until well blended.

Stir dry ingredients into banana mixture, stirring until all ingredients are moistened.

Divide evenly into 8 nonstick muffin cups or ones that have been sprayed with a nonstick cooking spray.

Bake 15 minutes, until firm and lightly browned.

Cool in pan 5 minutes; then transfer to a rack to finish cooling.

Each serving provides:

185 Calories*

1	Bread Serving	4	g	Protein
1	Fat Serving	6	g	Fat
1/2	Fruit Serving	29	g	Carbohydrate
9	Additional Calories	93	mg	Sodium
	(plus 20 more calories if sugar is used as sweetener)	34	mg	Cholesterol

*If sugar is used as sweetener

Pumpkin Raisin Bran Muffins

These spicy muffins are tempting at a holiday buffet or brunch.

Makes 6 servings

3/4 cup whole wheat flour
1/2 teaspoon baking soda
1 teaspoon *each* baking powder and ground cinamon
1/4 teaspoon *each* ground ginger, cloves, and nutmeg
1-1/2 ounces bran cereal flakes, slightly crushed
1 egg
2 tablespoons vegetable oil
1 teaspoon vanilla extract
1 cup canned pumpkin
1/4 cup sugar (or sweetener equivalent to 12 teaspoons sugar)
1/4 cup plus 2 tablespoons raisins

Preheat oven to 375°.

In a large bowl, combine flour, baking soda, baking powder, and spices. Stir in cereal.

In a medium bowl, combine remaining ingredients, *except* raisins. Beat with a fork or wire whisk until blended.

Add wet mixture and raisins to dry ingredients, stirring until all ingredients are moistened.

Divide batter evenly among 6 nonstick muffin cups or ones that have been sprayed with a nonstick cooking spray.

Bake 20 minutes, until a toothpick inserted in the center comes out clean. Remove to a rack to cool.

Each serving provides:

204 Calories*

1	Bread Serving	5	g	Protein
1/3	Vegetable Serving	6	g	Fat
1	Fat Serving	36	g	Carbohydrate
1/2	Fruit Serving	221	mg	Sodium
8	Additional Calories (plus	46	mg	Cholesterol
	32 more calories if sugar is			
	used as sweetener)			

*If sugar is used as sweetener

Bran Muffins

These are the best ever! They're super-moist and just sweet enough.

Makes 8 servings

1/2	cup whole wheat flour
1/2	cup plus 2 tablespoons all-purpose flour
1-1/2	ounces bran
1	teaspoon baking soda
1-1/2	teaspoons ground cinnamon
1-1/2	cups buttermilk
1	egg, slightly beaten
1/4	cup molasses
1	tablespoon plus 1 teaspoon vegetable oil
1	teaspoon vanilla extract

Preheat oven to 375°.

In a medium bowl, combine both flours, bran, baking soda, and cinnamon.

In a large bowl, combine remaining ingredients. Beat with a wire whisk until blended.

Add dry ingredients to liquid mixture. Stir until all ingredients are moistened. (Batter will be thin.)

Place mixture in 8 nonstick muffin cups or ones that have been sprayed with a nonstick cooking spray.

Bake 20 to 22 minutes, until a toothpick inserted in the center comes out clean.

Remove muffins from pan and cool, upside-down, on a rack.

Each serving provides:

154 Calories

1	Bread Serving	5	g	Protein
1/2	Fat Serving	4	g	Fat
1/4	Milk Servings	25	g	Carbohydrate
36	Additional Calories	162	mg	Sodium
		36	mg	Cholesterol

Cheddar Bean Muffins

Cheddar cheese and beans combined make these a real high-protein treat. For a real quick lunch, add a tossed salad and your meal is complete. They're small, so we figured 2 muffins per serving.

Makes 4 servings
(2 muffins each serving)

3/4	cup all-purpose flour
1	teaspoon baking powder
1/2	teaspoon baking soda
1	egg
1	tablespoon plus 1 teaspoon vegetable oil
2	teaspoons sugar (or equivalent amount of sweetener)
6	ounces cooked kidney or pinto beans
2/3	cup nonfat dry milk
1/4	cup plus 2 tablespoons water
2	ounces shredded lowfat Cheddar cheese
2	teaspoons minced onion flakes

Preheat oven to 350°.

Sift flour, baking powder, and baking soda.

In a blender container, combine remaining ingredients. Blend until smooth. Transfer to a large bowl.

Add dry ingredients to bean mixture. Stir until all ingredients are moistened.

Spoon mixture into 8 nonstick muffin cups or ones that have been sprayed with a nonstick cooking spray.

Bake 12 to 15 minutes, until firm and lightly browned.

Each serving provides:

286 Calories*

1-1/2	Protein Servings	14	g	Protein
1	Bread Serving	8	g	Fat
1	Fat Serving	39	g	Carbohydrate
1/2	Milk Serving	334	mg	Sodium
8	Additional Calories (if sugar is used as sweetener)	75	mg	Cholesterol

*If sugar is used as sweetener

Maple Corn Muffins

Maple extract makes these corn muffins "different." They're not too sweet, and go well with any meal.

Makes 8 servings

3   ounces yellow corn meal (1/2 cup)
1/2   cup all-purpose flour
1/4   cup whole wheat flour
1-1/2   teaspoons baking powder
1   egg, slightly beaten
1/2   cup skim milk
2   tablespoons honey
2   tablespoons plus 2 teaspoons margarine, melted
1/2   teaspoon maple extract

Preheat oven to 425°.

In a large bowl, combine corn meal, both flours, and baking powder. Mix well.

Place muffin pan in the oven to preheat for 5 minutes.

In a medium bowl, combine remaining ingredients. Beat with a wire whisk until blended. Add to dry ingredients, stirring until all ingredients are moistened.

Spray preheated pan with a nonstick cooking spray.

Place batter in pan.

Bake 15 minutes, until crisp and lightly browned.

Remove to a rack to cool.

Each serving provides:

146 Calories

1	Bread Serving	3	g	Protein
1	Fat Serving	5	g	Fat
28	Additional Calories	22	g	Carbohydrate
		142	mg	Sodium
		35	mg	Cholesterol

Oat Bran Muffins

Oat bran is found in the cereal section of most supermarkets and is believed by many health professionals to help lower blood cholesterol levels. (If you are watching your cholesterol, these muffins will work just as well with an egg substitute.) And, they just happen to be delicious.

Makes 10 servings

7-1/2 ounces oat bran
1   teaspoon baking powder
1-1/2 teaspoons ground cinnamon
2   eggs
1   cup skim milk
1/4   cup honey
1   tablespoon plus 2 teaspoons vegetable oil
1-1/2 teaspoons vanilla extract

Preheat oven to 400°.

In a large bowl, combine oat bran, baking powder, and cinnamon. Mix well.

In a medium bowl, combine remaining ingredients. Beat with a wire whisk until blended.

Add liquid mixture to dry ingredients. Stir until all ingredients are moistened.

Place in 10 nonstick muffin cups or ones that have been sprayed with a nonstick cooking spray.

Bake 15 minutes, until golden.

Remove to a rack to cool.

Each serving provides:

156 Calories

1	Bread Serving	6	g	Protein
1/2	Fat Serving	5	g	Fat
44	Additional Calories	21	g	Carbohydrate
		70	mg	Sodium
		55	mg	Cholesterol

Fruits

Hints For Fruits

- When buying canned or frozen fruit, choose only the unsweetened water-packed or juice-packed varieties.
- In gelatin molds, using the sugar-free varieties will greatly reduce the amount of calories in the recipe.
- Try using *half* the amount of sugar called for in a fruit recipe. Practice moderation and get used to foods being less sweet. You'll probably find that you can enjoy the taste of the fruits themselves without covering up their flavor with sugar.
- For added calorie reduction, you may want to use half sugar and half artificial sweetener.
- Honey will work as a sweetener in most fruit recipes, and has a delicious flavor, but be aware that it has as many calories as sugar.
- Choose the sweetest varieties of fruits and they will require less added sugar. For example, if an apple recipe calls for Granny Smith apples, choose the sweeter Golden Delicious instead, and less sugar will be needed.
- Using very ripe fruit will also enable you to cut back on the amount of sugar needed in a recipe.
- For a wonderful lunchbox treat, core a fresh apple or pear and fill the hole with peanut butter.
- Sauté sliced apples, pears, pineapple, or any combination of these fruits in a nonstick saucepan with vanilla extract and a small amount of reduced-calorie margarine. Sprinkle with cinnamon, and you have a delicious dessert or snack.
- Broil orange or grapefruit halves, sprinkled with cinnamon, for a great addition to breakfast.
- For a wonderfully elegant melon dessert or appetizer, cut a cantaloupe and a honeydew melon into wedges. Scoop several balls out of each wedge. Then place the cantaloupe balls in the holes in the honeydew, and vice versa.
- Make interesting fruit salads by adding unusual fruits, such as kiwi fruit or star fruit.

Peach Crisp

Peaches, oats, and cinnamon are combined for our flavorful version of this all-time favorite dessert. Try it for breakfast, too.

Makes 4 servings

4   medium, ripe peaches, peeled, sliced 1/4-inch thick
3   tablespoons all-purpose flour
2-1/4 ounces quick-cooking oats, uncooked
1   teaspoon ground cinnamon
1/2 teaspoon ground nutmeg
2   tablespoons plus 2 teaspoons reduced-calorie margarine
3   tablespoons firmly-packed brown sugar (or sweetener
      equivalent to 9 teaspoons brown sugar)

Preheat oven to 350°.
Toss peaches with 1 tablespoon of the flour and place in a 6 x 11-inch baking pan that has been sprayed with a nonstick cooking spray.
In a small bowl, combine remaining ingredients. Mix well until mixture is crumbly. Sprinkle evenly over peaches.
Bake 30 to 35 minutes, until crisp.
Serve warm or cold.

Each serving provides:

214 Calories*

1	Bread Serving	4	g	Protein
1	Fat Serving	5	g	Fat
1	Fruit Serving	40	g	Carbohydrate
36	Additional Calories (if	84	mg	Sodium
	brown sugar is used as	0	mg	Cholesterol
	sweetener)			

*If brown sugar is used as sweetener

Quick Peaches 'n Cream

Rich and delicious and so easy to do, this dish makes a great snack for after school or anytime.

Makes 1 serving

1/2	cup plain lowfat yogurt
1/2	teaspoon vanilla extract
1/4	teaspoon almond extract
1/4	teaspoon ground cinnamon
2	teaspoons sugar (or equivalent amount of sweetener)
1	medium, ripe peach, peeled and chopped (or 1/2 cup canned, unsweetened peaches)

In a small bowl, combine all ingredients. Mix well and enjoy right away or chill for a later serving.

Each serving provides:

172 Calories*

1	Fruit Serving	7	g	Protein
1	Milk Serving	2	g	Fat
32	Additional Calories (if sugar is used as sweetener)	32	g	Carbohydrate
		80	mg	Sodium
		7	mg	Cholesterol

*If sugar is used as sweetener

Peach Butter

What a delicious topping for toast or English muffins!

Makes 16 servings
(1-1/2 tablespoons each serving)

2 cups canned, sliced peaches (unsweetened), drained
1 tablespoon plus 1 teaspoon cornstarch
1/8 teaspoon ground allspice
1/8 teaspoon ground nutmeg
1/4 teaspoon ground cinnamon
   Dash ground cloves
1/2 teaspoon vanilla extract
1 tablespoon plus 1 teaspoon sugar (or sweetener equivalent
   to 4 teaspoons sugar)

In a blender container, combine all ingredients. Blend until smooth.

Pour mixture into a medium saucepan. Cook over medium-low heat, stirring frequently, until mixture comes to a boil.

Reduce heat to low and simmer, stirring, 2 minutes.

Pour into a jar and chill.

Each serving provides:

14 Calories*

1/4	Fruit Serving	0	g	Protein
3	Additional Calories	0	g	Fat
	(plus 4 more calories if	4	g	Carbohydrate
	sugar is used as	0	mg	Sodium
	sweetener)	0	mg	Cholesterol

*If sugar is used as sweetener

Mom Mom's Applesauce

This recipe was hard to duplicate, since Mom Mom doesn't measure her ingredients, but, thanks to her assistance, here is our favorite applesauce. The number of servings is approximate and may very slightly with the amount of water used and the length of cooking time.

Makes 12 servings
(1/2 cup each serving)

4   pounds apples, preferably Stayman Winesap, peeled, cut
        into large chunks
1   whole lemon, cut into thin strips (Include rind, but remove
        center membrane and seeds.)
1/2   cup raisins
1-1/2 teaspoons ground cinnamon
2   teaspoons sugar (or equivalent amount of sweetener)

Place all ingredients in a large saucepan. Add enough water to come halfway up the apples.

Cook, uncovered, over medium heat until mixture comes to a boil. Reduce heat to low.

Cook until apples are mushy and lemon is tender. Remove from heat.

Mash apples with the back of a spoon. (They will be a little lumpy.)

Chill and enjoy.

Each serving provides:

97 Calories*

1	Fruit Serving	0	g	Protein
3	Additional Calories (if	0	g	Fat
	sugar is used as	26	g	Carbohydrate
	sweetener)	1	mg	Sodium
		0	mg	Cholesterol

*If sugar is used as sweetener

Peanutty Apple Crisp

This unusual dessert combines the wonderful flavors of apples and peanut butter for an unforgettable taste.

Makes 8 servings

4	small, sweet apples, peeled and chopped
1	teaspoon ground cinnamon
1/2	teaspoon ground nutmeg
2	teaspoons vanilla extract
2	tablespoons sugar (or sweetener equivalent to 6 teaspoons sugar)
1/4	cup peanut butter
1	tablespoon plus 1 teaspoon reduced-calorie margarine
3	ounces quick-cooking oats, uncooked

Preheat oven to 350°.

In a medium bowl, combine apples, cinnamon, nutmeg, vanilla, and sugar. Toss until mixed well. Place in a 9-inch pie pan that has been sprayed with a nonstick cooking spray.

In a small saucepan, melt peanut butter and margarine over low heat, stirring until smooth. Remove from heat. Stir in oats.

Sprinkle oats mixture evenly over apples.

Bake, uncovered, 30 minutes, until crisp.

Each serving provides:

143 Calories*

1/2	Protein Serving	4	g	Protein
1/2	Bread Serving	6	g	Fat
3/4	Fat Serving	20	g	Carbohydrate
1/2	Fruit Serving	58	mg	Sodium
12	Additional Calories (if sugar is used as sweetener)	0	mg	Cholesterol

*If sugar is used as sweetener

Apple Creams

The delicate flavors of apples and "cream" make this a refreshing dessert. It can be served warm or cold, and also makes a tasty snack.

Makes 4 servings

2   small, sweet apples (such as Golden Delicious), peeled and chopped into 1/4-inch pieces
2   eggs
1   teaspoon vanilla extract
2   tablespoons sugar (or sweetener equivalent to 6 teaspoons sugar)
1   cup evaporated skim milk

Topping
1/4   teaspoon ground cinnamon
1   teaspoon sugar

Preheat oven to 350°.

Divide apple pieces evenly into 4 custard cups.

In a small bowl, beat eggs, vanilla, and sugar with a fork or wire whisk. Gradually whisk in milk. Pour mixture over apples.

Place custard cups in an 8-inch square baking dish. Pour 1 cup of boiling water into bottom of pan.

Bake 30 minutes, until set.

Combine cinnamon and sugar. When custard comes out of the oven, sprinkle each with the topping and place on a rack to cool.

Serve warm or chill and serve cold.

Each serving provides:

150 Calories*

1/2	Protein Serving	8 g	Protein
1/2	Fruit Serving	3 g	Fat
1/2	Milk Serving	23 g	Carbohydrate
24	Additional Calories (if sugar is used as sweetener)	108 mg	Sodium
		140 mg	Cholesterol

*If sugar is used as sweetener

Apple Tapioca Dessert

Using sweet apples, such as Golden Delicious, makes this succulent dessert taste even better. It's also a great breakfast treat.

Makes 4 servings

4   small, sweet apples, peeled, coarsely shredded
1   cup water
2   tablespoons plus 2 teaspoons quick-cooking tapioca, uncooked
1   teaspoon vanilla extract
1/2   teaspoon ground cinnamon
1/4   teaspoon ground nutmeg
1   tablespoon plus 1 teaspoon sugar (or sweetener equivalent to 4 teaspoons sugar)

Preheat oven to 350°.

Combine all ingredients in a large bowl and mix well.

Place in a 1-quart baking dish that has been sprayed with a non-stick cooking spray. Let stand 10 minutes. Smooth the top of the pudding with the back of a spoon.

Bake, uncovered, 40 minutes, until tapioca granules are clear.

Serve hot or cold.

Each serving provides:

101 Calories*

1	Fruit Serving	0	g	Protein
20	Additional Calories	0	g	Fat
	(plus 16 more calories if	25	g	Carbohydrate
	sugar is used as	0	mg	Sodium
	sweetener)	0	mg	Cholesterol

*If sugar is used as sweetener

Applesauce Ambrosia

Serve this fruit combo in pretty sherbet glasses for a delicious dessert, or serve it over vanilla ice milk for really elegant fare.

Makes 8 servings

2   cups applesauce (unsweetened)
2   medium, ripe bananas, sliced
1   cup canned mandarin oranges (unsweetened)
1   ounce slivered toasted almonds
2   tablespoons shredded coconut (unsweetened)

Combine all ingredients.
Chill.

Each serving provides:

91 Calories

1-1/4	Fruit Servings	1 g	Protein
29	Additional Calories	3 g	Fat
		18 g	Carbohydrate
		4 mg	Sodium
		0 mg	Cholesterol

Baked Apples and Creme

We've replaced the cream with evaporated skim milk in this "formerly fattening favorite," and we don't even miss it.

Makes 4 servings

4	small, sweet apples (such as Rome or Golden Delicious), peeled, cored, and sliced 1/4-inch thick
3	tablespoons firmly-packed brown sugar (or sweetener equivalent to 9 teaspoons brown sugar)
1	tablespoon plus 1 teaspoon reduced-calorie margarine
1/2	cup evaporated skim milk
2	teaspoons vanilla extract
1/4	teaspoon ground cinnamon
1/8	teaspoon ground nutmeg

Preheat oven to 350°.

Place apple slices in a shallow baking pan that has been sprayed with a nonstick cooking spray.

Sprinkle with *half* the brown sugar.

Dot with margarine.

Combine milk and vanilla extract and drizzle evenly over apples.

Sprinkle with cinnamon, nutmeg, and remaining brown sugar.

Bake, uncovered, 30 minutes, until apples are tender.

Each serving provides:

145 Calories*

1/2	Fat Serving	3	g	Protein
1	Fruit Serving	2	g	Fat
1/4	Milk Serving	29	g	Carbohydrate
36	Additional Calories (if brown sugar is used as sweetener)	80	mg	Sodium
		1	mg	Cholesterol

*If brown sugar is used as sweetener

Citrus Fluff

This light-as-air dessert has many variations. Just change the fruit juice and the extract and you have a new dessert.

Makes 4 servings

1	envelope unflavored gelatin
1/2	cup water
1/4	cup frozen orange juice concentrate (unsweetened), thawed
3	tablespoons sugar (or sweetener equivalent to 9 teaspoons sugar)
1/4	teaspoon lemon extract
15	small ice cubes (about 1-1/2 cups)
2	egg whites
1/4	teaspoon cream of tartar

In a small saucepan, sprinkle gelatin over combined water and orange juice concentrate. Heat over low heat, stirring frequently, until gelatin is completely dissolved.

Remove from heat. Stir in sugar and extracts, stirring until sugar is dissolved.

Add ice. Stir until mixture thickens. Discard any remaining pieces of ice.

Beat egg whites and cream of tartar on high speed of an electric mixer until stiff. Fold orange mixture into egg whites gently, but thoroughly.

Chill 1 hour before serving.

Each serving provides:

80 Calories*

1/2	Fruit Serving	4	g	Protein
10	Addittional Calories	0	g	Fat
	(plus 36 more calories if	16	g	Carbohydrate
	sugar is used as	27	mg	Sodium
	sweetener)	0	mg	Cholesterol

*If sugar is used as sweetener

Fruity Gel

Here's a gelatin dessert that's as easy to prepare as the kind in the box, but with no added sugar. And, you can make it any flavor you like.

Makes 4 servings

2   cups orange juice (unsweetened) or any other flavor fruit
        juice or combination of juices
1   envelope unflavored gelatin

Sprinkle gelatin over half of the juice in a small saucepan. Let soften a few minutes.

Heat, stirring frequently, over low heat, until gelatin is completely dissolved. Remove from heat.

Stir in remaining juice.

Pour mixture into 1 serving bowl or 4 individual bowls.

Chill.

Each serving provides:

62 Calories

1	Fruit Serving	2	g	Protein
		0	g	Fat
		13	g	Carbohydrate
		3	mg	Sodium
		0	mg	Cholesterol

Frozen Banana Yogurt

So cool and refreshing, this dessert is one of our summertime favorites.

Makes 4 servings

2	medium, ripe bananas, cut into chunks
1/4	cup orange juice (unsweetened)
1/2	cup plain lowfat yogurt
1/3	cup nonfat dry milk
3	tablespoons sugar (or sweetener equivalent to 9 teaspoons sugar)
1/4	teaspoon lemon extract
1	teaspoon vanilla extract
1	egg white

In a blender container, combine all ingredients. Blend until smooth.

Pour mixture into a 4 x 8-inch loaf pan. Place in freezer for 1 hour, until crystals form around edge of pan and mixture is slushy.

Remove from freezer. Beat with an electric mixer for 1 minute on medium speed and then 1 minute on high speed.

Return mixture to pan and freeze at least 1 hour.

Each serving provides:

143 Calories*

1	Fruit Serving	5	g	Protein
1/2	Milk Serving	1	g	Fat
11	Additional Calories	30	g	Carbohydrate
	(plus 36 more calories if	64	mg	Sodium
	sugar is used as	3	mg	Cholesterol
	sweetener)			

*If sugar is used as sweetener

Broiled Bananas

If you like bananas, you'll love this scrumptious recipe. Try it for dessert, with breakfast, or as a side dish with curried entrees.

Makes 6 servings

3	medium, ripe bananas
2	tablespoons lemon juice
2	tablespoons margarine, melted
2	teaspoons firmly-packed brown sugar (or equivalent amount of sweetener)
1/4	teaspoon ground cinnamon
1/8	teaspoon ground allspice
	Dash ground cloves

Slice bananas crosswise and then lengthwise. Place in a shallow baking pan that has been sprayed with a nonstick cooking spray. Brush both sides with lemon juice.

Drizzle margarine over bananas.

Combine remaining ingredients. Sprinkle evenly on bananas.

Broil 5 inches from heat about 5 minutes, until lightly browned. Serve hot.

Each serving provides:

94 Calories*

1	Fat Serving	1	g	Protein
1	Fruit Serving	4	g	Fat
5	Additional Calories (if	15	g	Carbohydrate
	brown sugar is used as	47	mg	Sodium
	sweetener)	0	mg	Cholesterol

*If brown sugar is used as sweetener

Blueberry and Apple Delight

We call this "Delight" because it is so versatile. Use it as a topping for cottage cheese or ice milk, spoon it over hot oatmeal, or enjoy it as is. Any way you try it, you're sure to fall in love with it.

Makes 12 servings
(1/2 cup each serving)

8   cups sweet apples (such as Golden Delicious), peeled, sliced
        1/4-inch thick
4   cups fresh or frozen blueberries (unsweetened)
1-1/2   cups water
1   teaspoon lemon juice
1/2   teaspoon ground cinnamon
1   tablespoon plus 1 teaspoon cornstarch
3   tablespoons sugar (or sweetener equivalent to 9 teaspoons
        sugar)

In a large saucepan, combine all ingredients. (If using Nutra-Sweet as sweetener, add it after cooking.) Cook over medium heat, stirring occasionally, until mixture comes to a boil.

Reduce heat to low and cook, stirring frequently, until apples are tender.

Serve warm or chill and serve cold.

Each serving provides:

90 Calories*

1	Fruit Serving	0	g	Protein
3	Additional Calories	0	g	Fat
	(plus 12 more calories if	23	g	Carbohydrate
	sugar is used as	3	mg	Sodium
	sweetener)	0	mg	Cholesterol

*If sugar is used as sweetener

Baked Pears with Cinnamon Creme Sauce

This dessert looks like a work of art and tastes just as good. Try the sauce over other fruits as well.

Makes 4 servings

4	small pears
2	tablespoons firmly-packed brown sugar (or sweetener equivalent to 6 teaspoons brown sugar)
1/2	cup water
1	tablespoon lemon juice
1/4	teaspoon ground cinnamon

Creme Sauce

1/2	cup plain lowfat yogurt
1/2	teaspoon ground cinnamon
1/2	teaspoon vanilla extract
1	tablespoon firmly-packed brown sugar (or sweetener equivalent to 3 teaspoons brown sugar)

Prepare creme sauce ahead of time. In a small bowl, combine all ingredients in creme sauce. Chill to blend flavors.

Preheat oven to 350°.

Peel pears, cut in half lengthwise and scoop out core. Place, flat-side down, in a small shallow baking dish. Combine brown sugar, water, lemon juice, and cinnamon. Pour over pears.

Cover and bake 45 minutes, or until pears are tender. Baste occasionally with pan juices while baking.

To serve, place 2 pear halves in each of 4 individual serving bowls. Spoon pan juices over pears; then top each serving with a dollop of creme sauce. Serve right away.

Each serving provides:

134 Calories*

1	Fruit Serving	2	g	Protein
1/4	Milk Serving	1	g	Fat
36	Additional Calories (if	32	g	Carbohydrate
	brown sugar is used as	24	mg	Sodium
	sweetener)	2	mg	Cholesterol

*If brown sugar is used as sweetener

Berries Romanoff

(Shown on Cover)

This dessert is so easy to do, and yet so elegant. Serve it in tall-stemmed champagne glasses for an even more festive touch.

Makes 2 servings

1   cup plain lowfat yogurt
1   tablespoon plus 1 teaspoon sugar (or sweetener equivalent
            to 4 teaspoons sugar)
1   teaspoon vanilla extract
1/2   teaspoon orange extract
2   cups fresh strawberries

In a small bowl, combine all ingredients, *except* strawberries. Mix well.

Chill to blend flavors.

To serve, divide berries into individual serving bowls. Stir yogurt mixture and spoon over berries.

Each serving provides:

162 Calories*

1	Fruit Serving	7	g	Protein
1	Milk Serving	2	g	Fat
32	Additional Calories (if	28	g	Carbohydrate
	sugar is used as	81	mg	Sodium
	sweetener)	7	mg	Cholesterol

*If sugar is used as sweetener

Strawberry Fruit Sherbet

When fresh strawberries are in season, freeze lots of them and you can enjoy this sherbet all year round. It's ready in an instant and makes a great after-school snack.

Makes 2 servings

1   cup frozen strawberries (unsweetened) (Do not thaw.)
1/2   medium, ripe banana
1/4   cup orange juice (unsweetened)
1   teaspoon honey

Combine all ingredients in a blender container. Blend until smooth, stopping blender several times to stir mixture.

Spoon into sherbet glasses and enjoy.

Note: To make this into a drink, add more juice.

Each serving provides:

77 Calories

1-1/4	Fruit Servings	1	g	Protein
10	Additional Calories	0	g	Fat
		20	g	Carbohydrate
		2	mg	Sodium
		0	mg	Cholesterol

Raspberry Tapioca

This is a real treat when fresh summer berries are available. It's absolutely delicious as it is, and even better over vanilla ice milk.

Makes 4 servings

2   cups fresh or frozen (thawed) raspberries (unsweetened)
3   tablespoons quick-cooking tapioca, uncooked
2   tablespoons plus 2 teaspoons sugar (or sweetener equivalent to 8 teaspoons sugar)

Place berries in a blender container. Blend until smooth. Pour through a strainer.

In a small saucepan, combine puréed berries with enough water to equal 2 cups.

Stir in tapioca and sugar. (If using NutraSweet as a sweetener, add it after cooking.) Let mixture stand 5 minutes.

Bring to a boil over medium heat, stirring frequently. Remove from heat.

Cool in pan 20 minutes. Then stir and place in 4 custard cups. Chill.

Each serving provides:

87 Calories*

1	Fruit Serving	1	g	Protein
23	Additional Calories	0	g	Fat
	(plus 32 more calories if	22	g	Carbohydrate
	sugar is used as	0	mg	Sodium
	sweetener)	0	mg	Cholesterol

*If sugar is used as sweetener

Baked Cranberry Relish

Baking seems to bring out the color and flavor of this popular holiday treat. Hot or cold, its zesty flavor is a perfect addition to a roast chicken or turkey dinner.

Makes 12 servings

3	cups fresh cranberries
2	small apples, peeled, cut into chunks
3	small oranges, peeled, sectioned
1/4	cup raisins
8	dried apricot halves
2	ounces chopped walnuts
1/4	cup sugar (or sweetener equivalent to 12 teaspoons sugar)
3	tablespoons quick-cooking tapioca, uncooked

Preheat oven to 350°.

Finely chop cranberries, apples, orange sections, raisins, and apricots. If using a food processor, all of these ingredients can be combined and chopped. If using a blender, chop a small amount at a time so that fruit is chopped and not puréed.

Stir in walnuts, sugar, and tapioca. Place mixture in a 1-1/2 quart casserole that has been sprayed with a nonstick cooking spray. Let stand 5 minutes.

Bake, uncovered, 40 minutes.

Serve hot or chill and serve cold.

Each serving provides:

107 Calories*

1	Fruit Serving	1	g	Protein
38	Additional Calories	3	g	Fat
	(plus 16 more calories if	20	g	Carbohydrate
	sugar is used as	1	mg	Sodium
	sweetener)	0	mg	Cholesterol

*If sugar is used as sweetener

Fruit Fritters

What a treat for dessert or breakfast! And, what a combination of fruits and flavors! Don't forget, if you're watching your cholesterol, use an egg substitute in place of the eggs.

Makes 8 servings
(2 fritters each serving)

4	eggs
1	medium, ripe banana
4	slices enriched white or whole wheat bread, crumbled
2/3	cup nonfat dry milk
2	teaspoons vanilla extract
1/4	teaspoon banana extract
1/4	teaspoon orange *or* lemon extract
1/2	teaspoon ground cinnamon
2	teaspoons baking powder
1	tablespoon plus 1 teaspoon vegetable oil
1	tablespoon plus 1 teaspoon sugar (or sweetener equivalent to 4 teaspoons sugar)
1/2	cup fresh or frozen (unsweetened) blueberries (If using frozen berries, thaw and drain well.)
1/2	cup canned crushed pineapple (unsweetened), drained

In a blender container, combine all ingredients, *except* blueberries and pineapple. Blend until smooth.

Pour mixture into a large bowl.

Stir in remaining fruit.

Preheat a nonstick skillet or griddle over medium heat, spraying lightly with a nonstick cooking spray. Spoon batter onto skillet, making 16 four-inch fritters. When edges are dry, turn fritters carefully, browning on both sides.

Note: To make turning fritters easier, spray spatula with nonstick cooking spray.

Each serving provides:

154 Calories*

1/2	Protein Serving	6	g	Protein
1/2	Bread Serving	6	g	Fat
1/2	Fat Serving	19	g	Carbohydrate
1/2	Fruit Serving	234	mg	Sodium
1/4	Milk Serving	138	mg	Cholesterol
8	Additional Calories (if sugar is used as sweetener)			

*If sugar is used as sweetener

Baked Fruit Medley

Slightly sweet and slightly tangy, this compote is delicious. It adds a tasty touch to any buffet and can be served hot or cold.

Makes 12 servings

6   small, sweet apples, unpeeled, cut into 1/2-inch chunks
4   small oranges, peeled and sectioned (Discard white
         membrane.)
1   cup canned crushed pineapple (unsweetened), drained
         slightly
1   cup water
2   tablespoons cornstarch
1   teaspoon ground cinnamon
1/2   teaspoon ground nutmeg
3   tablespoons firmly-packed brown sugar (or sweetener
         equivalent to 9 teaspoons brown sugar)
1   teaspoon freshly grated orange peel

In a large bowl, combine fruits. Toss gently until thoroughly mixed.

Preheat oven to 350°.

In a small bowl, combine remaining ingredients, mixing until cornstarch is completely dissolved. Add to fruit, mixing well.

Place in a 2-quart casserole that has been sprayed with a non-stick cooking spray.

Cover and bake 40 minutes, stirring once after 20 minutes.

Serve hot or cold.

Each serving provides:

81 Calories*

1	Fruit Serving	0	g	Protein
5	Additional Calories	0	g	Fat
	(plus 12 more calories if	21	g	Carbohydrate
	brown sugar is used as	1	mg	Sodium
	sweetener)	0	mg	Cholesterol

*If brown sugar is used as sweetener

Dried Fruit Compote

This compote has a delightfully strong cinnamon flavor. It can be made with any mixture of dried fruits and is tasty as a dessert over cottage cheese or on hot cereal.

Makes 16 servings
(1/4 cup each serving)

6	dried peach halves, cut into quarters
16	dried apricot halves, cut in half
10	pitted prunes, cut in half
1/2	cup raisins
1	tablespoon ground cinnamon
	Dash ground cloves
2	tablespoons honey
3-1/2 cups water	

Combine all ingredients in a medium saucepan. Bring to a boil over medium heat, stirring occasionally.

Reduce heat to low and simmer, uncovered, 15 minutes.

Cool slightly; then chill.

Note: An easy way to cut dried fruit is with kitchen shears.

Each serving provides:

55 Calories

1	Fruit Serving	1	g	Protein
8	Additional Calories	0	g	Fat
		15	g	Carbohydrate
		2	mg	Sodium
		0	mg	Cholesterol

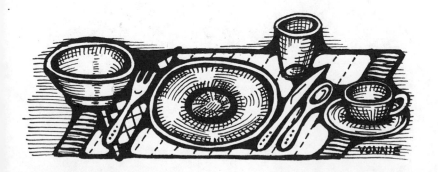

Hot Spiced Fruit

A winning combination of peaches and pineapple, this dish can be used as a dessert, or as a very pretty and flavorful accompaniment for roast chicken or turkey.

Makes 4 servings

4   slices canned pineapple (unsweetened), drained (Reserve 2
        tablespoons juice.)
1   cup canned, sliced peaches (unsweetened), drained
        (Reserve 2 tablespoons juice.)
1/4   teaspoon ground cinnamon
1/4   teaspoon ground cloves
1   tablespoon plus 1 teaspoon reduced-calorie margarine

Preheat oven to 350°.

Place pineapple in a shallow baking pan that has been sprayed with a nonstick cooking spray. Top with peach slices.

Combine reserved juices and pour over fruit.

Sprinkle evenly with cinnamon and cloves.

Dot with margarine.

Bake, uncovered, 20 to 25 minutes, until hot and bubbly.

Each serving provides:

67 Calories

1/2	Fat Serving	1	g	Protein
1	Fruit Serving	2	g	Fat
		13	g	Carbohydrate
		43	mg	Sodium
		0	mg	Cholesterol

Desserts

Hints for Desserts

- In most dessert recipes, you can use half the amount of sugar called for without affecting the texture of the dessert, and you'll be amazed at how good the desserts still taste. (In our dessert recipes we have already greatly reduced the amount of sugar.)

- While artificial sweeteners work well in pies and puddings, they can alter the texture of cakes, cookies, and pastries. If you use a sweetener, for best results we suggest that you use half sugar and half sweetener. All of our cakes were tested in this manner, as well as with all sugar, and we found that the taste and texture were consistently better than when we used all sweetener.

- NutraSweet should not be used in desserts when they will be cooked because prolonged exposure to heat causes the sweetness to break down and be lost. It can, however, be added immediately after cooking.

- Honey will work as a sweetener in most pies and puddings. However, it may alter the texture of cakes or cookies. Be aware that honey has as many calories as sugar.

- By adding vanilla extract to a recipe, or increasing the amount already called for, you can add a perceived sweetness that makes foods taste sweeter than they really are.

- You can add fiber, vitamins, iron, and protein to your desserts by replacing half the flour called for with whole wheat flour. If you substitute more than half, you will need to add a little more liquid to the recipe. As a general rule of thumb: To replace all of the white flour in a recipe, for each cup of white flour, use 1 cup minus 2 tablespoons of whole wheat flour. Or, use the same amount of whole wheat flour and add more liquid to the recipe.

- The amount of cholesterol in a recipe can be greatly reduced by either using an egg substitute in place of the eggs, or 2 egg whites in place of each egg.

- When vegetable oil is called for, be sure to choose a polyunsaturated oil such as safflower, sunflower, corn, or soybean oil.

- While coconut oil and palm kernel oil are vegetable oils, they are extremely high in saturated fat. (Your body turns this saturated fat into cholesterol.)

- Avoid animal fats, such as butter, lard, and suet. They are very high in saturated fat and cholesterol.
- Using margarine in place of butter will lower the amount of saturated fat and cholesterol in a recipe. The calories, however, will remain the same.
- When choosing a margarine, your best bet is one that lists a polyunsaturated oil in liquid form as its main ingredient. Examples would be liquid safflower oil or liquid corn oil.
- Be aware that the reduced-calorie, tub-style margarines usually have a high water content and may alter the texture of a recipe. Experimentation may be necessary.
- Use a nonstick cooking spray instead of greasing pans.
- Use lowfat cottage cheese and part-skim ricotta cheese in cheesecakes and other recipes that call for the higher fat varieties. The taste will be the same.
- In place of sour cream use plain lowfat or nonfat yogurt.
- Replace the cream in a recipe with evaporated skim milk. Add vanilla for a richer taste.
- Always use skim milk in place of whole milk.
- Whipped toppings often contain coconut oil, so read labels carefully and "go easy" when using them as a garnish.
- Making a pie with one crust instead of two will reduced the amount of calories in each slice.
- In dessert recipes that call for nuts or coconut, use only one half or one quarter the amount called for.
- When a recipe calls for ground nuts, use wheat germ instead.
- To save calories, use 3 tablespoons of cocoa in place of 1 ounce of solid chocolate.
- When a recipe calls for canned or frozen fruit, use only the unsweetened water-packed or juice-packed varieties.
- In order to cut back on the amount of sugar needed in fruit desserts, choose the sweetest varieties of fruits and the ripest fruits available.
- For additional dessert recipes, be sure to see our sections on Breads and Grains, Fruits, and Tofu.

Banana Cake Roll

Elegant enough for any party and so easy to make, this cake will delight the banana devotee. It also works well with an egg substitute in place of the eggs.

Makes 8 servings

3/4   cup all-purpose flour
1   teaspoon baking powder
1   teaspoon ground cinnamon
3   eggs
1   teaspoon vanilla butternut flavor
1/2   teaspoon banana extract
1   tablespoon plus 1 teaspoon vegetable oil
3   tablespoons plus 1 teaspoon sugar (or sweetener equivalent to 10 teaspoons sugar)
2   medium, ripe bananas, mashed

Filling
1-1/4 cups part-skim ricotta cheese
1   teaspoon vanilla extract
1/2   teaspoon vanilla butternut flavor
1/4   teaspoon banana extract
2   tablespoons sugar (or sweetener equivalent to 6 teaspoons sugar)

Preheat oven to 350°.

In a small bowl, sift flour, baking powder, and cinnamon.

In another bowl, beat eggs on medium speed of an electric mixer 3 minutes. Beat on high speed 2 minutes.

Reduce mixer to low speed and beat in extracts, oil, sugar, and bananas.

Add dry ingredients. Beat on low speed until all ingredients are moistened.

Spread batter in a 10 x 15-inch nonstick jelly roll pan that has also been sprayed lightly with a nonstick cooking spray.

Bake 10 minutes.

Cool in pan on rack for 3 minutes. Loosen sides of cake with a spatula and invert cake onto a kitchen towel. Roll up like a jelly roll and let cool completely.

Combine all filling ingredients in a small bowl.

When cake is cool, unroll and spread evenly with filling. Carefully roll cake again and chill.

Each serving provides:

210 Calories*

1	Protein Serving	8	g	Protein
1/2	Bread Serving	8	g	Fat
1/2	Fat Serving	27	g	Carbohydrate
1/2	Fruit Serving	128	mg	Sodium
32	Additional Calories (if sugar is used as sweetener)	115	mg	Cholesterol

*If sugar is used as sweetener

Fruit Medley Pudding Cake

This eggless dessert gets its flavor from quite a lineup of fruits and spices.

Makes 8 servings

3/4	cup orange juice (unsweetened)
1-1/3	cups nonfat dry milk
1/2	medium, ripe banana
1	small orange, peeled and sectioned
1/4	cup plus 2 tablespoons sugar (or sweetener equivalent to 18 teaspoons sugar)
1	teaspoon vanilla extract
1/2	teaspoon *each* baking powder and baking soda
1	teaspoon *each* grated orange peel and ground cinnamon
1	teaspoon ground allspice
1/2	teaspoon *each* ground cloves, nutmeg, and mace
8	slices white or whole wheat raisin bread, crumbled
1/2	cup canned crushed pineapple (unsweetened), drained
1	cup fresh or frozen blueberries (unsweetened)
2	small, sweet apples, peeled, finely chopped

Preheat oven to 350° (325° for glass pan).

In a blender container, combine orange juice, dry milk, banana, orange, sugar, vanilla, baking powder, baking soda, and spices. Blend until smooth. Add bread. Blend until combined, stopping the blender occasionally to stir. Continue to blend 1 more minute.

Pour batter into a large bowl. Add remaining ingredients. Stir until well mixed.

Place in an 8-inch square baking pan that has been sprayed with a nonstick cooking spray.

Bake 1 hour, until edges are brown and top is set. Cool on rack.

Each serving provides:

205 Calories*

1	Bread Serving	6	g	Protein
1	Fruit Serving	1	g	Fat
1/2	Milk Serving	44	g	Carbohydrate
3	Additional Calories (plus	233	mg	Sodium
	36 more calories if sugar is	3	mg	Cholesterol
	used as sweetener)			

*If sugar is used as sweetener

Double Lemon Pudding Cake

This cake is so moist and lemony, no one will ever guess the ingredients.

Makes 4 servings

2/3	cup lowfat cottage cheese
2	eggs, slightly beaten
1/2	teaspoon ground cinnamon
1	teaspoon *each* baking powder and vanilla extract
1/2	teaspoon lemon extract
2	tablespoons plus 2 teaspoons sugar (or sweetener equivalent to 8 teaspoons sugar)
1-1/2	ounces bran cereal flakes, slightly crushed

Lemon Sauce

1	cup water
1-1/2	tablespoons lemon juice
1	tablespoon plus 1 teaspoon cornstarch
2	drops yellow food color
2	tablespoons plus 2 teaspoons sugar (or sweetener equivalent to 8 teaspoons sugar)

Preheat oven to 350°. Combine all ingredients, *except* cereal, in a bowl. Mix well.

Stir in cereal. Place mixture in a 4 x 8-inch nonstick loaf pan. Smooth the top with the back of a spoon.

Bake 20 to 25 minutes, until set and lightly browned.

When cake is almost done, combine all sauce ingredients in a small saucepan. (If using NutraSweet as sweetener, add it after cooking.) Stir until cornstarch is dissolved. Cook, stirring, over medium heat, until mixture comes to a boil. Continue to cook and stir 1 minute. Remove from heat.

To serve, cut hot cake into squares, place in individual serving bowls, and spoon hot sauce over cake.

Each serving provides:

185 Calories*

1	Protein Serving	9	g	Protein
1/2	Bread Serving	3	g	Fat
10	Additional Calories (plus	30	g	Carbohydrate
	64 more calories if sugar is	395	mg	Sodium
	used as sweetener)	139	mg	Cholesterol

*If sugar is used as sweetener

Piña Colada Upside-Down Cake

This cake is incredibly moist and just bursting with flavor.

Makes 8 servings

Topping

2   cups canned crushed pineapple (unsweetened), drained
1/4   cup juice from pineapple
2/3   cup nonfat dry milk
2   tablespoons cornstarch
2   teaspoons shredded coconut (unsweetened)
1   teaspoon coconut extract
1   tablespoon sugar (or sweetener equivalent to 3 teaspoons sugar)

Cake

3/4   cup all-purpose flour
1   teaspoon baking powder
2   tablespoons plus 2 teaspoons reduced-calorie margarine
2   eggs
2/3   cup lowfat cottage cheese
2   teaspoons vanilla extract
3   tablespoons sugar (or sweetener equivalent to 9 teaspoons sugar)

Preheat oven to 350°.

Spray a 9-inch glass pie pan with a nonstick cooking spray. Line the pan with wax paper. Then spray again.

In a small bowl, combine all topping ingredients, mixing well. Spread evenly in pan.

In a medium bowl, combine flour and baking powder. Add margarine and mix with a fork or pastry blender until mixture resembles coarse crumbs.

Combine eggs, cottage cheese, vanilla, and sugar. Beat with a fork or wire whisk until blended. (Mixture will be lumpy.)

Add cottage cheese mixture to dry ingredients, stirring until all ingredients are moistened. Spoon batter evenly over topping in pan.

Bake 30 minutes, until golden.

Cool in pan on wire rack 15 minutes. Then loosen edges with knife and invert cake onto a plate. Peel off wax paper.

Each serving provides:

194 Calories*

1/2	Protein Serving	7	g	Protein
1/2	Bread Serving	4	g	Fat
1/2	Fat Serving	32	g	Carbohydrate
1/4	Milk Serving	220	mg	Sodium
10	Additional Calories	70	mg	Cholesterol
	(plus 24 more calories if			
	sugar is used as			
	sweetener)			

*If sugar is used as sweetener

Apple-Zucchini Coffee Cake

This is a perfect snack to have with a coffee break.

Makes 8 servings

1-1/2 cups all-purpose flour
1-1/2 teaspoons baking powder
1/2 teaspoon baking soda
1-1/2 teaspoons ground cinnamon
1/2 teaspoon ground nutmeg
1 egg
1 teaspoon vanilla extract
1/4 cup margarine, melted
1/4 cup plus 2 tablespoons sugar (or equivalent sweetener)
1 cup coarsely shredded zucchini, unpeeled
2 small, sweet apples, peeled and coarsely shredded
1/4 cup raisins

Preheat oven to 350°. In a large bowl, combine flour, baking powder, baking soda, and spices. In another bowl, combine egg, vanilla, margarine, and sugar. Beat with a fork until blended. Stir in zucchini, apples, and raisins.

Add zucchini mixture to dry ingredients, stirring until all ingredients are moistened.

Spread batter in an 8-inch round nonstick cake pan that has also been sprayed lightly with a nonstick cooking spray. Smooth the top of the cake with the back of a spoon.

Bake 35 minutes, until a toothpick inserted in the center of the cake comes out clean. Cool in pan on wire rack.

Each serving provides:

217 Calories*

1	Bread Serving	4	g	Protein
1/4	Vegetable Serving	7	g	Fat
1-1/2	Fat Servings	36	g	Carbohydrate
1/2	Fruit Serving	208	mg	Sodium
6	Additional Calories (plus	34	mg	Cholesterol
	32 more calories if sugar is			
	used as sweetener)			

*If sugar is used as sweetener

1-2-3 Brownies

We've greatly reduced the calories and fat in these quick and easy brownies.

Makes 8 servings

3/4	cup all-purpose flour
2	tablespoons cocoa (unsweetened)
1/2	teaspoon baking soda
2	tablespoons plus 2 teaspoons vegetable oil
1	teaspoon vanilla extract
1	teaspoon chocolate extract
1/2	teaspoon imitation butter flavor
1	tablespoon plain lowfat yogurt
1/4	cup plus 2 tablespoons cold water
1/4	cup plus 1 tablespoon sugar (or sweetener equivalent to 15 teaspoons sugar)

Preheat oven to 350°.

In a medium bowl, combine dry ingredients, mixing until blended. With a spoon, make a well in the center.

In a small bowl, combine remaining ingredients, mixing with a spoon. Pour into well in dry mixture. Stir until all ingredients are moistened.

Place batter in a 4 x 8-inch nonstick loaf pan or one that has been sprayed with a nonstick cooking spray.

Bake 15 minutes.

Cool in pan on wire rack.

Each serving provides:

122 Calories*

1/2	Bread Serving	2	g	Protein
1	Fat Serving	5	g	Fat
5	Additional Calories	18	g	Carbohydrate
	(plus 30 more calories if	53	mg	Sodium
	sugar is used as	0	mg	Cholesterol
	sweetener)			

*If sugar is used as sweetener

Honey Spice Cake

This old-fashioned tasting cake is so tender, moist, and spicy. For a special treat, try it warm, with vanilla ice milk or a dollop of whipped topping.

Makes 8 servings

3/4	cup whole wheat flour
1/2	teaspoon baking soda
1	teaspoon ground cinnamon
1/2	teaspoon ground nutmeg
1/4	teaspoon ground cloves
1/4	teaspoon ground allspice
2	tablespoons plus 2 teaspoons reduced-calorie margarine
1	egg
1	teaspoon vanilla extract
2	tablespoons honey
1/2	cup plain lowfat yogurt
2	tablespoons plus 2 teaspoons sugar (or sweetener equivalent to 8 teaspoons sugar)
1/4	cup raisins

Preheat oven to 350°.

In a medium bowl, combine flour, baking soda, and spices, mixing well.

Add margarine. Using a fork or pastry blender, mix until mixture resembles coarse crumbs.

In a large bowl, combine remaining ingredients, *except* raisins. Beat on low speed of an electric mixer until smooth.

Add dry ingredients. Beat 1 minute.

Stir in raisins.

Place batter in a 4 x 8-inch nonstick loaf pan or one that has been sprayed with a nonstick cooking spray.

Bake 25 minutes.

Cool in pan 10 minutes; then invert onto a rack to finish cooling.

Each serving provides:

122 Calories*

1/2	Bread Serving	3	g	Protein
1/2	Fat Serving	3	g	Fat
1/4	Fruit Serving	22	g	Carbohydrate
34	Additional Calories	111	mg	Sodium
	(plus 16 more calories if	35	mg	Cholesterol
	sugar is used as			
	sweetener)			

*If sugar is used as sweetener

Peanut Butter Banana Cake

Our favorite way to serve this great-textured cake is to cut it in half lengthwise and spread with a thin layer of reduced-calorie strawberry jam. Yum!

Makes 8 servings

1-1/2 cups all-purpose flour
1   teaspoon baking soda
1   teaspoon baking powder
1   egg plus 2 egg whites
1/4   cup plus 3 tablespoons peanut butter
3   tablespoons vegetable oil
1/4   cup plus 2 tablespoons sugar (or sweetener equivalent to 18 teaspoons sugar)
2   medium, ripe bananas, mashed
1   teaspoon vanilla extract

Preheat oven to 350°.

In a medium bowl, sift dry ingredients.

In a large bowl, combine remaining ingredients. Beat on medium speed of an electric mixer until blended.

Add dry ingredients to peanut butter mixture. Beat until all ingredients are moistened.

Place batter in a 9-inch round nonstick cake pan that has also been sprayed lightly with a nonstick cooking spray.

Bake 25 minutes, until a toothpick inserted in the center of the cake comes out clean.

Cool in pan 10 minutes; then invert onto a rack to finish cooling.

Each serving provides:

292 Calories*

1	Protein Serving	8	g	Protein
1	Bread Serving	13	g	Fat
2	Fat Servings	36	g	Carbohydrate
5	Additional Calories	244	mg	Sodium
	(plus 36 more calories if sugar is used as sweetener)	34	mg	Cholesterol

*If sugar is used as sweetener

Surprise Pudding Cake

You'll be astonished at the vegetable that gives this cake its special texture!

Makes 8 servings

1-1/2 cups all-purpose flour
1-1/2 teaspoons baking powder
2   teaspoons ground cinnamon
1/2   teaspoon ground nutmeg
1/8   teaspoon ground cloves
1   egg plus 1 egg white
1/4   cup vegetable oil
1/4   cup plus 2 tablespoons sugar (or equivalent sweetener)
1/3   cup nonfat dry milk
1/2   cup plain lowfat yogurt
1-1/2 teaspoons vanilla extract
1/2   teaspoon almond extract
1   teaspoon vanilla butternut flavor
2   cups eggplant, peeled, cut into 1/2-inch cubes
1/2   cup raisins

Preheat oven to 350°.

In a large bowl, combine flour, baking powder, and spices.

In a blender container, combine remaining ingredients, *except* raisins. Blend until smooth. Stir eggplant mixture and raisins into dry ingredients. Mix until moistened.

Place batter in a 6 x 10-inch baking pan that has been sprayed with a nonstick cooking spray.

Bake 25 to 30 minutes, until firm and golden. Cool on a rack.

Each serving provides:

253 Calories*

1	Bread Serving	6 g	Protein
1/2	Vegetable Serving	8 g	Fat
1-1/2	Fat Servings	39 g	Carbohydrate
1/2	Fruit Serving	123 mg	Sodium
1/4	Milk Serving	36 mg	Cholesterol
9	Additional Calories (plus 36 more calories if sugar is used as sweetener)		

*If sugar is used as sweetener

Tofu Chocolate Spice Brownies

How can a cake be so delicious and actually be good for you? If you have a sweet tooth, try this for breakfast instead of a doughnut.

Makes 8 servings

3/4	cup whole wheat flour
1	teaspoon baking powder
2	tablespoons plus 2 teaspoons cocoa (unsweetened)
1	teaspoon ground cinnamon
1/2	teaspoon ground nutmeg
1/8	teaspoon ground allspice
6	ounces tofu, sliced, drained well on paper towels
2	eggs
1/4	cup honey
2	tablespoons plus 2 teaspoons vegetable oil
2	teaspoons vanilla extract
1/2	cup skim milk

Preheat oven to 350° (325° for glass pan).

In a large bowl, combine dry ingredients. Mix well.

In a blender container, combine remaining ingredients. Blend until smooth.

Add tofu mixture to dry ingredients. Stir until mixture is well blended and all dry ingredients are moistened.

Spoon mixture into an 8-inch square baking pan that has been sprayed with a nonstick cooking spray.

Bake 20 minutes.

Cool in pan. Cut into squares to serve.

Each serving provides:

159 Calories

1/2	Protein Serving	5	g	Protein
1/2	Bread Serving	8	g	Fat
1	Fat Serving	19	g	Carbohydrate
28	Additional Calories	77	mg	Sodium
		69	mg	Cholesterol

Best Carrot Cake

The unbelievable taste and moistness make a hit whenever we serve this delicious cake. The surprise ingredient is tofu, and it makes the cake healthful as well as delicious.

Makes 8 servings

3/4	cup whole wheat flour
1	teaspoon *each* baking powder and ground cinnamon
1/2	teaspoon ground nutmeg
1/8	teaspoon *each* ground cloves and allspice
2	eggs
2	tablespoons plus 2 teaspoons vegetable oil
1/4	cup honey
1	teaspoon vanilla extract
6	ounces tofu, sliced, drained well between paper towels
2	tablespoons skim milk
1	cup finely shredded carrots
1/2	cup raisins

Preheat oven to 350°(325° for glass pan).

In a large bowl, combine flour, baking powder, and spices. Mix well.

In a blender container, combine eggs, oil, honey, vanilla, tofu, and milk. Blend until smooth. Stir in carrots and raisins.

Add tofu mixture to dry ingredients. Stir until moistened.

Spoon mixture into an 8-inch square baking pan that has been sprayed with a nonstick cooking spray.

Bake 25 to 30 minutes. Cool in pan.

Each serving provides:

184 Calories

1/2	Protein Serving	5	g	Protein
1/2	Bread Serving	7	g	Fat
1/4	Vegetable Serving	27	g	Carbohydrate
1	Fat Serving	81	mg	Sodium
1/2	Fruit Serving	69	mg	Cholesterol
32	Additional Calories			

Applesauce Wheat Bars

This moist, spicy dessert doubles as a very healthful snack, and makes a perfect lunch box treat.

Makes 10 servings

1	cup minus 1 tablespoon whole wheat flour
1	teaspoon baking soda
1	teaspoon ground cinnamon
1/4	teaspoon ground cloves
1/4	teaspoon ground allspice
1/2	teaspoon ground nutmeg
2	tablespoons skim milk
1	egg
1	cup applesauce (unsweetened)
3	tablespoons plus 1 teaspoon vegetable oil
2	teaspoons vanilla extract
3	tablespoons plus 1 teaspoon sugar (or sweetener equivalent to 10 teaspoons sugar)
1/4	cup plus 2 tablespoons raisins

Preheat oven to 350°.

Mix dry ingredients together in a large bowl.

In a blender container, combine remaining ingredients, *except* raisins. Blend until smooth.

Add applesauce mixture and raisins to dry ingredients. Mix until all ingredients are moistened.

Place batter in a 6 x 10-inch glass baking pan that has been sprayed with a nonstick cooking spray.

Bake 30 minutes, until a toothpick inserted in the center comes out clean.

Each serving provides:

134 Calories*

1/2	Bread Serving	2	g	Protein
1	Fat Serving	5	g	Fat
1/2	Fruit Serving	20	g	Carbohydrate
8	Additional Calories (plus	92	mg	Sodium
	16 more calories if sugar is	27	mg	Cholesterol
	used as sweetener)			

*If sugar is used as sweetener

Tender-Moist Bean Cake

This recipe makes one of the most wonderful pound cakes you'll ever sink your teeth into, and contains no flour–just high-protein soybeans instead.

Makes 4 servings

6	ounces cooked soybeans, drained (Canned may be used.)
2	eggs, separated
1/2	cup orange juice (unsweetened)
1/2	teaspoon orange *or* lemon extract
1	teaspoon vanilla butternut flavor
1/4	cup sugar
1/4	teaspoon cream of tartar
2/3	cup nonfat dry milk
1/2	teaspoon baking powder

Preheat oven to 350°.

In a blender container, combine soybeans, egg yolks, orange juice, extracts, and 3 tablespoons of the sugar. Blend into a paste. Place in a large bowl.

In a deep bowl, beat egg whites on low speed of an electric mixer until foamy. Add cream of tartar and beat on high speed until egg whites are stiff.

Slowly add dry milk to egg whites, continuing to beat. Beat in baking powder and remaining sugar.

Fold egg white mixture into soybean paste. Fold gently until both mixtures are combined.

Place in a 4 x 8-inch nonstick loaf pan or one that has been sprayed with a nonstick cooking spray.

Bake 25 to 30 minutes, until top is firm and golden.

Cool in pan on rack.

Note: Because of the interaction with beaten egg whites, artificial sweeteners do not work well in this cake.

Each serving provides:

223 Calories

1-1/4	Protein Servings	14	g	Protein
1/4	Fruit Serving	7	g	Fat
1/2	Milk Serving	27	g	Carbohydrate
48	Additional Calories	151	mg	Sodium
		139	mg	Cholesterol

Sweet Potato Cake

The wonderful blend of spices really adds zest to this unusual cake. If using canned sweet potatoes, be sure to avoid those packed in heavy syrup.

Makes 10 servings

1-1/2 cups all-purpose flour
1   teaspoon *each* baking powder and baking soda
1   teaspoon ground cinnamon
1/4   teaspoon ground ginger
1/8   teaspoon *each* ground cloves and nutmeg
1/2   cup plus 2 tablespoons reduced-calorie margarine
6   ounces cooked sweet potatoes, mashed
1   teaspoon vanilla extract
1/2   teaspoon orange extract
1   egg plus 2 egg whites
1/4   cup sugar (or sweetener equivalent to 12 teaspoons sugar)
1/4   cup skim milk

Into a large bowl, sift flour, baking powder, baking soda, and spices. Add margarine and mix with a fork or pastry blender until mixture resembles coarse crumbs.

Combine remaining ingredients in a large bowl. Beat on low speed of an electric mixer until well blended.

Add dry ingredients to potato mixture, beating until all ingredients are moistened. Beat on high speed 1 minute.

Place mixture in a 6 x 10-inch glass baking pan that has been sprayed with a nonstick cooking spray.

Bake 30 minutes, until a toothpick inserted in the center of the cake comes out clean.

Cool in pan on wire rack.

Each serving provides:

173 Calories*

1	Bread Serving	4	g	Protein
1-1/2	Fat Servings	7	g	Fat
12	Additional Calories (plus	24	g	Carbohydrate
	19 more calories if sugar is	268	mg	Sodium
	used as sweetener)	28	mg	Cholesterol

*If sugar is used as sweetener

Apple Creme Pie

We've blended cottage cheese and apples with cinnamon and nutmeg, and the result is spectacular!

Makes 6 servings

Crust
4-1/2 ounces Grape-Nuts® cereal, crushed
3 tablespoons margarine, melted
1/4 teaspoon ground cinnamon
Filling
3 small, sweet apples, peeled and sliced very thin
1/3 cup water
1/2 teaspoon *each* ground cinnamon and nutmeg
1/3 cup nonfat dry milk
3 eggs
1 cup lowfat cottage cheese
2 teaspoons vanilla extract
1/4 cup sugar (or sweetener equivalent to 12 teaspoons sugar)

Preheat oven to 350°.

In a 9-inch pie pan, combine crust ingredients. Mix until crumbs are moistened. Press crumbs onto bottom and sides of pan.

Bake 8 minutes. While crust is baking, place apples and water in a large nonstick skillet. Sprinkle with cinnamon and nutmeg. Simmer apples over medium heat until slightly tender, about 10 minutes. Drain, reserving liquid. Spread apples evenly over crust.

In a blender container, combine reserved apple liquid with remaining filling ingredients. Blend until smooth. Pour over apples.

Bake 25 minutes, until filling is set. Chill.

Each serving provides:

274 Calories*

1	Protein Serving	12 g	Protein
1	Bread Serving	9 g	Fat
1-1/2	Fat Servings	37 g	Carbohydrate
1/2	Fruit Serving	423 mg	Sodium
17	Additional Calories (plus	139 mg	Cholesterol
	32 more calories if sugar is		
	used as sweetener)		

*If sugar is used as sweetener

Most Versatile Coffee Cake

The variations of this moist, delectable cake are unlimited. In place of the peaches, try chopped apples, blueberries, cherries, or any combination of fruits. Add an extract that you like, such as almond extract if you use cherries or orange extract with blueberries. Or, leave off the fruit and just top the cake with sugar and cinnamon. The Piña Colada Upside-Down Cake on page 378 is yet another variation of this wonderful dessert.

Makes 8 servings

3/4   cup all-purpose flour
1   teaspoon baking powder
2   tablespoons plus 2 teaspoons reduced-calorie margarine
2   eggs
2/3   cup lowfat cottage cheese
2   teaspoons vanilla extract
3   tablespoons plus 1 teaspoon sugar (or sweetener equivalent
         to 10 teaspoons sugar)
4   medium, ripe peaches, peeled and sliced

Topping
2-1/2 teaspoons sugar (or equivalent amount of sweetener)
1/2   teaspoon ground cinnamon

Preheat oven to 375°.

In a medium bowl, combine flour and baking powder. Add margarine and mix with a fork or pastry blender until mixture resembles coarse crumbs.

Combine eggs, cottage cheese, vanilla, and sugar. Beat with a fork or wire whisk until blended. (Mixture will be lumpy.)

Add cottage cheese mixture to dry ingredients, stirring until all ingredients are moistened. Spoon batter into a 10-inch glass pie pan that has been sprayed with a nonstick cooking spray.

Arrange peach slices evenly over batter. Press them down slightly into the batter.

Combine topping ingredients and sprinkle evenly over peaches. (If peaches are very sweet, use less sugar.)

Bake 25 minutes.

Cool in pan on wire rack. Enjoy warm or cold.

Each serving provides:

150 Calories*

1/2	Protein Serving	6	g	Protein
1/2	Bread Serving	4	g	Fat
1/2	Fat Serving	24	g	Carbohydrate
1/2	Fruit Serving	188	mg	Sodium
25	Additional Calories (if	69	mg	Cholesterol
	sugar is used as			
	sweetener)			

*If sugar is used as sweetener

Blueberry Cheese Pie

Who said delicious had to be fattening? Unlike most cheesecakes, which call for cream cheese, ours uses part-skim ricotta cheese instead. To lower the cholesterol, use an egg substitute in place of the eggs. Enjoy!

Makes 8 servings

Crust

3   ounces graham cracker crumbs (twelve 2-1/2-inch graham cracker squares, crushed)

3   tablespoons margarine, melted

Filling

1-1/2 cups fresh or frozen blueberries (unsweetened) (If using frozen berries, thaw and drain well.)

2-1/4 cups part-skim ricotta cheese

3   eggs

1   tablespoon all-purpose flour

2   teaspoons vanilla extract

1/4 teaspoon lemon *or* orange extract

1/4 cup plus 1 tablespoon sugar (or sweetener equivalent to 15 teaspoons sugar)

Topping

1-1/2 cups fresh or frozen blueberries (unsweetened)

1   tablespoon cornstarch

1/2 cup water

2   tablespoons sugar (or sweetener equivalent to 6 teaspoons sugar)

Preheat oven to 350°.

Combine crust ingredients in a 9-inch pie pan. Mix well, until crumbs are moistened. Press crumbs onto bottom and sides of pan to form a crust. Bake 8 minutes.

Arrange 1-1/2 cups of blueberries evenly in crust.

In a blender container, combine remaining filling ingredients. Blend until smooth. Pour over berries.

Bake 30 to 35 minutes, until filling is set.

While pie cools slightly, prepare topping:

Place blueberries in a medium saucepan. Dissolve cornstarch in water and add to berries. Add sugar. (If using NutraSweet as sweetener in topping, add it after cooking.)

Cook over medium heat, stirring, until mixture boils. Boil 1 minute, stirring. Cool slightly; then spread over pie.

Chill.

Each serving provides:

292 Calories*

1-1/2	Protein Servings	11	g	Protein
3/4	Bread Serving	13	g	Fat
1	Fat Serving	33	g	Carbohydrate
3/4	Fruit Serving	233	mg	Sodium
14	Additional Calories			
	(plus 42 more calories if	124	mg	Cholesterol
	sugar is used as			
	sweetener)			

*If sugar is used as sweetener

Maple Buttercream Cheese Pie

This luscious pie was created to please a cheesecake-lover in our family. It's almost too good to be true. To lower the cholesterol, use an egg substitute in place of the eggs.

Makes 8 servings

Crust
3   ounces graham cracker crumbs (twelve 2-1/2-inch graham crackers, crushed
3   tablespoons margarine, melted

Filling
2   cups part-skim ricotta cheese
4   eggs
1   tablespoon all-purpose flour
2   teaspoons vanilla butternut flavor
1/2 teaspoon maple extract
1/4 cup plus 1 tablespoon sugar (or sweetener equivalent to 15 teaspoons sugar)

Topping
2   cups canned crushed pineapple (unsweetened), *un*drained
1/2 teaspoon vanilla butternut flavor
1   tablespoon cornstarch
2   tablespoons water
1   tablespoon sugar (or sweetener equivalent to 3 teaspoons sugar)

Preheat oven to 350°.

Combine crust ingredients in a 9-inch pie pan. Mix well, until crumbs are moistened. Press crumbs onto bottom and sides of pan, forming a crust. Bake 8 minutes.

Increase oven temperature to 375°.

In a blender container, combine all filling ingredients. Blend until smooth. Pour into crust.

Bake 25 to 30 minutes, until filling is set.

While pie cools prepare topping:

Combine all topping ingredients in a small saucepan. (If using NutraSweet in the topping, add it after cooking.) Cook over medium heat, stirring, until mixture boils. Boil 1 minute, stirring.

Spread topping over pie.

Chill.

Each serving provides:

293 Calories*

1-1/2	Protein Servings	11	g	Protein
3/4	Bread Serving	13	g	Fat
1	Fat Serving	33	g	Carbohydrate
13	Additional Calories	230	mg	Sodium
	(plus 36 more calories if	156	mg	Cholesterol
	sugar is used as			
	sweetener)			

*If sugar is used as sweetener

Mock Coconut Custard Pie

Eat this pie with your eyes closed and you'll think it's coconut! We've replaced the coconut, which is very high in saturated fat, with–of all things–carrots! To further lower the cholesterol, use an egg substitute in place of the eggs.

Makes 8 servings

2	cups skim milk
4	eggs
2	tablespoons plus 2 teaspoons reduced-calorie margarine
1/2	teaspoon vanilla butternut flavor
1	teaspoon coconut extract
1	teaspoon vanilla extract
1/4	cup plus 2 tablespoons all-purpose flour
2	teaspoons baking powder
1/4	cup plus 1 tablespoon sugar (or sweetener equivalent to 15 teaspoons sugar)
1	cup finely shredded carrots
	Ground nutmeg

Preheat oven to 350°.

In a blender container, combine all ingredients, *except* carrots and nutmeg. Blend 1 minute. Stir in carrots.

Pour mixture into a 9-inch glass pie pan that has been sprayed with a nonstick cooking spray. Sprinkle lightly with nutmeg. Let stand 5 minutes.

Bake 40 minutes, until set. Cool slightly; then chill.

Each serving provides:

139 Calories*

1/2	Protein Serving	6	g	Protein
1/4	Bread Serving	5	g	Fat
1/4	Vegetable Serving	18	g	Carbohydrate
1/2	Fat Serving	218	mg	Sodium
1/4	Milk Serving	138	mg	Cholesterol
30	Additional Calories (if sugar is used as sweetener)			

*If sugar is used as sweetener

Miracle Lemon Tofu Pie

There's enough protein in this pie to make it a nutritious breakfast or lunch, as well as a refreshing dessert. Imagine having a salad and a slice of pie for lunch, with no guilt!

Makes 8 servings

9	ounces tofu, sliced, drained well between paper towels
1/2	cup part-skim ricotta cheese
3	eggs
1	cup evaporated skim milk
1/4	cup plus 2 tablespoons all-purpose flour
2	teaspoons baking powder
1-1/2	teaspoons lemon extract
1	teaspoon vanilla extract
1/2	teaspoon vanilla butternut flavor
1/2	teaspoon ground cinnamon
1/4	cup plus 1 tablespoon sugar (or sweetener equivalent to 15 teaspoons sugar)

Preheat oven to 350°.

In a blender container, combine all ingredients. Blend 2 minutes.

Pour mixture into a 10-inch pie pan that has been sprayed with a nonstick cooking spray. Let stand 5 minutes.

Bake 30 minutes, until set.

Cool slightly; then chill.

Each serving provides:

160 Calories*

1	Protein Serving	10	g	Protein
1/4	Bread Serving	5	g	Fat
1/4	Milk Serving	18	g	Carbohydrate
30	Additional Calories (if	191	mg	Sodium
	sugar is used as	109	mg	Cholesterol
	sweetener)			

*If sugar is used as sweetener

Tofu Almond Creme Pie

This creamy, delectable pie has as many variations as there are flavors of extracts. In place of almond try coconut, lemon, orange, banana . . .

Makes 8 servings

Crust

12   2-1/2 inch graham cracker squares, crushed (3 ounces graham cracker crumbs)

3   tablespoons margarine, melted

Filling

9   ounces tofu, sliced, drained well between paper towels

1/2   cup part-skim ricotta cheese

3   eggs

1   cup evaporated skim milk

2   tablespoons all-purpose flour

1-1/2 teaspoons almond extract

1   teaspoon vanilla extract

1/4   cup plus 1 tablespoon sugar (or sweetener equivalent to 15 teaspoons sugar)

Preheat oven to 350°. Combine crust ingredients in a 9-inch pie pan. Mix well, until crumbs are moistened. Press crumbs onto bottom and sides of pan to form a crust.

Bake 8 minutes. Cool slightly.

In a blender container, combine all filling ingredients. Blend until smooth. Pour into cooled crust.

Bake 25 minutes, until set. Chill.

Each serving provides:

225 Calories*

1	Protein Serving	10	g	Protein
3/4	Bread Serving	10	g	Fat
1	Fat Serving	23	g	Carbohydrate
1/4	Milk Serving	202	mg	Sodium
13	Additional Calories			
	(plus 30 more calories if	109	mg	Cholesterol
	sugar is used as			
	sweetener)			

*If sugar is used as sweetener

"Beanana" Creme Pie

Yes, that's spelled correctly. We've combined soybeans and bananas for a nutritious, yet incredibly tasty, pie.

Makes 8 servings

Crust
4-1/2 ounces Grape-Nuts® cereal, crushed
3 tablespoons margarine, melted

Filling
10 ounces cooked soybeans, drained
2 medium, ripe bananas
1 egg plus 2 egg whites
1/4 cup plus 2 tablespoons all-purpose flour
1 teaspoon baking powder
2/3 cup nonfat dry milk
1/2 teaspoon ground cinnamon
2 teaspoons vanilla butternut flavor
1/2 teaspoon maple extract
1/4 teaspoon banana extract
1/4 cup plus 2 tablespoons water
1/4 cup plus 1 tablespoon sugar (or equivalent sweetener)

Preheat oven to 350°. In a 9-inch pie pan, combine crust ingredients. Mix until crumbs are moistened. Press crumbs onto bottom and sides of pan to form a crust.

Bake 8 minutes.

In a blender container, combine all filling ingredients. Blend until smooth. Pour into crust.

Bake 30 minutes, until set. Cool slightly; then chill.

Each serving provides:

273 Calories*

3/4	Protein Serving	12	g	Protein
1	Bread Serving	8	g	Fat
1	Fat Serving	39	g	Carbohydrate
1/2	Fruit Serving	268	mg	Sodium
1/4	Milk Serving	35	mg	Cholesterol
11	Additional Calories (plus 30 more calories if sugar is used as sweetener)			

*If sugar is used as sweetener

Pumpkin Pie

We've taken the traditional holiday pie, added a nutritious whole wheat crust, removed the egg yolks and half of the sugar, and it still tastes great!

Makes 8 servings

Crust

1/2	cup whole wheat flour
1/2	cup all-purpose flour
1/2	teaspoon baking powder
2	tablespoons plus 2 teaspoons margarine
1	tablespoon plus 1 teaspoon vegetable oil
1/4	cup ice water

Filling

1	1-pound can pumpkin
4	egg whites
1	teaspoon vanilla extract
1/4	cup plus 2 tablespoons sugar (or sweetener equivalent to 18 teaspoons sugar)
1	teaspoon ground cinnamon
1/2	teaspoon ground ginger
1/4	teaspoon ground cloves
1-1/2	cups evaporated skim milk

Preheat oven to 425°.

In a medium bowl, combine both flours and baking powder. Add margarine and mix with a fork or pastry blender until mixture resembles coarse crumbs.

With a fork, stir in oil, and then water.

Work the dough into a ball, using your hands. Roll dough between 2 sheets of wax paper into an 11-inch circle. Fit dough into a 9-inch pie pan, leaving a 1-inch overhang. Bend edges under and flute with a fork. Prick the bottom and sides of crust about 25 times with a fork.

In a large bowl, combine all filling ingredients, *except* milk. Mix well. Gradually add milk, stirring until mixture is well blended. Pour into pie crust.

Bake 15 minutes.

Reduce oven temperature to 350°.

Bake 45 minutes, until set.

Each serving provides:

212 Calories*

1/2	Bread Serving	8	g	Protein
1/2	Vegetable Serving	7	g	Fat
1-1/2	Fat Servings	31	g	Carbohydrate
1/3	Milk Serving	155	mg	Sodium
25	Additional Calories	2	mg	Cholesterol

(plus 36 more calories if sugar is used as sweetener)

*If sugar is used as sweetener

Mystery Custard Pie

The mystery ingredient is a very nutritious vegetable, and it helps to make this pie a healthful, moist, and delicious treat.

Makes 8 servings

Crust
3   ounces graham cracker crumbs (twelve 2-1/2-inch graham crackers, crushed)
3   tablespoons margarine, melted
Filling
3   cups zucchini, unpeeled, cut into 1/4-inch pieces
3   eggs
1   tablespoon all-purpose flour
1-1/3 cups nonfat dry milk
1   teaspoon ground cinnamon
1/2   teaspoon ground ginger
1/4   teaspoon ground cloves
1   teaspoon vanilla extract
1/4   cup plus 2 tablespoons sugar (or equivalent sweetener)
       A few drops *each* of yellow and red food color

Preheat oven to 350°.

Combine crust ingredients in a 9-inch pie pan. Mix well, until crumbs are moistened. Press crumbs onto bottom and sides of pan to form a crust. Bake 8 minutes.

In a blender container, combine all filling ingredients. Blend until smooth. Pour into crust.

Bake 30 minutes, until set. Cool slightly; then chill.

Each serving provides:

203 Calories*

3/4	Protein Serving	8 g	Protein
3/4	Bread Serving	7 g	Fat
3/4	Vegetable Serving	26 g	Carbohydrate
1	Fat Serving	207 mg	Sodium
1/2	Milk Serving	105 mg	Cholesterol
10	Additional Calories (plus 36 more calories if sugar is used as sweetener)		

*If sugar is used as sweetener

Mozzarella Bread Pudding

So unusual, this delicate bread pudding is a perfect brunch dessert. It's best served warm while the cheese is still soft.

Makes 2 servings

2   slices whole wheat bread, crumbled
1   small, sweet apple, peeled and diced
2   tablespoons raisins
2   ounces part-skim Mozzarella cheese, shredded
1/3   cup nonfat dry milk
1/2   teaspoon ground cinnamon
2   tablespoons firmly-packed brown sugar (or sweetener
          equivalent to 6 teaspoons brown sugar)
1/2   cup water
1   teaspoon vanilla extract
1   egg white
1/8   teaspoon cream of tartar

Preheat oven to 350°. In a medium bowl, combine bread, apple, raisins, and cheese. Toss to mix.

In a small bowl, combine dry milk, cinnamon, and brown sugar. Stir in water and vanilla, stirring until brown sugar is dissolved. In a small, deep bowl, beat egg white on low speed of an electric mixer until frothy. Add cream of tartar and beat until egg white is stiff.

Fold milk mixture into egg white until smooth. Pour over apples. Mix gently until combined.

Place in a 4 x 8-inch baking pan that has been sprayed with a nonstick cooking spray.

Bake 20 minutes. Serve warm.

Each serving provides:

292 Calories*

1	Protein Serving	15	g	Protein
1	Bread Serving	5	g	Fat
1	Fruit Serving	47	g	Carbohydrate
1/2	Milk Serving	345	mg	Sodium
10	Additional Calories	19	mg	Cholesterol
	(plus 48 more calories if			
	brown sugar is used as			
	sweetener)			

*If brown sugar is used as sweetener

Orange Dreamsicle Dessert

This one's a dream! It's an absolute must *for your next party.*

Makes 12 servings

Crust
4-1/2 ounces graham cracker crumbs (eighteen 2-1/2-inch
      graham crackers, crushed)
1/4   cup margarine, melted
1/2   teaspoon ground cinnamon
1/2   teaspoon freshly grated orange peel

Filling
2-1/4 cups part-skim ricotta cheese
3   eggs
1   tablespoon all-purpose flour
2   teaspoons vanilla extract
1/4   cup sugar (or sweetener equivalent to 12 teaspoons sugar)

Topping
3   tablespoons cornstarch
2   cups orange juice (unsweetened)
1   tablespoon lemon juice
1/2   teaspoon orange extract
1/4   cup sugar (or sweetener equivalent to 12 teaspoons sugar)
4   cups fresh orange sections, white membrane removed
      (Navel oranges make the best choice.)

Preheat oven to 350°.

Combine crust ingredients in a 9 x 13-inch baking pan. Press gently onto the bottom of pan to form a crust.

Bake 8 minutes.

In a blender container, combine all filling ingredients. Blend until smooth. Pour over crust.

Bake 18 to 20 minutes, until set. Cool completely.

In a saucepan, dissolve cornstarch in orange juice. Add lemon juice, orange extract, and sugar. (If using NutraSweet as sweetener, add it after cooking.) Bring mixture to a boil over medium heat, stirring constantly. Boil 1 minute, stirring. Remove from heat.

Allow to cool 5 minutes, then gently stir in orange sections. Spread mixture evenly over cooled cheese filling.

Chill. Cut into squares to serve.

Each serving provides:

255 Calories*

1	Protein Serving	9	g	Protein
3/4	Bread Serving	10	g	Fat
1	Fat Serving	33	g	Carbohydrate
1	Fruit Serving	188	mg	Sodium
8	Additional Calories	83	mg	Cholesterol

(plus 32 more calories if sugar is used as sweetener)

*If sugar is used as sweetener

Fruited No-Bake Bread Pudding

Unlike most bread puddings, this marvelous combination of bread and fruits contains no eggs. It can be made ahead and doubles as a great breakfast.

Makes 8 servings

4	slices whole wheat bread, cubed
1/2	cup orange juice (unsweetened)
1/4	teaspoon ground cinnamon
1	medium, ripe banana, sliced
1	small orange, peeled and sectioned
1	envelope unflavored gelatin
3/4	cup water
2/3	cup nonfat dry milk
1-1/3	cups lowfat cottage cheese
1	tablespoon vanilla extract
3	tablespoons sugar (or sweetener equivalent to 9 teaspoons)
10	small ice cubes (about 1 cup)

Place bread cubes in a large bowl. Pour orange juice over bread, sprinkle with cinnamon. Add banana and orange and toss.

In a small saucepan, sprinkle gelatin over water. Heat over low heat, stirring frequently, until gelatin is completely dissolved.

In a blender container, combine gelatin mixture with remaining ingredients. Blend until ice cubes are completely dissolved.

Pour mixture over bread. Mix well.

Place mixture in an 8-inch square casserole. Press bread and fruit down gently into liquid. Chill until firm.

Each serving provides:

129 Calories*

1/2	Protein Serving	9	g	Protein
1/2	Bread Serving	1	g	Fat
1/2	Fruit Serving	22	g	Carbohydrate
1/4	Milk Serving	246	mg	Sodium
18	Additional Calories (if sugar is used as sweetener)	3	mg	Cholesterol

*If sugar is used as sweetener

Lemon Dream Parfaits

These lemony parfaits are truly a dreamy dessert. To dress them up for a
party, add a dollop of whipped topping and a few slivered almonds.

Makes 4 servings

1   cup orange juice (unsweetened)
1   envelope lemon-flavored gelatin (sugar-free)
1   cup part-skim ricotta cheese
1   cup evaporated skim milk
1-1/2 teaspoons vanilla extract

In a small saucepan, bring orange juice to a boil over medium
heat. Remove from heat and stir in gelatin. Stir until gelatin is completely dissolved.

In a blender container, combine gelatin mixture with remaining
ingredients. Blend until smooth.

Pour mixture into 4 parfait glasses.

Chill.

Each serving provides:

176 Calories

1	Protein Serving	13	g	Protein
1/2	Fruit Serving	5	g	Fat
1/2	Milk Serving	18	g	Carbohydrate
8	Additional Calories	211	mg	Sodium
		22	mg	Cholesterol

Indian Carrot Pudding

Don't let the seemingly long cooking time deter you. This healthful dessert is unsurpassed in flavor and well worth the effort! After all, what could be more nutritious than a dessert made out of vegetables?

Makes 4 servings

2   cups grated or finely shredded carrots
2   cups evaporated skim milk
1   ounce graham cracker crumbs (four 2-1/2-inch graham
          crackers, crushed)
2   tablespoons plus 2 teaspoons reduced-calorie margarine
1/8   teaspoon ground nutmeg
1/8   teaspoon ground cinnamon
1   teaspoon vanilla extract
1/16   teaspoon saffron, crushed
2   tablespoons firmly-packed brown sugar (or sweetener
          equivalent to 6 teaspoons brown sugar)

In a medium saucepan, combine carrots and milk. Bring to a boil over medium heat, stirring constantly. Cook, stirring, until most of milk is absorbed, about 20 minutes.

Add remaining ingredients. Cook, stirring, 5 minutes.

Serve warm.

Each serving provides:

216 Calories*

1/2	Bread Serving	11 g	Protein
1	Fat Serving	5 g	Fat
1	Milk Serving	33 g	Carbohydrate
1	Vegetable Serving	293 mg	Sodium
24	Additional Calories (if brown sugar is used as sweetener)	5 mg	Cholesterol

*If brown sugar is used as sweetener

Quick Rum Raisin Pudding

This quick dessert is very easy and very rich. For a special treat, serve it in a champagne glass, drizzled with our hot Lemon Sauce on page 377.

Makes 2 servings

1	cup part-skim ricotta cheese
1-1/2	teaspoons vanilla extract
1/2	teaspoon rum extract
2	tablespoons sugar (or sweetener equivalent to 6 teaspoons sugar)
2	tablespoons raisins
1/4	ounce chopped walnuts

In a small bowl, combine all ingredients.
Chill.

Each serving provides:

283 Calories*

2	Protein Servings	15	g	Protein
1/2	Fruit Serving	12	g	Fat
23	Additional Calories	28	g	Carbohydrate
	(plus 48 more calories if	155	mg	Sodium
	sugar is used as	38	mg	Cholesterol
	sweetener)			

*If sugar is used as sweetener

Pumpkin Custard Cups

This moist, cheesecake-like dessert was so popular at Thanksgiving, they now ask for it all year round. Our favorite way to serve it is in a tall sherbet glass, garnished with a few orange slices and a sprig of mint. If you double the recipe it will fill a 9-inch pie crust.

Makes 4 servings

1   package orange-flavored gelatin (sugar-free)
3/4   cup boiling water
1/2   cup part-skim ricotta cheese
1   cup canned pumpkin
1   teaspoon vanilla extract
1/2   teaspoon ground cinnamon

In a small saucepan, dissolve gelatin in boiling water.

In a blender container, combine gelatin mixture with remaining ingredients. Blend until smooth.

Divide mixture evenly into 4 individual serving bowls or sherbet glasses.

Chill until firm.

Each serving provides:

76 Calories

1/2	Protein Serving	5 g	Protein
1/2	Vegetable Serving	3 g	Fat
8	Additional Calories	7 g	Carbohydrate
		102 mg	Sodium
		10 mg	Cholesterol

Magic Strudel Bars

These delightful bars, made from a familiar breakfast cereal, make a wonderful dessert or a great snack for any time of day. When you're in a hurry, add a glass of skim milk and you have a "quickie" breakfast.

Makes 6 servings

1/2	cup water
1/2	cup canned crushed pineapple (unsweetened), drained
2	tablespoons juice from pineapple
1-1/2	envelopes unflavored gelatin
2	tablespoons sugar (or sweetener equivalent to 6 teaspoons sugar)
1/4	teaspoon orange extract
1/4	teaspoon coconut extract
1/4	teaspoon ground cinnamon
1/2	cup plus 2 tablespoons raisins
1	tablespoon shredded coconut (unsweetened)
4-1/2	ounces Grape-Nuts® cereal

In a medium saucepan, combine water and pineapple juice. Sprinkle with gelatin and let stand a few minutes. Heat over low heat, stirring frequently, until gelatin is completely dissolved.

Add sugar. Stir until dissolved.

Add remaining ingredients, *except* cereal. Mix well.

Stir in cereal. Mix until cereal is moistened.

Place mixture in a 6 x 11-inch baking pan that has been sprayed with a nonstick cooking spray. Press firmly in pan.

Chill.

Cut into squares to serve.

Each serving provides:

165 Calories*

1	Bread Serving	5	g	Protein
1	Fruit Serving	1	g	Fat
5	Additional Calories	38	g	Carbohydrate
	(plus 16 more calories if	152	mg	Sodium
	sugar is used as	0	mg	Cholesterol
	sweetener)			

*If sugar is used as sweetener

Banana Oat Breakfast Bars

Imagine having your cereal, milk, and banana all rolled into one moist and tasty bar. You'll want to make extras and freeze them for when you have to have breakfast "on the run."

Makes 4 servings

3	ounces quick-cooking oats, uncooked
2/3	cup nonfat dry milk
1/2	teaspoon ground cinnamon
1/2	teaspoon baking soda
1/2	teaspoon baking powder
2	medium, ripe bananas, mashed
1	teaspoon vanilla extract
1/2	teaspoon vanilla butternut flavor
1/4	teaspoon banana extract
2	tablespoons plus 2 teaspoons sugar (or sweetener equivalent to 8 teaspoons sugar)

Preheat oven to 350°.

In a medium bowl, combine dry ingredients.

In another bowl, combine remaining ingredients. Add to dry mixture, mixing until all ingredients are moistened.

Spread mixture in an 8-inch square baking pan that has been sprayed with a nonstick cooking spray.

Bake 20 minutes, until lightly browned.

Cool in pan on wire rack.

Cut into squares to serve.

Each serving provides:

214 Calories*

1	Bread Serving	8	g	Protein
1	Fruit Serving	2	g	Fat
1/2	Milk Serving	43	g	Carbohydrate
32	Additional Calories (if sugar is used as sweetener)	219	mg	Sodium
		2	mg	Cholesterol

*If sugar is used as sweetener

Cinnamon Whirls

These attractive pinwheels are definitely party fare!

Makes 6 servings

1   cup plus 2 tablespoons all-purpose flour
1-1/2 teaspoons baking powder
1/4   teaspoon baking soda
2   tablespoons margarine
2   tablespoons sugar (or sweetener equivalent to 6 teaspoons)
1-1/2 teaspoons vanilla extract
1/4   cup plus 1 tablespoon plain lowfat yogurt

Topping
1   tablespoon sugar (Sweeteners do not work well here.)
3/4   teaspoon ground cinnamon

Preheat oven to 425°. In a large bowl, combine flour, baking powder, and baking soda. Add margarine. Mix with a fork or pastry blender until mixture resembles coarse crumbs.

Stir the 2 tablespoons of sugar and the vanilla into yogurt. Add to flour mixture, stirring until most of the flour is moistened. Knead dough with hands until mixture holds together.

Roll dough between 2 sheets of wax paper into a rectangle 1/4-inch thick. Combine remaining sugar and cinnamon and sprinkle evenly over dough.

Starting with one long side, roll dough tightly into a log. With a sharp knife, cut into 18 even slices.

Place slices on a nonstick baking sheet or one that has been sprayed with a nonstick cooking spray.

Bake 10 minutes, until lightly browned.

Remove from pan and cool on rack. Serve warm for best flavor.

Each serving provides:

156 Calories*

1	Bread Serving	3	g	Protein
1	Fat Serving	4	g	Fat
18	Additional Calories (plus	26	g	Carbohydrate
	16 more calories if sugar is	194	mg	Sodium
	used as sweetener)	1	mg	Cholesterol

*If sugar is used as sweetener

Mandarin Chocolate Slices

We've combined the tastes of chocolate and orange in a tender, low-fat pastry.

Makes 6 servings
(2 slices each serving)

1	cup plus 2 tablespoons all-purpose flour
1/2	teaspoon baking powder
1/4	teaspoon baking soda
3	tablespoons sugar (or sweetener equivalent to 9 teaspoons)
2	tablespoons margarine, melted
1	egg, slightly beaten
1/2	teaspoon *each* vanilla extract and imitation butter flavor
1	tablespoon plus 1 teaspoon water
3	tablespoons reduced-calorie orange marmalade
2	teaspoons cocoa (unsweetened)

Preheat oven to 400°. In a large bowl, combine flour, baking powder, and baking soda. Mix well.

In a small bowl, combine sugar, margarine, egg, extracts, and water. Beat with a fork or wire whisk until dough holds together. With your hands, work the dough into a ball.

Place dough between 2 sheets of wax paper and roll into a rectangle about 6 inches by 12 inches.

Combine marmalade and cocoa and spread over dough, keeping it 1 inch away from edges of dough.

Starting with one long side, roll dough into a log, lifting the wax paper as you roll. Pinch sides and edges closed.

Place seam-side down on a nonstick baking sheet.

Bake 15 minutes, until lightly browned.

Remove to a rack to cool. Slice into 12 even slices.

Each serving provides:

172 Calories*

1	Bread Serving	4	g	Protein
1	Fat Serving	5	g	Fat
22	Additional Calories (plus	28	g	Carbohydrate
	24 more calories if sugar is	126	mg	Sodium
	used as sweetener)	46	mg	Cholesterol

*If sugar is used as sweetener

Cheese Pastries

These rich pastries are reminiscent of those made with sour cream, but we've really lowered the fat.

Makes 4 servings
(2 pastries each serving)

3/4   cup all-purpose flour
1/3   cup lowfat cottage cheese
2   tablespoons plus 2 teaspoons reduced-calorie margarine
1   tablespoon plus 1 teaspoon sugar (Sweeteners do not work
        well here.)
1/2   teaspoon ground cinnamon

Preheat oven to 375°.

In a medium bowl, combine flour, cottage cheese, and margarine. Mix well with a fork until dough holds together.

Divide dough evenly and roll into 2 balls.

One at a time, place each ball of dough between 2 sheets of wax paper. With a rolling pin, flatten each ball into a circle about 1/8-inch thick.

In a small bowl, combine sugar and cinnamon. Sprinkle 1-1/2 teaspoons of this mixture evenly over each circle of dough.

Cut each circle into 4 pie-shaped wedges. Starting with the wide end, roll up each wedge. Sprinkle with remaining sugar and cinnamon.

Place pastries on a nonstick baking sheet or one that has been sprayed with a nonstick cooking spray.

Bake 15 to 18 minutes, until lightly browned.

Remove to a rack to cool.

Each serving provides:

149 Calories

1/4	Protein Serving	5	g	Protein
1	Bread Serving	4	g	Fat
1	Fat Serving	23	g	Carbohydrate
16	Additional Calories	156	mg	Sodium
		1	mg	Cholesterol

Almost Apple Strudel

When you're in the mood for something sweet, these quick "mock" strudels can be put together in no time.

Makes 2 servings

2   slices thin-sliced whole wheat bread
2   teaspoons reduced-calorie margarine

Filling
1/4   cup applesauce (unsweetened)
2   teaspoons reduced-calorie orange ma 'malade
1/4   teaspoon *each* coconut extract and grc und cinnamon
1/4   teaspoon ground cinnamon
1   teaspoon sugar (or equivalent amoun! of sweetener)

Topping
1/4   teaspoon ground cinnamon
1   teaspoon sugar (Sweeteners do not work well here.)

Preheat oven to 350°.

Place bread between 2 sheets of wax paper and flatten with a rolling pin. Spread 1 side of each slice with margarine. Place margarine-side down on a sheet of wax paper.

In a small bowl, combine all filling ingredients. Divide evenly onto the bread. Spread filling, staying 1 inch away from the edges.

Gently roll each piece of bread like a small jelly roll. Sprinkle with the combined remaining sugar and cinnamon.

Place rolls in a shallow baking pan. Bake 10 minutes, until lightly browned. Remove from pan and serve warm.

Each serving provides:

96 Calories*

1/2	Bread Serving	2 g	Protein
1/2	Fat Serving	2 g	Fat
1/4	Fruit Serving	19 g	Carbohydrate
16	Additional Calories	136 mg	Sodium
	(plus 8 more calories if	0 mg	Cholesterol
	sugar is used as		
	sweetener)		

*If sugar is used as sweetener

Cinnamon-Orange Rolls

*These luscious orange- and cinnamon-flavored goodies are made in a snap
from refrigerator biscuits.*

Makes 10 servings

1   tablespoon plus 2 teaspoons margarine, melted
3   tablespoons sugar (or sweetener equivalent to 9 teaspoons
         sugar)
1   tablespoon frozen orange juice concentrate (unsweetened),
         thawed
1/2   teaspoon ground cinnamon
1   10-ounce package refrigerator biscuits (10 biscuits)

Preheat oven to 350°.
   In a 9-inch pie pan, combine margarine, sugar, orange juice con-
centrate, and cinnamon. Spread evenly over bottom of pan.
   Arrange biscuits evenly in pan.
   Bake 20 to 25 minutes, until golden.
   Cool in pan 1 minute; then invert onto a serving plate.
   Serve warm for best flavor.

Each serving provides:

110 Calories*

1	Bread Serving	2	g	Protein
1/2	Fat Serving	3	g	Fat
3	Additional Calories	18	g	Carbohydrate
	(plus 14 more calories if	264	mg	Sòdium
	sugar is used as	0	mg	Cholesterol
	sweetener)			

*If sugar is used as sweetener

Peanut Butter Meringues

These peanut buttery gems will definitely become a favorite.

Makes 8 servings
(4 cookies each serving)

1	egg white
1/8	teaspoon cream of tartar
3	tablespoons plus 1 teaspoon sugar (Sweeteners do not work well here.)
1/4	cup creamy peanut butter

Preheat oven to 300°.

In a small, deep bowl, beat egg white on low speed of an electric mixer until frothy. Add cream of tartar and beat on high speed until stiff. Gradually beat in sugar.

Fold in peanut butter until well blended.

Drop mixture by teaspoonfuls onto a nonstick cookie sheet or one that has been sprayed with a nonstick cooking spray.

Bake 25 minutes, until lightly browned.

Remove to a rack to cool.

Each serving provides:

70 Calories

1/2	Protein Serving	3	g	Protein
1/2	Fat Serving	4	g	Fat
23	Additional Calories	6	g	Carbohydrate
		44	mg	Sodium
		0	mg	Cholesterol

Coconut Wheat Crispies

We've used our old-time favorite puffed wheat cereal to make these nutritious cookies. They're a great lunch box treat.

Makes 4 servings
(4 cookies each serving)

1-1/2 ounces puffed wheat cereal
1/2   teaspoon baking powder
2   tablespoons plus 2 teaspoons reduced-calorie margarine
1   teaspoon coconut extract
1/2   teaspoon vanilla extract
1   tablespoon shredded coconut (unsweetened)
3   tablespoons plus 1 teaspoon sugar (Sweeteners do not work
        well here.)

Preheat oven to 375°.

Place cereal in a blender container and blend until fine crumbs are formed. Pour into a bowl.

Add remaining ingredients. Mix with a fork or pastry blender until mixture resembles coarse crumbs. Roll crumbs tightly into balls, making 16 in all.

Place balls on ungreased cookie sheet. Flatten each cookie to 1/4-inch thick, using the bottom of a glass that is first dipped in water.

Bake 10 minutes, until lightly browned.

Remove to a rack to cool.

```
Each serving provides:

                    122 Calories

1/2  Bread Serving          2  g  Protein
1    Fat Serving            5  g  Fat
48   Additional Calories   20  g  Carbohydrate
                          134 mg  Sodium
                            0 mg  Cholesterol
```

Almond Macaroons

Wheat germ replaces the ground nuts in these crispy macaroons. It reduces the fat and calories, adds more nutrition, and still gives a delicious, nutty flavor.

Makes 10 servings
(5 cookies each serving)

1	egg white
1/4	cup sugar (Sweeteners do not work well here.)
1	teaspoon almond extract
1/4	cup wheat germ

Preheat oven to 325°.

In a deep bowl, beat egg white on low speed of an electric mixer until frothy. Beat on high speed until stiff.

Gradually beat in sugar and then almond extract.

Fold in wheat germ.

Drop mixture by 1/2 teaspoonfuls onto a cookie sheet that has been sprayed with a nonstick cooking spray and dusted lightly with flour.

Put the cookies in the oven and immediately reduce the temperature to 200°.

Bake 1 hour.

Turn off heat and leave cookies in oven to cool.

Each serving provides:

33 Calories

33	Additional Calories	1	g	Protein
		0	g	Fat
		6	g	Carbohydrate
		5	mg	Sodium
		0	mg	Cholesterol

Peanut Butter Chews

Peanut butter lovers are in for a real treat. These soft, moist morsels are almost cookies, almost candies, and entirely delicious.

Makes 8 servings
(2 cookies each serving)

1/4	cup peanut butter
1/2	cup evaporated skim milk
1/2	teaspoon vanilla extract
1	tablespoon plus 2 teaspoons sugar (or sweetener equivalent to 5 teaspoons sugar)
2	teaspoons shredded coconut (unsweetened)
1/4	cup raisins
3	ounces corn or oat flakes cereal (unsweetened)

Preheat oven to 375°.

In a medium bowl, combine all ingredients, *except* cereal. Mix well.

Stir in cereal. Mix well, crushing cereal lightly with the back of the spoon.

Drop mixture by rounded teaspoonfuls onto a nonstick cookie sheet or one that has been sprayed with a nonstick cooking spray.

Bake 12 minutes, until lightly browned.

Remove to a rack to cool.

Each serving provides:

126 Calories*

1/2	Protein Serving	5	g	Protein
1/2	Bread Serving	4	g	Fat
1/2	Fat Serving	18	g	Carbohydrate
1/4	Fruit Serving	188	mg	Sodium
15	Additional Calories	1	mg	Cholesterol
	(plus 10 more calories if sugar is used as sweetener)			

*If sugar is used as sweetener

Raspberry-Filled Almond Cookies

There's something about the taste of almond and raspberry that seems to form the perfect combination.

Makes 4 servings
(4 cookies each serving)

3/4	cup all-purpose flour
1/2	teaspoon baking powder
1/4	cup reduced-calorie margarine
1	tablespoon plus 2 teaspoons sugar (or sweetener equivalent to 5 teaspoons sugar)
1/2	teaspoon almond extract
1/2	teaspoon vanilla butternut flavor
1	tablespoon plus 1 teaspoon reduced-calorie raspberry jam (8 calories per teaspoon)

Preheat oven to 350°.

In a small bowl, combine flour and baking powder.

Add margarine, sugar, and extracts. Mix well with a fork until dough is formed.

Using your hands, work dough into a ball. Divide dough into 16 pieces and roll each into a ball. Place balls between 2 sheets of wax paper. With a rolling pin, roll each into a circle 1/8-inch thick.

Place 1/4 teaspoon of the jam in the center of each circle. Fold in half and pinch ends together. Place on a nonstick cookie sheet or one that has been sprayed with a nonstick cooking spray.

Bake 12 minutes, until bottoms are lightly browned.

Remove to a rack to cool.

Each serving provides:

167 Calories*

1	Bread Serving	2	g	Protein
1-1/2	Fat Servings	6	g	Fat
8	Additional Calories	25	g	Carbohydrate
	(plus 20 more calories if	174	mg	Sodium
	sugar is used as	0	mg	Cholesterol
	sweetener)			

*If sugar is used as sweetener

Peanut Butter Raisin Balls

The kids will love making these easy candies.

Makes 8 servings
(2 candies each serving)

1/2   cup peanut butter
1/2   cup raisins, chopped
1/3   cup nonfat dry milk
1   teaspoon vanilla extract
1   tablespoon water

Combine all ingredients and mix well. Shape into 16 balls.
Chill.

Each serving provides:

134 Calories

1	Protein Serving	6	g	Protein
1	Fat Serving	8	g	Fat
1/2	Fruit Serving	11	g	Carbohydrate
13	Additional Calories	92	mg	Sodium
		1	mg	Cholesterol

Chocolate Coconut Kisses

For variation, try replacing the coconut extract with another flavor, such as almond, orange, or banana.

Makes 2 servings
(2 candies each serving)

1/3   cup nonfat dry milk
2   teaspoons cocoa (unsweetened)
2   tablespoons sugar (or sweetener equivalent to 6 teaspoons sugar)
2   teaspoons shredded coconut (unsweetened)
1/2   teaspoon vanilla extract
1/2   teaspoon coconut extract
1-1/4 teaspoons water (If you are using a sweetener in place of the sugar, use 2 teaspoons water.)

In a small bowl, combine dry milk and cocoa. Mix well, pressing out any lumps with the back of the spoon.
Add remaining ingredients, adding water last. Mix well.
Divide mixture and roll into 4 balls.
Cover and chill.

Each serving provides:

107 Calories*

1/2	Milk Serving	4 g	Protein
15	Additional Calories	1 g	Fat
	(plus 48 more calories if	20 g	Carbohydrate
	sugar is used as	62 mg	Sodium
	sweetener)	2 mg	Cholesterol

*If sugar is used as sweetener

Crunchy Peanut Candy Bar

This easy candy has such a great flavor!

*Makes 2 servings
(1 candy each serving)*

2	tablespoons crunchy peanut butter
1/3	cup nonfat dry milk
2	teaspoons cocoa (unsweetened)
3/4	ounce Grape-Nuts® cereal
1	teaspoon honey
2	tablespoons water
1	tablespoon plus 1 teaspoon sugar (or sweetener equivalent to 4 teaspoons sugar)

Combine all ingredients in a small bowl. Mix well.

Divide mixture evenly and shape into 2 logs. Place on wax paper and flatten each slightly to resemble a candy bar.

Chill at least 30 minutes.

Each serving provides:

221 Calories*

1	Protein Serving	10	g	Protein
1/2	Bread Serving	9	g	Fat
1	Fat Serving	29	g	Carbohydrate
1/2	Milk Serving	201	mg	Sodium
15	Additional Calories	2	mg	Cholesterol
	(plus 32 more calories if sugar is used as sweetener)			

*If sugar is used as sweetener

Pineapple Fudge Drops

These super-rich candies are sure to satisfy any sweet tooth.

Makes 2 servings
(4 candies each serving)

1/4   cup canned crushed pineapple (unsweetened), drained
1/3   cup nonfat dry milk
2   teaspoons cocoa (unsweetened)
1/2   ounce graham cracker crumbs (two 2-1/2-inch graham
          crackers, crushed)
2   teaspoons sugar (or equivalent amount of sweetener)

In a small bowl, combine all ingredients, mixing well.
Drop by tablespoonfuls onto wax paper, making 8 candies.
Chill until firm, about 30 minutes.

Each serving provides:

110 Calories*

1/2	Bread Serving	5	g	Protein
1/4	Fruit Serving	1	g	Fat
1/2	Milk Serving	21	g	Carbohydrate
5	Additional Calories	107	mg	Sodium
	(plus 16 more calories if	2	mg	Cholesterol
	sugar is used as			
	sweetener)			

*If sugar is used as sweetener

Butter Rum Drops

These buttery, rich candies literally melt in your mouth. You'll want to make extras to keep in the freezer.

Makes 2 servings
(5 candies each serving)

1/3 cup nonfat dry milk
2 tablespoons water
1/4 teaspoon vanilla butternut flavor
1/8 teaspoon rum extract
2 teaspoons sugar (or equivalent amount of sweetener)

In a small bowl, combine all ingredients, mixing until blended.

Line a small pan with wax paper and drop mixture by teaspoonfuls onto the paper, making 10 candies.

Freeze until firm, about 20 minutes.

Eat candies frozen.

Each serving provides:

59 Calories*

1/2	Milk Serving	4	g	Protein
16	Additional Calories (if	0	g	Fat
	sugar is used as	10	g	Carbohydrate
	sweetener)	62	mg	Sodium
		2	mg	Cholesterol

*If sugar is used as sweetener

Snacks and Dips

Hints for Snacks and Dips

Yes, there are snacks that are low in calories and fat. One of the secrets is to use flavorful combinations of the right ingredients. Another secret is to make snacks that can be prepared quickly so you won't eat the wrong things while waiting for the right things to cook. Following are some hints that will help you in planning delicious, satisfying snacks.

- Plan ahead and have healthful snacks on hand. For example, keep a plastic bag of cut vegetables in your refrigerator. If you don't have time to prepare them, pick them up at any salad bar.

- Try lots of different raw vegetables, such as fresh pea pods, sliced turnip, and broccoli stems. (Peel stems before eating.)

- Always keep fresh fruit handy. Many salad bars offer a variety of fresh fruits, but some have sugar added, so be sure to check with the attendant.

- Make dips from lowfat yogurt and cheeses.

- Try our dips for fruits and vegetables (in this chapter) and keep your favorite one on hand.

- Don't keep high-calorie snack foods in the house. If they're not there, you can't eat them.

- Nuts are a "risky" snack food to have around. They're very high in fat, and it's hard to eat just one.

- If you like pretzels, try the whole wheat varieties. If your supermarket doesn't carry them, it's definitely worth a trip to the health food store.

- Be aware that most packaged snack foods such as potato chips and taco chips are deep fried. In addition to the calories they contain, many are fried in saturated oil, such as coconut or palm oil.

- Combinations of fruits and juices in the blender make wonderful fruit slushies.

- Add nonfat dry milk to your slushy and you can whip up a delicious fruit shake.

- Many of the cookies, candies, fruits, and muffins in this book also make wonderful snacks. Please see our sections on Breads and Muffins, Fruits, and Desserts.

Granola

This crunchy snack is made commercially by many companies. However, most brands contain large amounts of sugar and fats. Our version uses extracts for flavor and the results are outstanding. Snack it plain, sprinkle it over sliced, cooked peaches or apples for an instant fruit crisp, try it over ice milk, cook it just like oatmeal, or enjoy it cold with milk and raisins.

Makes 6 servings
(1/4 cup per serving)

4-1/2 ounces rolled oats, uncooked (1-1/2 cups)
1/2   ounce slivered almonds
1-1/2 teaspoons ground cinnamon
2   tablespoons honey *or* maple syrup
1/2   teaspoon almond extract
1/2   teaspoon coconut extract
1   teaspoon vanilla extract
2   tablespoons vegetable oil
1/4   cup apple juice (unsweetened)

Preheat oven to 300°.

In a large bowl, combine oats, almonds, and cinnamon. Mix well.

In a small bowl, combine remaining ingredients. Drizzle over oats. Mix well until all ingredients are moistened.

Spread mixture in a 10 x 15-inch baking pan that has been sprayed with a nonstick cooking spray.

Bake 20 minutes.

Stir granola and return to oven for 5 minutes.

Stir again and return for another 5 minutes.

Cool in pan, stirring occasionally. Store in an airtight container.

Each serving provides:

168 Calories

1	Bread Serving	4	g	Protein
1	Fat Serving	7	g	Fat
41	Additional Calories	23	g	Carbohydrate
		2	mg	Sodium
		0	mg	Cholesterol

Cinnamon Bread Sticks

These crisp snacks are so easy to make. Why not make a lot of them, so they'll be handy to munch. And, for an interesting variation, omit the sugar and cinnamon and lightly sprinkle with garlic powder instead.

Makes 4 servings
(6 sticks each serving)

4	slices thin-sliced whole wheat bread
2	teaspoons reduced-calorie margarine
1	teaspoon sugar
1/4	teaspoon ground cinnamon

Preheat oven to 300°.

Spread margarine on bread, using 1/2 teaspoon for each slice.

Combine sugar and cinnamon and sprinkle evenly on bread.

Cut each slice into 6 even strips. Place on a baking sheet that has been sprayed lightly with a nonstick cooking spray.

Bake 18 minutes, until crisp. Remove to a rack to cool.

Each serving provides:

53 Calories

1/2	Bread Serving	2	g	Protein
1/4	Fat Serving	1	g	Fat
4	Additional Calories	10	g	Carbohydrate
		115	mg	Sodium
		0	mg	Cholesterol

Roasted Chestnuts

You'll love the "homey" smell of chestnuts roasting. One reason why they make such a good snack is that they're delicious. Another reason is that it takes some time to peel and eat each one.

Makes 4 servings
(6 chestnuts each serving)

24   small chestnuts

Preheat oven to 425°.

With a sharp knife, cut an X through the flat side of each chestnut. Place in a shallow baking pan.

Bake 15 to 20 minutes, or until the X begins to separate.

Enjoy warm for best flavor.

Each serving provides:

78 Calories

1	Bread Serving	1	g	Protein
		1	g	Fat
		17	g	Carbohydrate
		8	mg	Sodium
		0	mg	Cholesterol

Nutty Frozen Banana

When our children were small, this was one of their favorite snacks. It's a wonderful alternative to an ice cream bar.

*Makes 2 servings
(1/2 banana each serving)*

1   medium, ripe banana
1/2   ounce finely chopped walnuts

Peel banana and cut in half, crosswise.

Spread chopped nuts on a piece of wax paper. Roll the banana in the nuts, carefully pressing the nuts into the banana.

Roll up the banana in the wax paper and freeze 1 hour. (If you have 2 ice cream sticks, insert 1 into the cut end of each banana before freezing.)

Enjoy them right from the freezer.

Each serving provides:

98 Calories

1	Fruit Serving	2	g	Protein
46	Additional Calories	5	g	Fat
		15	g	Carbohydrate
		1	mg	Sodium
		0	mg	Cholesterol

Frozen Juice Cubes

When you crave something sweet, why not try a frozen juice cube. They're icy cold and delicious, and take a while to eat. For a special "reward", place a raisin or an almond in the center of each cube.

Makes 6 servings
(2 cubes per serving)

1-1/2 cups orange juice, or any flavor unsweetened fruit juice

Pour juice into an ice cube tray. Freeze. When cubes are solid, place them in a plastic bag and return to freezer.

Enjoy them right from the freezer.

Each serving provides:

28 Calories

1/2	Fruit Serving	0	g	Protein
		0	g	Fat
		7	g	Carbohydrate
		0	mg	Sodium
		0	mg	Cholesterol

Frozen Strawberry Pops

On a warm summer night, or as a different kind of a TV snack, we give these a five-star rating.

Makes 6 servings

1-1/2 cups plain lowfat yogurt
2   cups fresh strawberries
2   tablespoons reduced-calorie strawberry jam (8 calories per
         teaspoon)

In a blender container, combine all ingredients. Blend 1 minute.
Spoon mixture into six 4-ounce paper cups that have been
sprayed lightly with a nonstick cooking spray. Freeze 30 minutes;
then stand a wooden stick in the center of each pop.
Freeze until solid.
To eat, peel off paper cups.

Each serving provides:

59 Calories

1/3	Fruit Serving	3	g	Protein
1/2	Milk Serving	1	g	Fat
8	Additional Calories	10	g	Carbohydrate
		40	mg	Sodium
		3	mg	Cholesterol

Peanutty Date Treats

These easy treats were always our kids' favorite lunchbox surprise.

Makes 4 servings

4   pitted dates
1   tablespoon peanut butter

Divide peanut butter evenly and stuff into dates. Pinch closed. Enjoy right away or chill for later servings.

Each serving provides:

47 Calories

1/4	Protein Serving	1	g	Protein
1/4	Fat Serving	2	g	Fat
1/2	Fruit Serving	7	g	Carbohydrate
		19	mg	Sodium
		0	mg	Cholesterol

Potato Chips

Who said potato chips have to be fried? Our baked version is a far cry from the 170-calorie-per-ounce commercial chips.

Makes 4 servings

1   6-ounce baking potato, unpeeled
     Salt to taste

Preheat oven to 350°.

Using a food processor, vegetable peeler, or grater/slicer, slice potato into very thin, uniform slices.

Place, in one layer, on a baking sheet that has been sprayed with a nonstick cooking spray.

Spray potatoes lightly with the spray. Sprinkle with salt to taste.

Bake 12 to 14 minutes, until light brown. Remove to a rack to cool. (Note: Baking time may vary according to thickness of potato slices. Potatoes need to be light brown all over, or they will be soggy when cooled.

Enjoy right away or store in an airtight container.

Each serving provides:

31 Calories

1/2	Bread Serving	1	g	Protein
		0	g	Fat
		7	g	Carbohydrate
		3	mg	Sodium
		0	mg	Cholesterol

Tortilla Chips

These crispy, crunchy chips are a wonderful alternative to the deep-fried nacho chips.

Makes 4 servings
(6 chips each serving)

4   corn tortillas
     Garlic powder
     Ground cumin
     Salt

Preheat oven to 300°.

Cut each tortilla into 6 pie-shaped wedges. Place in a single layer
on a cookie sheet that has been sprayed with a nonstick cooking spray. Spray chips lightly with the spray. Sprinkle with spices.

Bake 12 to 15 minutes, until crisp.

Remove to a rack to cool. Store in an airtight container.

Each serving provides:

67 Calories

1	Bread Serving	2	g	Protein
		1	g	Fat
		13	g	Carbohydrate
		53	mg	Sodium
		0	mg	Cholesterol

Bagel Crackers

These crispy crackers are best when made with the large, bakery-style bagels.
For variations, try different flavored bagels, such as onion, garlic, or sesame.
For a delicious snack, enjoy them plain or spread lightly with reduced-calorie
jam.

Makes 4 servings
(6 crackers each serving)

1   4-ounce plain bagel

Preheat oven to 300°.

Cut bagel in half lengthwise, and then cut each half into 4 quarters. Slice each quarter into 3 slices.

Place on a baking sheet that has been sprayed lightly with a nonstick cooking spray.

Bake 25 minutes, until crisp. Remove to a rack to cool.

Each serving provides:

75 Calories

1	Bread Serving	3	g	Protein
		0	g	Fat
		15	g	Carbohydrate
		175	mg	Sodium
		0	mg	Cholesterol

Cinnamon Popcorn

This truly nutritious snack is low in calories and high in protein and fiber. Unfortunately, most of the popcorn available in the grocery store, even the type for microwaves, has fat added. The best popcorn is made with a hot air popper. That way, you can control the toppings. In this recipe we've added cinnamon for an unusual flavor.

Makes 4 servings
(1 cup each serving)

1/2	teaspoon ground cinnamon
2	teaspoons sugar
4	cups freshly popped popcorn
	Nonstick cooking spray

Combine cinnamon and sugar.

Spread popcorn on a baking sheet. Spray lightly with cooking spray. Sprinkle with cinnamon and sugar.

Enjoy!

Each serving provides:

35 Calories

1/2	Bread Serving	1	g	Protein
8	Additional Calories	1	g	Fat
		7	g	Carbohydrate
		0	mg	Sodium
		0	mg	Cholesterol

Cottage Cheese and Olive Dip

This recipe is an adaptation of one that's been in the family for 3 generations. We love it with raw vegetables, especially celery sticks.

Makes 6 servings
(3 tablespoons each serving)

1	cup lowfat cottage cheese
2	tablespoons reduced-calorie mayonnaise
1	tablespoon horseradish mustard
1/2	teaspoon vinegar
1	tablespoon minced onion flakes
6	pitted black olives, chopped
6	stuffed green olives, chopped
1/8	teaspoon pepper
	Salt to taste

In a blender container, combine cottage cheese, mayonnaise, mustard, vinegar, and onion flakes. Blend until smooth. Spoon into a bowl.
Add remaining ingredients. Mix well.
Chill to blend flavors.

Each serving provides:

58 Calories

1/2	Protein Serving	5	g	Protein
1/2	Fat Serving	3	g	Fat
10	Additional Calories	2	g	Carbohydrate
		375	mg	Sodium
		3	mg	Cholesterol

Dijon Dip

Mustard lovers, here it is! This unusual dip doubles as a spread for chicken or fish sandwiches.

Makes 8 servings
(3 tablespoons each serving)

1/2	cup reduced-calorie mayonnaise
1/2	cup part-skim ricotta cheese
1/3	cup Dijon mustard
1	teaspoon dill weed
1/8	teaspoon garlic powder

In a small bowl, combine all ingredients. Chill to blend flavors.

Each serving provides:

74 Calories

1/4	Protein Serving	2	g	Protein
1-1/2	Fat Servings	6	g	Fat
		3	g	Carbohydrate
		426	mg	Sodium
		10	mg	Cholesterol

Creamy Bacon Dip

We've used imitation bacon bits and yogurt in place of the bacon and sour cream in this creamy dip, and it tastes the same as its more fattening forerunner.

Makes 8 servings
(3 tablespoons each serving)

1	cup plain lowfat yogurt
1/4	cup plus 4 teaspoons reduced-calorie mayonnaise
1	tablespoon minced onion flakes
1	tablespoon imitation bacon bits

In a small bowl, combine all ingredients. Chill to blend flavors.

Each serving provides:

50 Calories

1	Fat Serving	2	g	Protein
1/4	Milk Serving	3	g	Fat
4	Additional Calories	3	g	Carbohydrate
		111	mg	Sodium
		5	mg	Cholesterol

Spinach Dip

This is our low-fat version of a classic dip. It's great for dipping veggies or crackers.

Makes 8 servings
(1/4 cup each serving)

1	10-ounce package frozen chopped spinach, thawed and drained well
1	cup plain lowfat yogurt
1/4	cup plus 2 tablespoons reduced-calorie mayonnaise
1/4	teaspoon garlic powder
1	teaspoon dill weed
1/4	cup finely chopped green onions

In a medium bowl, combine all ingredients, mixing well. Chill to blend flavors.

Each serving provides:

58 Calories

1/3	Vegetable Serving	3	g	Protein
1	Fat Serving	4	g	Fat
15	Additional Calories	4	g	Carbohydrate
		131	mg	Sodium
		5	mg	Cholesterol

Dilly Dip

This is a great dip to keep on hand for dipping veggies, or try it as a salad dressing or as a baked potato topper.

Makes 8 servings
(2 tablespoons each serving)

1	cup plain lowfat yogurt
1	teaspoon dill weed
1	tablespoon minced onion flakes
1/8	teaspoon celery seed
1	teaspoon dried chives

In a small bowl, combine all ingredients. Chill to blend flavors.

Each serving provides:

20 Calories

1/4	Milk Serving	2 g	Protein
		0 g	Fat
		2 g	Carbohydrate
		20 mg	Sodium
		2 mg	Cholesterol

Yogurt Marmalade Dip

Make this dip with any flavor jam or marmalade you like. They're all luscious over fresh fruit or spread on rice cakes. (Our favorites are apricot and raspberry.)

Makes 8 servings
(2 tablespoons each serving)

1   cup plain lowfat yogurt
1/4   cup reduced-calorie jam or marmalade (8 calories per
           teaspoon)
1   teaspoon vanilla extract

In a small bowl, combine all ingredients and chill.

Each serving provides:

32 Calories

1/4	Milk Serving		1	g	Protein
12	Additional Calories		0	g	Fat
			5	g	Carbohydrate
			20	mg	Sodium
			2	mg	Cholesterol

Creme Topping

This creamy topping is delicious as a dip for any fresh fruit, especially fresh berries. It's also a good topper for any of our pies or fruit desserts. For variations, in place of the lemon extract try another flavor, such as coconut, almond, or orange.

Makes 6 servings
(3 tablespoons each serving)

1	cup lowfat cottage cheese
2	tablespoons skim milk
2	teaspoons vanilla extract
3	tablespoons sugar (or sweetener equivalent to 9 teaspoons sugar)
1/4	teaspoon lemon extract

In a blender container, combine all ingredients. Blend until smooth. Chill.

Each serving provides:

59 Calories*

1/2	Protein Serving	5	g	Protein
26	Additional Calories	0	g	Fat
	(plus 12 more calories if	8	g	Carbohydrate
	sugar is used as	156	mg	Sodium
	sweetener)	2	mg	Cholesterol

*If sugar is used as sweetener

Brown Sugar Dip

This delicious dip for fruit can also be used to top any of our fabulous desserts.

Makes 8 servings
(2 tablespoons each serving)

1   cup plain lowfat yogurt
3   tablespoons brown sugar (or sweetener equivalent to 9
           teaspoons brown sugar)
1   teaspoon vanilla butternut flavor
1/4   teaspoon ground cinnamon

In a small bowl, combine all ingredients. Chill.

Each serving provides:

39 Calories*

1/4	Milk Serving	1	g	Protein
18	Additional Calories (if	0	g	Fat
	brown sugar is used as	7	g	Carbohydrate
	sweetener)	21	mg	Sodium
		2	mg	Cholesterol

*If sugar is used as sweetener

Index

FILL IN AND MAIL ... TODAY

PRIMA PUBLISHING & COMMUNICATIONS
P.O. Box 1260MLL
Rocklin, CA 95677

USE YOUR VISA/MC AND ORDER BY PHONE
(916) 624-5718
Mon.–Fri. 9–4 PST (12–7 EST)

Dear People,

I'd like to order copies of the following **Lean and Luscious** titles:

_____ copies of the original **Lean and Luscious**
at $13.95 each for a total of . . . . _____

_____ copies of **More Lean and Luscious**
at $14.95 each for a total of . . . . _____

Subtotal	_____
Postage & Handling	$3.00
Sales Tax	_____
TOTAL (U.S. funds only)	_____

☐ Check enclosed for $_____, payable to Prima Publishing
 Charge my ☐ Mastercard ☐ Visa

Account No. _____ Exp. Date _____

Signature _____

Your Name _____

Address _____

City/State/Zip _____

Daytime Telephone _____

GUARANTEE
YOU MUST BE SATISFIED!
You get a 30-day, 100% money-back guarantee on all books.

Thank you for your order.